WHAT PEACE THERE MAY BE

To Gigi,
Any friend of Susan's
is a friend of mine.
Thank you for reading;
for touching my life in your
unique way. I hope to meet
you soon.

Susanna

WHAT PEACE THERE MAY BE

A MEMOIR

SUSANNA BARLOW

iUniverse, Inc.
New York Lincoln Shanghai

WHAT PEACE THERE MAY BE
A MEMOIR

Copyright © 2007 by Susanna Barlow

All rights reserved. No part of this book may be used or reproduced by any means, graphic, electronic, or mechanical, including photocopying, recording, taping or by any information storage retrieval system without the written permission of the publisher except in the case of brief quotations embodied in critical articles and reviews.

iUniverse books may be ordered through booksellers or by contacting:

iUniverse
2021 Pine Lake Road, Suite 100
Lincoln, NE 68512
www.iuniverse.com
1-800-Authors (1-800-288-4677)

The views expressed in this work are solely those of the author and do not necessarily reflect the views of the publisher, and the publisher hereby disclaims any responsibility for them.

ISBN-13: 978-0-595-40777-4 (pbk)
ISBN-13: 978-0-595-67832-7 (cloth)
ISBN-13: 978-0-595-85141-6 (ebk)

Printed in the United States of America

This book is dedicated to my children.
May you inherit a different legacy and pass on a new flame to the torch of the next generation.

CONTENTS

Preface xiii

Part I   The Inside World

Chapter 1	 3
Chapter 2	 7
Chapter 3	 9
Chapter 4	 12
Chapter 5	 15
Chapter 6	 17
Chapter 7	 21
Chapter 8	 24
Chapter 9	 27
Chapter 10	 30
Chapter 11	 32
Chapter 12	 35
Chapter 13	 38
Chapter 14	 40
Chapter 15	 43
Chapter 16	 46

Chapter 17	49
Chapter 18	52
Chapter 19	55
Chapter 20	58

Part II   Endings

Chapter 21	63
Chapter 22	66
Chapter 23	69
Chapter 24	74
Chapter 25	77
Chapter 26	79
Chapter 27	82
Chapter 28	86
Chapter 29	88
Chapter 30	92
Chapter 31	94
Chapter 32	97
Chapter 33	100
Chapter 34	103
Chapter 35	105
Chapter 36	107
Chapter 37	109
Chapter 38	111
Chapter 39	113

Chapter 40	115
Chapter 41	117
Chapter 42	120
Chapter 43	123
Chapter 44	125
Chapter 45	128
Chapter 46	130
Chapter 47	133
Chapter 48	135
Chapter 49	137
Chapter 50	139
Chapter 51	142
Chapter 52	145
Chapter 53	147
Chapter 54	150
Chapter 55	152
Chapter 56	155
Chapter 57	157

Part III *Beginnings*

Chapter 58	163
Chapter 59	166
Chapter 60	168
Chapter 61	171
Chapter 62	174

CHAPTER 63	176
CHAPTER 64	181
CHAPTER 65	183
CHAPTER 66	185
CHAPTER 67	188
CHAPTER 68	190
CHAPTER 69	193
CHAPTER 70	195
CHAPTER 71	198
CHAPTER 72	201
CHAPTER 73	203
CHAPTER 74	205
CHAPTER 75	207
CHAPTER 76	210
CHAPTER 77	212
CHAPTER 78	215
CHAPTER 79	217
CHAPTER 80	220
CHAPTER 81	224
CHAPTER 82	226
Epilogue	229
Author's Note	231
Note to the Reader	233

ACKNOWLEDGMENTS

There are many individuals to whom I would like to give thanks for the conception and completion of this book.

I would first like to thank my husband and companion. You have stood by my side, sometimes leading, sometimes pushing, sometimes silently observing, but you have always been there. Your belief in me and your willingness to see me succeed is an inspiration. To my wonderful husband I extend a heartfelt thank-you. Your support has been my staff.

To my children I feel a deep gratitude because of your pure love and devotion. Without having held each one of you in my arms when you were born I would have lacked the conviction to write at all. It was because of my desires for you that I tell this story. The truth, no matter how personal or ugly it may be, will always set you free. Thank you, my angel children.

A big thanks goes to my sisters. A more devoted group of women I could never find. You have given me a gift of love and friendship that I will always treasure.

A special thanks goes to my sister Maryanne. You were there in the beginning and you stayed until the end. You gave me the encouragement I needed and the belief in myself when I wavered. I couldn't have written this book without you. You are my dearest friend.

I would also like to thank Mother and Father. Thank you for your willingness to grow and change after all these years. Thank you for all the things you gave me that aren't part of this book. Your humility and goodness have blessed my life.

A huge thank-you goes to my dear friend Anne Marie. Without your wisdom and encouragement this book would be an unfinished stack of papers. Your amazing editorial abilities saved the book. Your love and commitment to me and this project propelled me forward. You are and always will be a vital part of my life.

I would also like to thank my Aunt Geri. Thank you for convincing me to write an honest book. Thank you for your support and for loving me in your very special way. The seeds you planted grew. Thank you.

To Joseph Walker, I hope this book speaks for itself. Thank you for choosing kindness.

To Walt, thank you, friend, for seeing me through. You made a difference.

Thanks to my writing group: Peter, Michelle, Sandra, Michael, Jackie, and Carol. You helped me to grow and develop as a writer. I thank each of you for your encouragement and writing advice.

I'd also like to thank each individual who reads this book. Without you I would have had no reason to write it. The idea that others would read this book kept me going. It pushed me to exceed my own expectations. For this I offer you my gratitude. Thank you.

PREFACE

Run, run, run!

Even the word has a sense of urgency, like the pounding of my feet on the snow-crusted sidewalk. I can't breathe. The cold air burns my lungs. I don't turn back and look but I push my legs a few strides more into the darkness. The full moon offers light enough that I have no trouble navigating my way through the streets, but the force behind me bears down upon me like a tidal wave, the roar of its comportment in my ears. The buzzing of telephone lines in the air and the swoosh of wheels on wet asphalt at the intersection ahead are amplified by the leafless trees that line the streets like guardians in front of sleeping houses. I stop to rest on the curb but there isn't time. I have to *run*. It will catch me soon, washing over me, wetting and weighing me down again. For now the adrenaline keeps my body in forward motion and the voice in my head is screaming *Go!* So I run. After a while I forget about breathing or the aching in my legs; all I can feel is the rhythm, like a marionette dancing on invisible strings that command the movement of every limb.

As swiftly as it came, the rhythm is gone. I fall to the pavement, a stumble, a crash to my knees. It's over. There's no use trying to escape. I stand up and brush the slush from my hem and turn around to face it. There is the house, still hovering over me, its unshapely appearance like a cutout in the velvety darkness, its veiled eyes hiding the secrets inside.

I turn around and walk back in the direction I came. Trudge. Drag. My cold feet plod forward and I have no other choice but to follow them. I pull my collar up to my nose, suddenly aware of the freezing temperature and my insane lack of a coat. My breathing regulates and reason fills my head. I rub both arms vigorously and stomp my feet. A slight breeze picks up from the north and flurries of snow swirl about me. What am I doing? Why can't I simply accept the life I have been given?

I have no answers, only more questions.

It must be past midnight. I stand at the gate and face the house that holds all of me within its intangible reach. This is where I was born. I belong to this tiny patch of earth, to the pine trees that shade both the house and the neighboring apartments. I belong here; a small portion of an acre and everything inside the tall white fence that borders my space is master over me. I belong to the house, like a structural wall supporting the framework of generations. I belong to the past, to the duty of memory and the beliefs of the dead.

I don't want to go inside and leave the outside world.

Fifth East runs perpendicular to the house and although it is relatively quiet at this time of night, it hums with activity during the day. I am on the outside tonight. Being here feels a bit surreal, like standing in a painting, in a place I am certain I don't belong.

I belong behind the glass, watching people and cars from the inside, through a finger-smudged pane. I have watched, many times, old Mrs. Harsh from across the street pulling a trash can to the curb, and little Colette from next door running to the park in her lime green swimsuit or the postman, in his khaki shorts and blue shirt, fishing in his brown knapsack and stuffing the mailbox full of letters. I cannot conceive of the vast world beyond the window, beyond the view of the mountains that press into the sky. My world, the inside world, has its own vastness, its own outer limits, its own mountains waiting to be conquered. But in spite of its uncertainties, the outside world appears more tolerable than the inside.

I stand beneath the orange glow of a street light. Tiny snowflakes dance in the beam. I don't feel the wind anymore, or the cold. I can feel every fiber of me in the shaft of light. I am completely here.

It is the house that finally calls me back. It is the pull of the inside world that tears at the fabric of my illusions. But for one brief moment the force of rebellion holds me to the spot, grounding me into myself.

It doesn't matter.

I cross the street and feel my way through the blackness of the lean-to. My hand bumps into the knob of the basement door. It's unlocked. Just the way I left it. The door squeaks just enough to cause me to bite my lip and hold statue-still. I wait for voices, but silence tells me I am alone. The warmth of the basement is both welcome and startling as I slip out of my wet clothes and into a flannel nightgown. Sleep will come quickly on the rickety bunk bed.

PART I

THE INSIDE WORLD

I

Lillian leaves me sitting on the kitchen stairs. The heavy, stained walnut door closes behind her with a heave and a groan. I root myself to the bottom stair to wait it out.

I can barely hear snippets of the conversation. There is mostly the sound of Mother Kay's voice. It's the voice of authority, the voice of the uncontested. I pretend I have x-ray vision and I can see right through the door, through the dark varnish and the molecules of planed wood and into the dining room.

Mother Kay is sitting at the head of two long and narrow dinner tables, connected only by a white cloth. Every chair is pushed into its proper place, obediently hidden. Her light brown hair is pulled tightly away from her face, sharpening her features. Her hands, smooth and untouched by either sun or dish water, rest on the table in a serious fold. Her words fill the room like the odor of steaming broccoli. A diatribe pours out of her, with Lillian in its path.

Lillian stands in front of Mother Kay, looking directly at the bridge of her nose, careful to avoid intimate contact. She wears dirty gym shoes and a yellow dress that comes just below the knees, barely covering a tiny hole in her tights.

I tell myself I don't care what Mother Kay is saying; still, I find myself straining to hear her words.

Claire plops down next to me. "Whatcha doin'?" Her dark braids, looped up and fastened with hair bands, rest comfortably on her shoulders.

"Waitin' for Lillian."

Claire looks over at the closed door. "She's talkin' to Lillian again?"

"Yep."

Claire says nothing but arches her left eyebrow suspiciously. I squint a little and nod knowingly at the space in front of me. Neither of us dares to wield words at such a dangerous intersection, in such a public place.

The door gives a warning creak.

"Well, I'm supposed to be helping Charlotte with wash duty," Claire says, standing up and putting the laundry basket on her hip. She wisely disappears.

Lillian appears, and I think perhaps Mother Kay stayed behind. But Lillian walks right past me, only giving me a glance. I start to follow her when I feel Mother Kay's presence behind me. Her knuckles rap the back of my head.

"You leave Lillian alone," she says. "She has things to do." Mother Kay slowly walks up the stairs and disappears into the darkened hall. I don't move for a moment, imagining the pleasure it would give me to rap Mother Kay's head with a certain cast iron skillet. There's a whistle at the top of the stairs. It's for me. I poke my head around the staircase. Mother Kay's figure is ominous from down below. She keeps one hand on the railing and one foot dangling off the top step.

"What's your job today?" she asks, her chin tilted upward.

"I'm on house duty." The words come out slippery. Two loose strands of hair tickle my nose but I don't make any sudden moves.

"Why aren't you doing it?" she says, tapping her fingernails on the banister.

"I was … just using the bathroom." We both know it's a perfectly valid excuse. Mother Kay pauses.

"You better get to it, then, ya hear?"

"Yes."

Mother Kay turns away and shuts herself in Father's bedroom.

I'm glad she didn't want to take me with her to Father's bedroom for a talk. I would rather take a beating than sit through one of her talks. They are psychological twistery that she uses to break me down by whatever means she can. I know how to handle myself, saying enough but not too much. When I convince Mother Kay of her own brilliance, she releases me from her claws. I know how to play her games as well as she does. Lillian, on the other hand, does not. Her unassuming nature makes her easy prey and a container for holding secrets that keep her captive.

Lillian is washing the sliding glass door in the playroom when I track her down.

"Did ya get in trouble?" I whisper.

"No, not really," she says coolly.

"Did she say anything about me?"

"Please … don't ask me." Her eyes are empty cones, her voice anxious as the call of pigeons.

"Just tell me if it was about me."

"I can't."

"Why not?"

"I just can't. Please, don't keep asking me." She turns her attention to the squirt bottle of vinegar water that she sprays generously over the window, distorting the figures of playing children on the other side.

"Just answer yes or no. Was she talking about me?"

Lillian whirls around, flipping her short black hair.

"Just leave me alone, please." Her eyes are flashing through the tears that teeter on the brink of release.

"Okay, I guess you're on her side now." Lillian's face splinters and I pretend to turn away.

"I'm not supposed to say anything, okay?! I'll probably get in trouble for saying that much." She turns back to the window to sop up the streaks of vinegar water running down to the carpet. I don't know what to say.

"Sorry ... I know you're not really on her side."

"It sure feels like it sometimes," she says bitterly, and without looking at me. She turns back to the window, excluding me from her silent inner turmoil.

I've heard enough. It's enough to know she has been expressly forbidden to tell me what the exchange was about. It tells me more than a verbatim recall of the conversation; but a part of me remains unremittingly curious. And fearful. Mother Kay's influence takes a greater and greater hold of Lillian's loyalties every day. The real Lillian is being whittled away, leaving someone that is entirely Mother Kay's creation. Lillian has become Mother Kay's servant and confidante. I watch Lillian let Mother Kay change her and I don't understand why Lillian seems helpless to stop her.

Lillian has always had troubles. She sleepwalks regularly and complains of dark hallucinations. She floats through the house, zombie-like, in her white nightgown in the middle of the night, placing a dry bath towel on her head like a veil. She rarely speaks in this trance-like state between sleep and wakefulness, but stares straight ahead as if she can see something no one else can. It would be an entertainment of sorts if I believed for a second she was putting on an act. Instead it unnerves me to see her possessed by this strange semiconscious behavior, with the real Lillian tucked away behind the unblinking eyes. While I know that Lillian is only nine years old, when she sleep walks it seems to me that she is not a child at all but a one-hundred-year-old woman and my curiosity impels me and the other sisters to follow her through the house and then back to her bed where she promptly closes her eyes.

Sometimes she tells me of the things she sees in her delusional state: a hand reaching around corners and out of dark closets; a hand crawling with spiny fingers up the side of her bed to grab her in her sleep. She refuses to sleep without a nightlight. I'd have trouble believing her stories if Lillian had any other disposition than that of impeccable honesty. Claire and I joke among ourselves that Lillian doesn't even know how to lie. I don't know how Lillian has survived without such a skill.

I lie without conscience and Claire seems equally competent. We save ourselves from useless punishments, though it is I who carry the reputation of liar. Claire is softer and more compliant in her demeanor. Claire can meld into her circumstances with the grace of a magician, while I find myself standing in the heat of every suspicion with a big red X on my back. Lillian is safe on the sidelines but trapped between alliances. We are The Three Girls. Claire is the balance that holds Lillian and me, the two extremes, from disaster. I am the oldest of the three and I don't let Lillian and Claire forget that my eighteen months seniority places me in charge. Claire and Lillian are both nine years old and are so close in age to each other that it doesn't really matter that Lillian is two months older than Claire. Lillian will do whatever I want her to but Claire is a bit bossier and we often get into arguments. Otherwise, we are inseparable.

There is one thing that divides our threesome apart, aside from Lillian's wavering devotions. Claire and I have the same mother, a fact we are none too hesitant to remind ourselves of. I am very jealous of Mother, my own mother, and I am glad she stays home with us, a white apron tied around her waist, available in some fashion, even if just for a hug. Lillian has no such security. Mother Helen leaves her and goes to work every day. It's the only thing Lillian has ever known. She expects this routine abandonment and dreads it. I expect my mother's presence with the same audacity that I expect the sun to rise. I forget that it brings order and sanity and predictability to my world.

I don't consider Mother Helen and Mother Kay as my mothers. I have only one mother. That's why I don't call her Mother Mary. She isn't just one of the three mothers; she is my own mother. Claire and I share Mother's blood, while Lillian will always be outside of it despite the similarities of our appearance. I told Lillian that she could pretend that Mother was her own mother. She smiled weakly at me, unable to find words for her daily loss.

I want to feel pity and compassion for Lillian when she stands at the window every morning holding a stack of dirty dishes that she has cleared from the breakfast table, watching Mother Helen drive the car out of the lean-to and down the street. I want to pretend that she isn't crying. But I can see her tears even before they well up in her eyes, before she wipes them on her sleeve and I turn away in guilt because my own suffering may not be in equal proportion to Lillian's. It's a gap I cannot bridge with my scheming use of words. I cannot rescue Lillian and I feel the inadequacy in my bones.

II

The big white house on Fifth East. That's what the neighbors call it. It's a big house that started small. It was added to as needed and now it is tight, stuffed with people. There's hardly room for all of us and the small yard keeps shrinking with each new addition. There is a large lean-to on one side where cars once parked. Now half of it has been converted into bedrooms. From the street the house looks almost normal. Well, if you stand at the right angle, anyway. There is a tiny porch on the front and a dark solid wood front door. No one really uses the front door. When the doorbell rings the whole house stops. We know we are supposed to hide if the doorbell rings and most of us do just that, but I am not afraid of the outside world or the Gentiles.

I try to reach the door before Mother does or one of the Big Girls because I like to get a taste of the outside world. I talk to the person through the screen door. I can't offer much but a smile and my overabundant conversation. There's a wide range of folks who come knocking: Mormon missionaries, the occasional salesperson, Girl Scouts selling cookies, Jehovah's Witnesses. Sometimes it's terribly exciting. Once a man in a black trench coat and dark glasses who said he was from the FBI came looking for our neighbor and asked me when I had seen him last. The man had suddenly moved two days before. We had watched him regularly from the upstairs window, sitting on the patio in his backyard with a needle hanging out of his arm. He looked to be in a daze. Other times he was with a group, standing around a pit burning things. Until the man in the dark glasses appeared, I hadn't the faintest idea that our neighbor was doing hard drugs, maybe selling drugs too. I suppose it is people like drug addicts and gang members and the FBI that make Father nervous. If a policeman comes to the door and sees all the kids running around and all the mothers and our long sleeves and dresses they will know about us and Father will get taken to jail.

But I am sure that everyone already knows about us. It's really obvious by the way we dress and comb our hair. The contrast between me and Colette the neighbor girl is like night and day. Colette never combs her hair and mine is always in tight, wet braids from the top of my head to the ends of my hair. Colette wears short sleeves or worse, no sleeves at all. I always wear sleeves that come down to my wrists. We aren't supposed to even roll up our sleeves. Colette wears pants and shorts and I must wear dresses and uncomfortable tights and shoes that cover the entire foot. Mother says I should be proud of the way I look. But I don't feel pride. It isn't that I want to be like Colette I simply don't want the differences between me and her, between me and the world. I don't want the Gentiles to look at me and think that I am different from them. I don't feel different although Mother says that I most certainly am different.

We live in an inner-city neighborhood and sometimes the outside world looks terrifying with its drug users and gangs that possessively crowd sidewalks and street corners and I can see why Mother wants me to be different.

Once, during the middle of the night, a drunk driver rammed into Glenn's car, which was parked out on the street, with such velocity that Glenn's car ended up on its nose, leaning precariously against a telephone pole. Glenn was pretty upset about it. He is one of the only brothers to have his own car at sixteen. The drunken man came stumbling into our lean-to, blood oozing out of the hundreds of tiny holes made from the shards of glass protruding from his head. His own vehicle lay steaming in the street like a crumpled soda can. I was awakened from sleep by the sound of the basement door flinging open and a bloody stranger staggering into the entry. He took off his jacket, rolled it up, and laid himself on the cement floor like he had done it fifty times before, and waited for the paramedics to come. Mother wasn't too far behind the man, looking anxious in her robe and slippers. With her arms folded tight she peered into the street, hoping the ambulance would hurry and take the man away. It was an intrusion into the inside world and it wasn't appreciated.

I know the parents are trying to keep the outside world from seeping into the inside world. But some of it leaks in anyway every time the doorbell rings and someone on the other side thinks we're regular folks. That door is a portal to the outside world. I want to be a part of the outside world but I don't want to be shut out of the inside. I can imagine the big front door locked, and no matter how many times I ring the bell no one will come and let me in, only small pathetic faces peeking at me through the sheers at the window. I am afraid if I ran away I would never be allowed to come back.

I won't leave the inside for now. I don't want to be wishing I could get back in.

III

The exquisite woman peers into my face. A grayish blue aura surrounds her angelic robes and fine, pale hair that swirls in an imaginary breeze. Everything in the background is blurry and indistinguishable and only her face is clear. She is speaking words to me but there is no sound, only her lips moving and the urgency I feel to hear her speak.

I am sinking. Into what, I don't know; I only know that I am sinking, dissolving into whatever lies beneath me. With an expression of sadness, her face begins to fade. I feel the slippery grip of water fold over my body and the air exhausted out of my lungs. I frantically flail my arms against a hopeless opposition. The woman is gone. Death seems as near to me as my last breath, when I bolt upright.

There is nothing about me but deep blackness. I slowly realize I have been dreaming. It's the same dream I have been having for months. I can hear Claire and Lillian sleeping in the bunk beside mine and I lie back down and fight the temptation to close my eyes again. I can feel the water rushing over me, and the slow descent to depths that have no end. It's true, I'm somewhat afraid of drowning, but this dream feels different and I wonder about the woman who is trying to help me.

When I was baptized I was worried about drowning. I worried that Father would lose his grip on my arm and I would slide mercilessly to the bottom of a great river.

He didn't let go of me. I was baptized by Father and Gerald, who held onto my left and right side before dunking me in the cool water. Mother was there too. She had prepared me for this day by reading about baptism and what it meant. She said from the day I was baptized henceforward I would be accountable for my actions. I would have to atone for my sins with heaps of repentance. She warned me that Satan would try to tempt me to do evil. She said baptism would wipe my slate clean and that all my sins would be erased and I would be perfected.

She said I had been an especially valiant spirit before I was born when we all lived in heaven or what Mother calls the preexistence. She said there was a war in heaven. I had fought on the side of Jesus and had been a rather great warrior otherwise I would not have been born into such a righteous family where the true gospel was taught. I wouldn't have been born to a family that was in the Work.

You are either born into the Work or you are a Gentile or an Apostate. You can join the Work if you want to but you have to believe the same way that we believe. Mother said it was a privilege being born into the Work and apparently I was a good soldier in heaven to earn this right. Mother made it sound rather exciting: being valiant and fighting in a war. I'd like to believe it even now. Me, up in heaven riding on a great white stallion, charging against the forces of the devil in a great war that challenged the fate of the world before it ever got started. It's nice to think I might have been a hero in another world, but I don't remember any of it.

But with baptism I had a chance at my former glory. I am ten years old now and so far, I haven't been much of a hero. I don't feel valiant or even particularly good. Sometimes I wonder if I am the only baptized person around for the devil to tempt.

I was only eight when I was baptized and Mother explained it all to me. I didn't understand everything she told me but I did understand the picture in the big Bible book of Jesus being dipped into the River Jordan by John the Baptist, a perfect white dove waiting in the background to perch on Jesus' shoulder. Mother told me that the dove symbolized the Holy Ghost and that the Holy Ghost was the Spirit of God. She said I would receive the Gift of the Holy Ghost at my own baptism, which I was quite anxious to experience. At the time I really believed that a dove would land on my shoulder and a perfect flashlight beam of light would envelop me, while the voice of God proclaimed me a beloved child.

It all turned out a bit differently than I expected. There was no river, no grassy bank, and no flowers in perfect bloom. There was no bright light, no voice of God. There were no spectators to witness the event and record it in their personal diaries. I was baptized in a swimming pool in someone's basement. It was over in fifteen minutes and we drove home in the rain, all so much the same. Except nothing was the same, and never would be again. Childish simplicity was drowned in the chlorinated waters and perfection was just out of reach—where it belonged.

There is a new picture in my head, one of Christ high on the mountaintop, the wind whipping his robes. Nearby is a red-skinned Satan, horned and cloven-hoofed, tempting him to turn his allegiance to the dark side. It took all of Jesus' power to resist the devil ... what hope do I have?

Mother says I can repent of my sins when the devil gets the better of me, but repentance isn't without its limitations. All my sins will be erased again, sort of like a mini-baptism, but if I should commit those sins again all past sins will be multiplied by seven and written on my clean slate. It's a terrible risk. I wonder if it isn't better to hold off on the repenting and just deal with the sins that I have.

I wonder what time it is. It feels like the very center of night. I think again of the woman in my dream. Maybe she is an angel assigned to watch over me. She is looking at the world through my eyes and when I look in the mirror I will see her there. I can never be entirely alone because she will be with me. I like to believe that.

I have considered all the sins that have accumulated since that night I was baptized. I think of the few times I summoned all the humility I possessed and begged for forgiveness. I can imagine all the inky black marks of my sins, times seven, reappearing like magic on a blank page in the book of life.

Points for the devil.

IV

"Don't do it," I whisper. It's dark in the kitchen and I can hear the TV on in the playroom. Tom and I are crouched down in the hallway.

"I'll be fine," Tom says so softly I can hardly make out the words. He tiptoes across the kitchen toward the corner cupboard. He moves with precision and stealth and manages to reach the cabinet soundlessly. We're supposed to be doing homework. I have two English assignments that have to be rewritten and a book report. Tom has to finish a history assignment and twelve pages in his phonics book. Mother Kay gives us so much to do that it cannot be done in a day. School is so long too. It starts at eight in the morning and ends at five in the afternoon. If we don't get the assignments done by lunch then we have to skip lunch and get them finished. After lunch we get all our afternoon assignments. If we don't get those done then we skip dinner until we are finished.

Neither of us has eaten since breakfast.

Mother Kay has to pass off our assignments with a big stroke of her red pen before we can go to bed. Ruby, Emily, and Danny finished their homework about an hour ago. All of us are in the same grade even though Ruby and Emily are thirteen, that's three years older than I am, and Danny twelve, a year and half older. Mother Kay wants us all in the same grade to make teaching easier. I can't imagine what is so hard about writing a bunch of stuff for us to do on the chalkboard and then disappearing. But I don't complain about the disappearing part.

I watch Tom with a kind of raw admiration as he plunges his hand into the bag of brown sugar while keeping one eye on the playroom.

Tom is my twin. Well, not exactly my twin but we are the same age, born just months apart. Tom likes to boast about being older than me and he thrives on teasing me. He likes to make me laugh or cry, enjoying both in equal proportions.

There's a rustling sound upstairs.

"Tom, someone's coming!" I hurry back to my desk in the schoolroom but I know it's too late for Tom.

"What do you think you're doing?" says Mother Kay standing on the bottom step, one hand on her hip, the other on the railing. Tom's face drops, his hand still clutching a lump of brown sugar. Mother Kay reaches for the stick from on top of the refrigerator. Tom can see his fate glinting in Mother Kay's green eyes.

He makes a daring escape right past her and into the hall toward the bookcase. He climbs to the top shelf, just inches below the ceiling, like a squirrel scurrying up a tree. It's empty and he crawls inside it. Mother Kay bangs her stick on the bookcase trying to hit him through the shelf; her anger surfaces and bursts forth like the birth of a living thing.

"Get down from there right now or you're gonna get it!" she barks. "You think you're so smart that you can get away with stealing? Get down here right now!" Her voice booms through the house and she looks as if she might climb the bookcase and drag him down herself when Father appears.

"What's going on here?" Father is perturbed.

"Tom's trying to get out of a whipping." Mother Kay's face is red and flushed.

"What did he do?"

"I caught him *stealing sugar*." She raises an eyebrow, expecting Father to realize the severity of Tom's crime.

"Well," he says, "he's probably hungry."

"That's his fault; he didn't get his schoolwork done and missed his meals."

"Leave him alone, Mother," he says, a surprising firmness in his voice.

"But Father! He was …"

Father cuts her off short.

"I said, leave him alone." Father's voice is steely. In that moment I love Father more than I thought was possible.

Mother Kay tries to hide her bewilderment, trying to convince Father all the way upstairs and into his bedroom. Father doesn't say a word. I am convinced that if Father was around more he would see the way things really are. He would make Mother Kay change.

It's all wishful thinking. I know it's not the end for Tom. Mother Kay will find a way to make him pay for what he did. I can only hope I'm nowhere around when it happens. I've watched her hit him. She doesn't let me leave. She makes him lean over his desk while she hits him with the stick on his back over and over and over. The sound of the stick hitting his spine and ribs leaves me feeling nauseous. I can't count how many times I have had to witness with either my eyes or my ears, or both, the relentless and unpredictable beating of another human being with the fearsome white stick. Each time is fresh like the first time, and the feeling of helplessness reasserts itself. That is why I turn my face away and hold my head in my hands. I cannot stop it. I want to be his friend and it feels like when she beats Tom and not me she is trying to take our friendship away.

So far she hasn't been able to take it away. Tom tells me things he doesn't tell anyone else. He has a radio and sometimes he takes me in his closet under the basement stairs and we listen to Def Leopard or Alice Cooper. I pretend to like his music but when he and Danny go to the garden with Mother Helen to work in the evening after we are done with our schoolwork, I sneak into his closet and listen to Ronnie Millsap and Michael Martin Murphy. There are magazines in his closet, hiding under a coat. He gets them from old Mrs. Larsen. She pays him five dollars a week to walk her dog, a little black terrier named Toby. He tricked Mrs. Larsen into ordering a subscription for him under her name and he picks them up right out of her mailbox and hides them in a sack under his shirt. I want to look inside the magazines but I don't dare. I've seen one before. Danny and Tom had found it in a dumpster. Ruby and Emily looked at it with us. It was disgusting and exciting all at once. It was a big deal when Father found out. Emily talked me into going with her to testify about the magazine. I thought I was doing the right thing, but when I saw the boys being humiliated in front of the family and getting in so much trouble from Father and the mothers, I decided I was on the wrong side. Emily said we were doing it for their salvation and one day they would thank us, but the feeling of ratting on them was one I wasn't willing to live with.

Tom trusts me now.

V

"I can't" is a slugger too lazy to try.

That's what Mother tells me, but she doesn't understand. It's not that I can't, but that I won't. She wants me to be like her when she knows, deep down, I'm not. I know Mother is worried about me. She doesn't say it, but I can feel her concern pulsing out from her body to mine, like electrical shocks.

Mother says I'm being stubborn. I must be stubborn not for the sake of being stubborn but because I have to; for some overwhelming urge to protect myself, I must. For Mother's sake I pretend I don't need to be stubborn. She says I can turn it around and be stubborn about being a righteous person; I can be stubborn about being good. I want to be good but I want something else more. I don't want to make sacrifices in hopes of being rewarded for it in the life hereafter. I don't want to wait for God to execute final justice when my life is over. What I want is here, right now.

Sometimes I think that Mother believes I belong to her, that she *knows* me. But I feel severed from her, like a genetic displacement. I am urged away from her in a blind direction and I know when I am grown up I will follow this urge, I will follow it like the wind, uncertain of a destination.

I don't know why this is so difficult to do what Mother is telling me to do. But the thought of it feels like I'm feeding my own flesh to wolves. Mother says it's the right thing to do but it feels like the most wrong thing possible. She talked to me for a couple of hours, trying to bend my mind into seeing it her way. I indulge in her distress over me, but the payoff is just too small. "It will make you feel better" isn't enough. Besides, I know it won't make me feel better, it will make *Mother* feel better. She said I can have until tonight to do it. She didn't say I could decide but I know that, at some cost, I can.

I just want it to be over. Mother hasn't spoken to me since this morning.

Mother says it is the nature of man to lie and that children are born liars. It is the job of the parents to lead the *born liars* back to innocence. I try not to lie but when the stakes are high, I find a falsehood irresistible. I've lied before and succeeded in avoiding punishment. But there are times when even lying is just the least painful choice. I know when Mother Kay asks me if I'm the one who took the breath mints out of Father's sock drawer, she wants me to say yes and thinks

I'll say no. The decision to be predictable rather than submissive is an easy one. It doesn't matter what actually happened, I'll say whatever I need to, to minimize the end result. As long as I stick with my answer 100 percent, she can't prove a thing. She can accuse me of lying and try to intimidate me into telling her what she wants to hear, but unless I say otherwise, it's her word against mine. Sometimes it feels like a tug of war with the odds stacked against me but I'd rather go down with a fight than give in and join the other side.

I hadn't touched anything from Mother Kay's closet. It was somebody else, but I was the one accused. Mother believes Mother Kay in spite of my pleading of innocence. She said I need to tell the truth in order to redeem myself. She says the truth will set me free.

Mother Kay's pretty certain it was me, otherwise it would have turned into a Session. Usually when something happens and there aren't any obvious suspects, Mother Kay sends all of us to the playroom where we're sequestered and pressured into either fussing up or ratting on someone else. Some of the Sessions have lasted all day. Eventually, hunger, guilt, or fear will break the silence and someone will be appropriately punished while the rest are free to go. After a Session, I'm not sure who I can trust.

Father should be home any minute and by then it will be too late. I don't want to do this in front of Father, and I know once he comes home Mother Kay will be glued to him all evening.

I stand at the top of the playroom stairs and watch Mother Kay on the couch, reading the newspaper. Every part of my physical being is telling me to turn and run the other way but I force my feet down the stairs.

"I'm sorry."

Her eyes appear neatly over the top of the newspaper.

"What are you sorry for?" It's not really a question but more of a test.

"I'm sorry for getting in your closet and looking at your stuff."

"Why did you lie about it?"

"I guess I didn't want you to know."

"Well, you know you're getting two whippings for that don't you? One for getting into things without asking and the other for lying."

I nod.

It's the worst kind of lie.

VI

I'm not used to being alone. The hunger inside of my body is loud. I can't hear anything else. I have been locked up before, when I didn't finish my report on the Cayuga Indians. It was only for a day and a night. I don't know how long I am going to be in here. I really can't write very fast. But I wrote the rule wrong and now I have to write it the proper way.

It's the K rule. Five hundred times. Something about K not being used alone at the end of a sentence but spelled with a CK instead. The rule is written in the most complicated way possible. It is a long rule and takes up three and a half lines. Of course my handwriting has to be perfectly neat, with each letter formed according to her specifications. Mother Kay is very picky about how my handwriting looks. It takes me a long time to write the whole rule even once. I can't imagine how long it will take me to write it five hundred times. It feels impossible. I have written furiously all night. It was scary being here alone last night, writing and writing, with the quiet, smothering sound of silence and the knowledge that everyone else is sleeping sweetly in their beds.

I wait for Rumpelstiltskin to come and offer to help me in exchange for my firstborn, but no one comes, not even Claire or Lillian peeking under the door to cheer me on. I think I fell asleep a few times on my desk. I wrote the K rule fifty times last night. I have so much more to go. I force my eyes to stay open. Write, write, write.

The last time I was in here, I was with Danny. He made it fun, like we weren't being punished. We played encyclopedia. He would browse through an encyclopedia for pictures of famous people and then I would try to guess what that person looked like. Sir Isaac Newton, Albert Schweitzer, Margaret Meade. I tried to guess outrageously so he would laugh. Our favorite game is Map, shooting spit wads at various continents on the world atlas that hangs on the wall and memorizing European countries and their capitals. We also read Mother Kay's *American Health* magazine. There are at least one or two subscriptions on the shelf behind the door. She's into *health*. She reads *Prevention Magazine, Organic Gardening,* and buys cookbooks with recipes for tofu stir-fry and soybean cookies. I don't think she reads *American Health* though because Danny read something once about men having sex with other men. I didn't believe it but he showed me the article. Sex is still an undigested topic for me.

When Mother Kay locked me in with Tom and Danny, they showed me a sketched figure of a man lying on top of a woman in a medical encyclopedia. They let me read the article on human reproduction. I was mortified. Pictures of the Big Girls who recently married older men flashed, unwanted, across my mental screen. "It can't be true!" I wailed. Danny and Tom laughed. I never wanted to be shocked again so I decided to learn anything I could about the subject. I cross-referenced everything I read about sex in the magazines with the medical dictionary. I learned all that the available information could teach me, but it wrestles uncomfortably in my stomach.

I'm so hungry. I think about the pictures of Ethiopians I had seen in *National Geographic*, their stomachs distended, their eyes haunted for want of basic human needs. I don't want my stomach to look like that. When I was a little bit younger, like six or seven, I threw food away that I didn't like such as eggplant, spinach, beans. I was pretty good at hiding the food I didn't want in a napkin and asking to use the bathroom. I would then flush it down the toilet. Today, I imagine all that food I didn't want, sitting on my desk right now.

My hand is starting to shake so much that writing is difficult. I wrote another twenty-five. I don't know how much longer I can go. When I stand up my whole body is dried wood and rusty hinges. I stretch and walk over to the window to get some snow from the shed roof. It feels good going down into my stomach. But my hands are shaking uncontrollably now. I sit down on them to keep them still. My hair is messy; strands that have nowhere to go tickle my chin. I've never been a whole day without combing my hair and it has been two days. My braids are coarse and rough, with the hair coming out. I've never been this long without talking to someone. It's Saturday afternoon and I can hear all the hubbub going on through the house. I stand next to the door and press my ear lightly against it. I ache to be out there doing all the jobs I hate to do. I can hear Claire and Mother doing Saturday cleaning, talking, laughing. I imagine the curtains on the dining room windows are taken down and an unmuffled brightness fills the room, the mist of window cleaner falling gently to the floor. I can smell dinner—meatloaf and baked potatoes, I'm sure of it—and I can hear more voices and clanging dishes. If I really strain I can hear kids in the playroom playing games. I am angry and hungry and so tired. I wonder if I have been forgotten or if this is the punishment that I am meant to have.

I go back and sit at my desk, pick up my pencil, which desperately needs sharpening, and try to force my hand to obey. I write five more. I reward myself with a treat by taking a peek in the teachers' edition at Monday's English lesson and copy the answers on a piece of scratch paper. If I make it to one hundred, I'll copy down the answers to one page of division.

Mother Kay comes to check on me. She seems a little nicer, like maybe she knows she overreacted but can't admit it yet. I have to use the bathroom; she follows me inside and locks the door. At first I wonder what she is going to do to me. Then I realize she is going to watch me. I pretend not to be embarrassed. When I am done, she follows me back to the schoolroom. The hardest part is hearing the keys lock out the rest of the world.

Whenever I'm locked in the schoolroom, I sleep in the closet. There's a heater vent in there and I can fit perfectly under the shoe rack next to the vent. For some reason I don't feel so alone in there. When Danny and I were in here last time, it was really cold because the window's broken, and I was sick and shivering with chills. Danny crawled through the window and snuck into the basement and got a blanket. I was so touched by his willingness to risk getting in trouble for me. I don't think I will ever forget that. Mother Kay caught us the next morning, asleep in the closet with the blanket wrapped around us, and Danny immediately 'fessed up and took a whipping for it. I feel bad for Danny; it seems he's always getting in trouble. His mouth is full of canker sores and it makes it hard for him to talk. Mother says it's because he worries so much. And he has lost a lot of weight since we started doing home school. We went to a private school for a few years. I went only for one year. Mother called the private school a priesthood school because it was run by the Priesthood Council. I think Father decided to start home school because of the split, and the people that were running the school decided to follow Brother Davidson. Father doesn't believe in Brother Davidson's authority anymore so we weren't invited to the priesthood school anymore.

Danny is so thin now that his pants would fall to his ankles when he stood up if he didn't gather them up in his hands and hold them. It feels like we never get to eat. I know I am thin, but I don't know if I am as thin as Danny is. I wish Danny was in here with me.

I thought Sunday would never get here but it's here. It's been three whole days. At least I think it has. I don't have a calendar in here. A schoolroom without a calendar, how do you like that? I guess there is no reason for us to use it. Every day just fuses into the next; what's the point of cutting it all up in pieces like a birthday cake you know you will never get to eat? Mother Kay let me out this afternoon. I nearly wrote two hundred. I think that is amazing. Though I am sure I would never have been able to reach five hundred. I'm not sure why she let me out before I was finished. Maybe Father told her to. Maybe she didn't realize how long it would take me. Maybe because school starts again for everyone else in the morning and it simply isn't convenient to have me tying up the schoolroom. Whatever her reason, she's not too angry and she said I could eat Sunday dinner. It's been three days since Mother Kay locked the schoolroom door and I finally get to eat. We're having spaghetti squash and peas. And bread. I will eat until it hurts.

VII

"Throw it out!"

Ruby gets plenty of encouragement as she stands at the window, holding the white stick in her hand above her head.

"Do it ... hurry, before Mother Kay comes back!" Danny looks nervously at the locked door. Ruby gives a long toss and the piece of poly tubing flies straight over the fence and lands on the roof of the single floor apartment building next door.

"Oh, no! She'll see it there!" Ruby covers her hand with her mouth. Tom stands guard with his ear on the door, listening for suspicious sounds while the rest of us crowd around the window. The stick rolls toward the rain gutter.

"C'mon ... faallll!" says Emily. Gradually the stick slides in jerky movements until it dangles over the rain gutter.

"She's coming!" Tom says, taking his seat at the desk next to mine. I can see his hand is shaking slightly as he picks up his pencil and starts working on his spelling words. I have my handwriting book open to page 134. The lock rattles. I touch my cheek with my hand. It's hot and flushed: the look of guilt. Ruby is bent over her history book and the stick is still balanced on the rain gutter. The door opens and Mother Kay comes in holding the padlock and keys in her hand. Her light brown hair is pulled straight back, a few reckless hairs at her temples. I glance over at Tom to see if he noticed her hair. But he doesn't risk looking up at me. Mother Kay is wearing the same peach-colored maternity dress with its white yoke and cuffs that she wore yesterday. I hope she doesn't notice what page I'm doing because I am ten pages behind.

She maneuvers her way between our desks and I can feel her dress brush past me on her way to the front of the room. Her slow methodic movements make it difficult to know what she is going to do next, but she slides into her seat and opens the top drawer. A thick orange notebook comes out of her desk and she flips it open and sighs.

"You guys missed a good lunch. Whew. I'm full." None of us look up at her. I can hear the scratch of her pen as she sorts through the piles of assignments, marking them up. She is correcting papers. She looks like a judge sitting on an elevated platform, passing sentences on criminals as she flings unsatisfactory papers back on our desks.

"Danny?" her voice startles me.

Danny looks up from his desk through the tops of his eyes, his straight brown hair falling neatly to his eyebrows.

"What?" he squeaks. His face is splotchy red and I can hear him breathing.

"Where are your spelling words?"

He scrambles through his desk looking hopelessly for what he knows is unfinished.

"Well?"

"Uh … I guess … um …"

"Just spit it out, Danny. It can't be that hard."

"I … guess I don't have it done."

"Why not? Didn't I tell you to have them finished before you went to bed last night?"

"Yeah."

I can't stand seeing Danny so nervous. I am sure the canker sores in his mouth are multiplying.

"What am I going to do to get you to finish the work I give you? Huh?"

Danny holds his head low.

"Well?"

"I dunno," he says.

"I do." Mother Kay reaches across her desk for the stick. I drop my head. Danny is on trial and I hold my breath.

"Where's my stick?"

He shrugs.

"Ruby?"

"I haven't seen it today," she says in her expert voice.

"It was here this morning. It didn't just disappear. Now where is it?"

None of us say anything.

"Don't just sit there like a bunch of dummies! Emily, go find me another one!"

Emily comes back empty handed, saying she couldn't find one.

"You're going to get it tomorrow when I find my stick." She turns back to her stack of papers; her irritation makes me nervous.

I've looked at the clock a hundred times since Mother Kay left to eat dinner. We are supposed to work on our war reports until she comes back. They are due at the end of the month. When she gave us the assignment, she wrote the names of five major wars on the chalkboard. I picked the American Revolution, Danny and Tom picked the two World Wars, and Emily chose the Civil War. That left Ruby with the Spanish-American War. I am sure glad I didn't get stuck with that one. There is no way I could find enough information to fill the required ten pages.

I knew I wanted to do my report on the American Revolution the minute she wrote it on the board. I like the idea of the ragged underdog colonists defeating the tyrannical King George III and his world-renowned armies. I can't decide which hero I like better: Nathan Hale, who said, "I only regret that I have but one life to lose for my country," or Patrick Henry and his speech he gave at the convention. I read his entire speech over and over. I have memorized the last paragraph and I have decided that my favorite line is not his famous quote, "Give me liberty or give me death," but the line just before that: "Is life so dear and peace so sweet as to be purchased at the price of chains and slavery? Forbid it, Almighty God!"

Peace. What a funny word that is. Mother is telling me all the time to keep the peace. "Don't rock the boat or cause ripples in the pond." Someday I'm going to ask her if life is so dear and peace so sweet as to be purchased at the price of chains and slavery.

I can hear the tinkle of silverware in the kitchen. I can smell corn on the cob, fresh bread, and I'm not sure what else. My hand is cramped from writing all day and there's a dent in my forefinger where the pencil has pressed against it. It's dark outside. The stick is long forgotten.

There are voices at the door and the unlocking of the padlock. Father and Mother Kay come in carrying bowls of hot cherry cobbler in their hands.

"So Mother Kay tells me that you guys aren't doing your schoolwork very good? Is that true?" Father's voice is pleasant. I can see the steam from the bowl in his hand rising in swirls up toward the ceiling.

"Susanna?" Father puts his big hand on top of my head.

"I guess."

"Guys, is it true?"

Everyone nods, looking away from Father's face.

"Well, Mother, I guess you were right. They will have to go without a few more meals to help them learn."

He put the bowl of cobbler under my face, and after sufficiently allowing me to view and smell it, he moves the bowl around the room and under every nose. Mother Kay stands at the doorway, eating spoonfuls in front of us.

"See what you're missing?" she says after she swallows the last bite.

The two of them walk out of the room locking the door behind them.

VIII

Emily told me a secret.

She made me follow her to the basement before she would tell me a word. The basement is the most obvious place to go, a container of secrets already. It is separated from the rest of the house by an old style door, with a worn, dull brass knob that feels loose when you turn it. The yellowing white paint is chipped and scratched and looks especially chewed on at the edges, and the hinges creak appropriately. There's thin carpeting on one wall of the staircase and it is dark, the way basements are supposed to be. Even with the light on it's dim and dank smelling.

The stairs make noise, each stair a signature sound. They are slabs of two-inch particleboard nailed to the frame. I've banged my knees on countless occasions while trying to take them in twos. The stairs have a black smudge right in the middle, where everyone walks. Mother has me scrub the stairs with a bucket of soapy water. I don't mind this job; the fragrance of the wet wood smells like the beginning of something new.

I sleep in the basement with the other middle kids. The parents with babies and small children sleep upstairs, and the Big Girls rotate sleeping in the bed of whichever mother spends the night with Father. The other Big Girls sleep on the sofas. I've been up early enough in the morning to see Maria or Ella, in weathered-looking robes, gather up the previous day's clothes in a wad while morphing the bed back into a couch. Maria and Ella are married now and it's Camille and Charlotte who share the sofas.

I sleep on the top bunk in a three-walled room. One wall is concrete, the other two sheetrock. I sleep on the sheetrock side. Lillian sleeps on the single bed by the concrete wall, and Claire sleeps underneath me. Ruby and Emily sleep on folding beds that are covered with a thin blanket during the day. The closet is the small space under the basement stairs with a copper pipe mounted to the wall for hanging our dresses. The cement floor is painted a blue-gray. The room next over is the boys' room: Danny, Tom, Glenn, and Albert. It has a door on it and a small window up near the ceiling. It used to be the schoolroom when we first started home school but the schoolroom has been moved to the main floor.

I like the basement. I like that its walls are uncovered and everything is exposed: wires slithering up the two-by-fours, a maze of copper pipes that run water through the house, and black PVC that makes a lot of noise when a toilet flushes upstairs. Spider webs are strung like pale string in the corners and behind boxes of old clothes. Everything is right out in the open. Mother told me once that your guardian angel will not follow you underground; she said it's the devil's territory and he has great power over the underworld. The basement is underground. I remember when Father and Gerald dug out the dirt by hand with shovels and buckets to make the room where I sleep. I think Mother is wrong. The basement is the safest place in the house.

Emily looked over her shoulder to make sure I was following and no one was watching us. She walked casually over to the water softener and motioned for me to come. She was wearing a green-checkered dress with a tiny black ribbon tied at the neck. Emily has jet-black hair that's as thick as it is long and nicely contrasts with her pale olive skin. She parts it in the middle and pulls it back into two braids. Her round and somewhat bulgy blue eyes give her a sleepy look. She carries her body in a slump like she's holding an invisible world on her shoulders. Once we were seated on the cold cement floor between the water softener and the brine barrel, Emily peeked out of the hiding place and looked both ways before she spoke.

"You can't tell a soul."

It seems Emily always has a secret, and is always telling me I can't tell a soul. But she unburdens herself on me. I don't mind. I like knowing things that others don't. I like being trusted and Emily reveals herself to me like the handwriting on the basement walls.

The basement has been the place where secrets are told and have been told for a long time. People have been writing on these walls since long before I was born. Melinda, Sheri, Heidi, and Don. There are names, dates, and height measurements of brothers and sisters who were grown up and gone before I started writing my name on the basement walls. But most intriguing are the messages. Short cryptic messages meant only for others who might, at some future point, share an understanding about the words.

Emily keeps looking around the storage room, jittery, like she's about to be captured.

"Promise?" she pleads when her story is finished.

"I promise. Cross my heart, hope to die." I do the motions over my heart.

The light in the basement flashes on and off. It's someone at the top of the stairs. Emily whispers "Not a soul," on her way to the stairs. I stay hidden between the softener and the brine barrel, hardly breathing. I can hear Mother Kay's voice. I can hear Emily's answer. "Of course I'll come and work on your feet. I'll be right there."

I decide to write my own message to future secret seekers and holders. "I am not a robot," I write in blue pen behind the furnace. I squint at the words and mouth them back to myself as if reading them for the first time. I want to write Emily's secret on the wall; the weight of it is like pressure on my lungs. But a promise is a promise.

IX

"You missed some crumbs," says Danny.

"Where?"

"Over on the other table, at the end."

I pull the sandwich baggie from my apron pocket, its menagerie of scraps bouncing loosely inside. I use my free hand to scrape the breadcrumbs from the cloth and into my bag. The smell of the food remnants on the plates is driving me crazy. Once I'm out of sight of the others I can lick the plates streaked with spaghetti sauce and gobble up any stray peas. I wipe my chin with a wadded up napkin already stained by someone else's mouth, and carry the stacked plates over to the sink where Ruby is making suds in the hot water with her hand. When the tables are cleared and the cloths are in the laundry basket, I turn over the bag of crumbs to Danny.

"This will be perfect for tomorrow," he says tucking the baggie in his desk. Danny is the only one of us with enough self-control to keep food in his desk and not eat it all himself. He will divvy it out among us for lunch tomorrow. Between the crumbs and the snow from the shed roof it should be a better day. If we have to do the dishes alone again tomorrow, I hope someone makes cornbread. It's really crumbly.

I don't think about my stomach too much anymore, except when we are called to prayer. We have to walk right past dinner on the stove. Last week there was a pan full of steamed red potatoes and a tray of meatloaf sitting on the counter; I couldn't help myself. The kitchen was empty, with everyone kneeling in the playroom waiting for the five of us to come to prayer. I stuffed a potato in my mouth and swiped a corner off the meatloaf, gulping everything whole on my way out. The hunger awakens and the desire to eat is a persistent moaning inside of me. But the best way to forget about being hungry is to be with the others, to see the same pale skin, the sad, hollow eyes. It helps when we make fun of each other. I look like an ostrich with a big head, and Danny can touch his thumb and forefinger through his armpit and collar bone. Then we can laugh; then it's all right.

"Hey, Sus, if you'll help me dry the dishes I'll finish telling you about the movie." Emily extends a dishtowel in my direction. I take it and drape it over my hand.

"Which one?"

"*Raiders of the Lost Ark.*"

"Ooh, is that the one with Indiana Jones and the pretty girl?"

"Yes, ya wanna hear what happens next?" I grab a plastic plate and start drying. "Okay, where was I?"

"You were at the part were Indiana Jones gets hurt." I know she already knows this.

"Oh yeah," she can't even think about what comes next without smiling.

"So he's laying there, and the girl, I forgot her name … oh well. Anyways, he's laying there and the girl is leaning over him with this worried look on her face when he opens his eyes and tries to smile. She comes in close and you can see her," Emily points to her bosom, "her you know what and says, 'Shhhh, tell me where it hurts.' And Indiana Jones points to his head and she leans over his face and kisses his head. He's likin' this so he picks up his arm and points to his elbow. She kisses his elbow and they gaze into each other's eyes."

"Oh, they did not!" Ruby says. "Quit makin' stuff up!"

"They did too! You just didn't notice."

"I watched it too, ya know!"

"Pleeease," I say, "let her finish. I don't care if they gazed in each other's eyes or not."

Emily looks over at Ruby and continues. "Anyways, so then after she kisses his elbow he points to his eye and she kisses his eye. Now he's *really* likin' it."

"More like you're really likin' it," says Ruby.

"Oh hush up!"

"Sorry, Susanna," says Emily, "I'll be able to finish if Ruby ever lets me." She goes on. "Then he points to his mouth and raises his eyebrows. Ohmyheck, you shoulda seen how cute he was when he did that." Emily starts a giggle. "Then she kisses him really good on the lips." She sighs and her gaze disappears somewhere between the wall and the window.

"What happens next?"

"I'll tell ya some more tonight after we go to bed," she says, still in a trance. She turns back around to the drainer and doesn't say another word.

Emily doesn't finish the story even though I have been waiting in bed for her. Mother Kay is talking to her at the top of the basement stairs. I can almost tell exactly what Mother Kay is saying by the waving pitch of her voice—up and down, likes she's asking a lot of questions that she doesn't want the answers to. I keep peeking up the stairway to see if she is almost done so Emily can come to bed, but it looks like it might be a while the way Emily is twitching her mouth and playing with the buttons on her robe.

Mother Kay takes Emily upstairs to Father's room all the time and talks to her for hours. I have to do Emily's work while she's gone. I don't like the way she comes back all quiet and depressed, and I don't bother asking her what Mother Kay said.

The next day Emily is a goody-two-shoes during school. Ruby leans back on her chair when Mother Kay's not looking and does devil horns over Emily's head.

X

I am glad I got sick, especially for the fever. No one can fake a fever. Mother let me sleep on the floor in her bedroom. Strep throat, she called it. I like the sound of it: dangerous like Hante virus or a staph infection. Grandpa died of a staph infection when I was eight. I wonder if you can die from strep throat. I didn't move from the little mattress on the floor for two weeks. It took my full attention just to swallow my own saliva. I eventually started to feel better but there was a constant ache in my bones and I felt an unusual fatigue. I didn't bother telling anyone. You can't see tired, you can't rest your hand on it or hear it like a rattle in the chest.

After the two weeks of sickness the swelling started. My feet looked like balloons when I woke up in the morning. I couldn't walk. Besides being painful, my feet were no longer flat on the bottom and I fell each time I tried to stand. Mother was wonderfully worried. She made Father come and see my feet and I could hear her whispering to him about taking me to the hospital. The hospital. That sounded like a great idea. Please rush me to the emergency room, preferably in an ambulance. But Father doused the idea. "Don't overreact," he chided her. The next day my other joints had started to swell. I had wet myself during the night while trying to get to the bathroom, crawling up the basement stairs on my knees. Mother's concern was palpable. "She'll be fine," Father said before leaving for work. I didn't want to be fine and I didn't like Father jeopardizing the amount of attention I was getting from Mother.

Mother was undaunted. She called someone on the telephone as soon as Father left for work, running through my symptoms and nodding her head. Mother Kay was eating breakfast at the table, listening to the conversation. When Mother got off the phone I could plainly hear their brief argument from behind the door in Mother's bedroom. Mother said she was now certain I had rheumatic fever. Mother Kay was certain I did not have rheumatic fever and that I was faking it. Mother was a little upset and asked Mother Kay if she wanted to see my feet and tell me how I could fake swelling. Mother Kay just said, "Don't let her fool you into thinking it's worse than it really is." It was an argument that Mother won and I was put on bed rest and milk and aspirin three times a day until further notice. No stairs allowed. I moved back into Mother's bedroom.

Each day it got a little worse until just breathing seemed to get my heart rate up; so I slept and slept and slept. I lost more weight although the regular milk allowed me to feel nourished. Some days my bones hurt so much I couldn't sleep, so I laid on Mother's bed, eyes wide open, listening to the world just beyond the bedroom door.

I like looking at myself in Mother's bedroom mirror, my face as pale as the moon and dark rings under my eyes. I feel like Tiny Tim Cratchet. I have to stay in Mother's bedroom until she says I have completely recovered. When I'm not sleeping Mother brings me baskets of laundry to fold because I can do it while sitting on her bed. I'm getting behind on my schoolwork so Mother has been bringing me math pages to work on. I wish I could do all my school like this, sitting in the safety of Mother's bedroom. I wish I could be sick for the rest of my life. I keep trying to be sicker than I really am, telling Mother I am tired when I'm really starting to get my energy back.

I know I'm going to be fine. I knew it from the very first day. I don't know how I know this, but I'm not telling anyone.

XI

Father says we should all try to be policemen. He says if we see someone doing something they're not supposed to be doing that we should tell on them. He said we need to weed out the wickedness that is creeping into our family. He had the whole family gather in the playroom to discuss it. He said there are people who are being directly disobedient and he needs us to come forward if we have any information. He didn't exactly say the word spy, but I know he is asking us to spy on each other. I won't do it. The idea of being a policeman just makes me mad. The parents just assume that we are all up to something bad. It's a pretrial verdict: guilty until proven innocent.

Some of us are convicted before we have a chance to prove ourselves. Mother Kay told us in morning class that some spirits are born into the family to persecute the more valiant ones and that the Lord knows who they are and that they aren't going to make it to heaven. So he sends them as opposition to the family members being tested. Like Tom, she said. Tom was sitting next to me with his head down, looking at his shoes. I don't know why she hates Tom.

She didn't even have to say Ruby's name for me to know she thinks that about her. She doesn't just hate Ruby, she despises her. I have to admit, Ruby doesn't try to be nice to her either. She smarts off and gets herself in trouble all the time. I've learned that I need to pretend I like Mother Kay. I'm good at pretending. I'll even pretend to be a policeman. But I am worried about Lillian and Emily. They'll feel like they have to tell, even when they don't want to. I don't know why they do what the parents tell them to do or believe everything Mother Kay tells us in morning class. Morning class is like Sunday school only shorter and we have one every morning after breakfast when Father and Mother Helen have left for work. Mother Kay thinks she is in charge of the whole family, telling us what Father wants us to do. I don't think Father knows half of what Mother Kay is saying to us. She just wants to control everyone and everything. Like yesterday, when I said the opening prayer and Mother Kay corrected me in front of the whole family. I guess I said the prayer wrong because I asked Heavenly Father to help everyone in the family to have a good attitude. Mother Kay said that I was practicing universalism, like the word *attitude* was some form of witchcraft. She said I am not to deviate from the way the Priesthood Council has taught us to pray. I know she wanted me to ask her what universalism meant so she could lecture me some more, but I just said, "You're right. I'm sorry, it won't happen again." After class I looked up "universalism" in the dictionary.

After my prayer yesterday, Mother Kay took it upon herself this morning to go over the proper way to pray, to say things in the right order.

"Please bless the Priesthood Council.

Please bless Father and the mothers that they will be blessed with the spirit of God to teach us right.

Please bless those who are traveling on the roads and highways that they will come home in peace and in safety.

Please bless the sick and afflicted that they will get well and strong again.

Thank you for our many blessings.

Please help us to do what is right and mind Father and the mothers.

We say these things in the name of Jesus Christ. Amen."

Pronounced "amen" and not "ahmen." "Ahmen" is for *Little House on the Prairie* and Billy Graham, not for people in the Work. Sometimes I want to say it "ahmen" just to see what everyone would do but I haven't worked up the nerve yet.

Father called on me to talk in Sunday school. I was half expecting it and came prepared. I stood up in front of the family and told everyone how I needed to do better and how important it was to listen to the parents and that the Lord had placed them over us to guide and protect us. I said I needed to be a better example for my little brothers and sisters. I said I knew the Lord would protect those who chose the right. I could tell Mother was boring a hole straight through me, but I kept my gaze on Father's shoes. Before I sat down I glanced over at Mother Kay sitting by the window. She was checking Father's reaction and I was checking hers.

Except for Sunday school, Sundays are the best day of the week. I get to sleep in until seven thirty, there's no regular school, and everyone is home, including all the Big Boys. In the evening, Charlotte plays the piano and we sing songs to Father and whomever he brings home from Meeting with him. Most of the time it's Aunt Liesel. She isn't really our aunt; in fact, she is a German immigrant, but Father told us to call her Aunt Liesel out of respect. Charlotte taught us "Brahms' Lullaby" in German. Aunt Liesel had taught it to her when Charlotte had spent the week at her house. Now, when Father brings Aunt Liesel home with him from Meeting, she insists we sing it to her in German. It goes like this:

"Guten Abend gute nacht, von engline bewacht

Die zeigen im traum, dir christkindleins baum
Schlaf nun selig und sus, shau im traums paradies
Schlaf nun selig und sus, schau im traums paradies."

Aunt Liesel says the first line means something like "Good evening, good night." And the last line means "Sleep in peace and paradise." I think it's beautiful and I like hearing the new sounds in my throat and mouth. She says when we can sing the song without an accent, she will teach us more.

Aunt Liesel has been old since I have known her but she reminisces to me about her younger days, of the carefree years before the war. She boasts to me of nude pictures of her and her girlfriends diving into the Rhine. She tells me that her coarse gray hair, twisted in a knot with a stick in it, was once a luxurious chestnut brown and the envy of all the girls her age. She says when I see the picture I will notice her large and firm breasts. She cups her aging ones in her hands and sighs. In spite of the creased heavy skin of her face and the deeply streaked gray and white of her hair, I believe her. I believe that she was once young and beautiful. I think she is the first adult who I can envision as a child or young person. There is something in her eyes and manners that tells me she was strong and intelligent in her native land. But here, in the United States, she is just an old woman, a refugee that says "be" instead of "am." "I be okay," she says when I ask her how she is doing. She promises someday to tell me her story but says that for now I am too young to understand. I know she cannot speak of it right now.

Aunt Liesel joined the Work a long time ago. The rest of her family members are Gentiles and some of them still live in Germany. She is different than any adult I know. Aunt Liesel would never keep secrets and I would tell her anything.

XII

Mother Kay says I'm a liar and a thief and a bad example to Claire and Lillian. She thinks I'm going to criticize her behind her back and make Lillian and Claire hate her. She has a paper taped to the inside of her bedroom door: the ten rules of criticism. It goes something like this: "First you hear something you don't understand, then you murmur about it, then you complain, and then you criticize, and all kinds of terrible things happen all because you didn't understand." It's something like that but I think it's stupid. It's like she hung it up on her door just to make me mad. It was written by one of the Priesthood Council. She says criticism is an abomination in the eyes of the Lord and points our attention to the saying that hangs in an oval frame on the playroom wall.

> These six things doth the Lord hate;
> Yea, seven is an abomination unto him:
> 1. A proud look
> 2. A lying tongue
> 3. Hands that shed innocent blood
> 4. A heart that deviseth wicked imaginations
> 5. Feet that are swift in running to mischief
> 6. A false witness that speaketh lies
> 7. He that soweth discord among his brethren

She says sowing discord is worse than shedding innocent blood. She said all of us kids need to be aware of anyone sowing discord, and she looked straight at me when she said it. I'd be hard pressed to sow discord because Mother hardly lets me say Mother Kay's name without jumping all over me. Last time I talked to Mother about her, Mother Kay had put two heaping teaspoons of dry cayenne pepper in my mouth. I asked Mother what I did wrong. She said, "You'd better not criticize her."

"I'm not, Mother, I just need you to help me know what to do so I don't get in trouble again."

"You'll have to talk to her about it." And she walked away from me and went with Mother Kay up to Father's bedroom and they talked for hours with the door shut. They do it all the time, probably every day. I've put a glass on the door before, trying to hear what they were talking about, but I couldn't understand enough words. Mother's different when they come downstairs, like she doesn't want me around. She's nice to Claire even after her talks with Mother Kay. I asked her once if she loved Claire more than me and she said, "Don't be ridiculous. I love you all exactly the same." I don't really believe her.

Mother has been extra nice to Claire lately because last week when she was doing dishes, she broke a gallon milk jar and it slit her wrist wide open. The doctor who stitched her arm told Mother that it came really close to cutting the tendons, which would have rendered her hand useless. When Claire came home from the hospital her arm was all wrapped up in gauze and resting in a sling. She was as white as a sheet, and Mother told her she didn't have to do her work and let her lay down on the couch for a few days.

Mother Kay told us in morning class that the reason Claire got cut was because of the disobedience in the family. She said there's been a bad spirit in the home. "There are evil spirits right here in the room, all around us, trying to get in our bodies." She said we need to keep the spirit of God in our home to combat the evil around us. "When you're disobedient, you have an evil spirit with you and you need to go to your room, kneel down, and ask the Lord for his forgiveness and to take the evil spirit away." I felt bad for Claire; she was curled up in the recliner after morning class, crying, her looped up braids resting on the shoulders of her green and yellow dress. I could see her toe poking out of a hole in her tights.

Last year, when Glenn fell out of a tree and broke both wrists and gouged his face on a stretch of asphalt, he was in the hospital for a week. Mother Kay said the same thing about him. She said he deserved it for being disobedient to Father and it was a blessing in disguise. Mother was crying a little. Mother Kay can talk that way because she thinks her kids will be perfect when they get older. Jacob is a goody-goody and complete tattletale. She never spanks him like she does Carl and Jonathon. It's like she hates Mother Helen's kids, except for Lillian and Emily because they work on her feet.

Mother says I have to be careful or I'll be taken over by a rebellious spirit. I need to make sure I say my prayers every day, morning and night and during the day, if I lose the spirit of God. It's hard for me to say my prayers. Sometimes I forget, but mostly I'm just too lazy. Mother prays all the time. I have found her in her bedroom on her knees, leaning over her bed, praying for ten or fifteen minutes at a time. I can't imagine what she has to say that takes so long. When she comes out her face is all red. I can't tell if it was because she had her face in her clasped hands for a long time or if she had been crying. It seems like being good is so hard. It takes your whole life. Mother says if you sacrifice and keep the peace, it doesn't matter how unfair things are. God will bless you for everything you've done after you die. That seems like a long time to wait. Besides, there's always a chance that Mother is wrong; maybe you don't get something in heaven for being good on earth.

XIII

The schoolroom is thick with the silence. Mother Kay strums her red pen on the edge of her desk. The fluorescent light above us begins to flicker. She puts one of her smooth, white hands to her forehead.

"Uuugh, I've gotta get those lights fixed. This headache is killing me." She sets her pen down and puts both arms on the desk, gently laying her face down onto her arms. I keep reading Gilbert and Sullivan out of my English textbook and try not to wish she would go upstairs and lay down. It's early evening and my hand is tired from writing and my stomach is growling in emptiness. Camille pokes her head around the doorjamb as if she's in a huge hurry.

"Which of the kids are supposed to do the dishes?"

Mother Kay lifts her head and blinks rapidly.

"Uhmm ... let me check." Mother Kay turns a couple of pages in the orange notebook that sits on her desk. Camille looks impatient. Mother Kay turns a few more pages and then looks up.

"Tom, Ruby, aaaand ... Emily. Go on! Get in there and do the dishes." She stands up from her seat. "Susanna, you come with me." She takes me upstairs into Father's room.

"Do you know what you're here for?" I shake my head no, but I have a pretty good idea. She opens Father's closet and gets the belt from the hook.

"Turn around and lift up your dress. How old are you?"

"Twelve."

"What's three times twelve?" It takes me minute to calculate.

"Thirty-six."

"We'd better get started then, hadn't we?"

Danny's turn is next. I sit at my desk and cry the tears I won't give her the satisfaction of seeing and remind myself how much I hate her. When Danny comes back he sits down and acts like nothing happened.

"Can I see?"

Danny shuts the door and rolls up his loose pants to his thighs. I can't believe how bad his legs look. The blood vessels are broken and it's all black and red and looks swollen. I go behind the desk to see if mine looks as bad. I can't see because the pain is mostly on my lower back.

"Come tell me how big it is."

"It's big."

I reach my hand to feel if it is swelling. It's hot.

"I hate her."

"I know."

"I HATE HER!!" I start crying again.

Danny scoots his chair over closer to mine.

"Ya know what? Ya can't hate her. Okay?"

"Why not? She's a horrible, horrible witch!"

"Ya just can't."

"How can you say that after what she just did to you?!"

Danny takes a deep breath.

"It's like this: If ya hate her, that hate is inside of you. Why do ya think she's hitting us so hard? The same kind of hate is in her. Do ya get it? Ya can't hate her; that makes you just like her."

I can see for the first time that Mother Kay doesn't control Danny the same way she controls me. He is so passive and lets her beat him without getting mad, but she doesn't have any hold on him.

"Besides, the way I see it? She's a schizophrenic."

"What's that?"

"A split personality. I read about it in *American Health*. It's like there are two people inside of one. There's the good Mother Kay, who tells us stories at the lunch table and doesn't get mad at us, and then there's the bad Mother Kay. It's not the good Mother Kay's fault if the bad one does mean things. She can't help it. If nothing else, ya gotta feel sorry for her."

I'm not sure I fully understand what Danny is saying but he believes it. I only know how much I love him for making me feel better.

"That's what I do, anyway," he says with a grin.

I don't know if I can do it. I can't see two people, just one really mean one. The hate is so much a part of me that I don't know where it is or how to separate it from myself. I'll just hate the only Mother Kay I know of, the bad Mother Kay.

XIV

"Hey, guys, get a load of this." Ruby climbs on top of Mother Kay's desk. "Ya wanna see my Shirley Temple impression?" She doesn't wait for an answer but lifts her dress to mid-thigh and starts a tap dancing attempt. She bobs her head from side to side.

"Du-da, du-da, du-da du-da du-da."

Ruby is definitely the class clown. Sometimes during math she'll put the ends of her hair so that they are sticking out of a hole in the sleeve of her underarm. Then she'll raise her hand and wait for Mother's reaction. Ruby can hold a straight face, but the rest of us are holding back snickers of laughter.

She's risky too, pushing things to the last second. Yesterday she stole a whole piece of bread *and* butter … during lunch! She was showing us her prize when Mother Kay came in, obviously suspicious of something. Ruby threw the slice of bread in her desk and slammed the top down.

"What do your desks look like today?" Mother Kay liked to do random checks on how organized we kept our desks. Her timing seemed a bit too coincidental. "Ruby?"

I don't think Ruby has ever been caught red-handed at anything before. She hardly glanced at me before she braced herself and slowly lifted the lid. Her back was toward Mother Kay but I could see her eyes were squeezed shut. I kept my eyes on my own desk, making sure there was nothing incriminating in it.

"That looks pretty good," she said, sounding more than a little surprised. Ruby put her desk top down very slowly, looked at me and shrugged. We all got lucky. Mother Kay was called to the telephone and we were relieved to hear her say, "Oh, hello, Mother."

As soon as we were sure she wasn't on her way back, Ruby lifted the top of her desk. Lo and behold, the bread was *gone!* There wasn't a crumb of evidence left behind. Ruby kept blinking and saying, "It's a miracle." And it was; nothing like that had ever happened to us before. It was like a sign from heaven telling us that we would be protected, just like the Israelites in Moses' day when they smeared the lamb's blood on their doors. It was an omen of good things to come. Then I saw it.

"Ruby, look!" That perfect piece of buttered white bread was neatly glued to the inside lid of her desk. When she had tossed it in there so casually, it had been butter side up. I actually think Ruby was relieved that it wasn't a miracle after all, a sign from God. It was easier having good luck. Ruby has become a bit of a celebrity since then, our four-leaf clover, our lucky charm.

Mother Kay lets us out of the schoolroom at nine o'clock to take a bath before we go to bed. Ruby has been stealing bread and peanut butter every night. She is tired of stealing meager crumbs and has started taking bigger prizes. Last week she stole a whole package of graham crackers, tore the plastic wrapping, and dumped the entire thing in her bath water. Then she ate them. I was kinda mad she didn't share it with us, so now she's been getting us whole loaves of bread and hiding them behind the toilet, wrapped in a towel, accompanied by peanut butter and jam and a serrated edge knife. We take our baths in order of age, oldest to youngest, which means I usually get the crust.

The bathroom is a safe haven of sorts to do all kinds of illegal things, like shaving your legs. Mother Kay caught Emily shaving her legs. Ruby has confessed to me that she uses Father's electric shaver to do the job but Emily was using a disposable razor she had found in the garbage in Mark's bedroom. Mother Kay dragged me and Emily and Ruby up to Father's bedroom for the interrogation. Emily broke down and said it was because of wicked vanity that she shaved her legs and because of the thick black hair that showed through her nylons. Ruby denied ever touching a razor and challenged Mother Kay by asking her if she wanted to see for herself. She said no, but she was going to be watching them. Then she turned on me. I didn't realize that women shaved their legs at all until Mother Kay accused me of it.

"I would never do such a stupid thing. I like the hair on my legs."

"Well, that's good. I always thought you weren't as vain as some of the other girls."

Mother Kay thinks she knows everything about us. The other day she told us how we loved to see men's naked chests. She looked a little flushed when she said it, too. Then she looked straight at Emily and said, "You like Tom Selleck, don't you? See, I'm not so dumb. Ruby? You like Christopher Reeve." Ruby looked more angry than surprised. I could tell she didn't like Mother Kay saying his name.

She looked at me and said, "I'm not sure who you like. Oh, wait a minute, you like that guy on *How the West was Won*, that Bruce what's-his-name." I gave her my best phony laugh.

"You guys better watch yourselves. It's not good to fall in love with even a movie star." Then she proceeded to tell us her life story, how she married Father. We'd heard it many times before but we let her tell it again anyway. It made her forget everything else.

XV

Something is going on today.

I can feel it even behind the closed schoolroom door. There have been whispers that it's presents. It's happened before. When I was seven, the parents surprised us with a brand new huge wooden toy box. Inside, it was filled with wrapped presents. It was the first present I'd ever received. It was watercolors, a coloring book, and paintbrushes. Claire got a doll, which she still has. She keeps it in Mother's closet and says she is never going to let anyone play with it; she is keeping it for her own kids. I have never been one for dolls. Claire and Lillian love playing house, but I have more fun rigging up a swing for their dolls out of wire coat hangers and an empty box and hanging it from the copper pipes in the basement ceiling, than pretending I have a baby made of plastic. I love to make things. Last summer I made a chariot out of an empty cardboard brine barrel, two metal lids, and some twine. I took Lillian and Claire for rides around the backyard in it. When Mother Kay looked out the upstairs window she was really mad and I got a spanking for touching things that didn't belong to me. "You must really love whippings," she says whenever she is hitting me. If I get a D or an F in school, that's the punishment, a beating and doing the dishes by myself. I know Mother feels bad that I am always in trouble with Mother Kay because she says to me, "Why do you do that to yourself?" She thinks I am being bad on purpose just to be stubborn.

Last September Father took the whole family to Disneyland and the beach for a week. They left us five school-kids home with Mother Helen and the babies. We didn't have our schoolwork done. I knew we wouldn't get to go when Mother Kay first told us about it. I could tell by the way she said, *"We* are going to the beach in September," like, "we" somebody else and not us. Then she gave us two reports: last year's unfinished curriculum, which was quite a bit, and worst of all, memorizing the Declaration of Independence, the Gettysburg Address, the Preamble to the Constitution, the presidents of the United States, the dates they held office, the states where they were born and the dates of their births and deaths, the states and capitals, the abbreviations, and the date and number they entered the Union. I'll be surprised if I ever learn all of it. Mother was so frustrated with me because she thought I refused to do it just to be rebellious. She said I deserved to stay home. I can't convince her that I really tried. She doesn't believe me and probably never will.

Sometimes I wonder why Mother Kay makes school so hard. Everything has to be perfect. Handwriting has to be perfect. I can get an F on a paper based on handwriting alone. We have to make our pencils last a long time: we only get three pencils. Our writing has to be perfect so we have to sharpen them a lot. We get a whipping if we use up our pencils too fast. Danny invented a pencil extender so that we can write with a pencil all the way to the end 'til it's just a pink eraser and a black lead. He makes a narrow funnel out of paper and tape and then drops the pencil in the hole at the base so that we can hold even the tiniest pencil with ease. It has saved all of us much stress and worry. I don't know why Mother Kay can't let us have a few more pencils; they can't be *that* expensive. I wonder if she thinks making school so difficult will make us smarter.

She likes to tell us the story of a basketball coach who had his team practice on a hoop that was a few inches smaller in diameter. When they played with a standard size hoop it seemed to be so much easier and they won all their games. Maybe she wants to make our school so hard that if we ever have to go to a public school, it will be easy.

I wish we could go to a public school but Mother Kay says it's the devil's breeding ground. She says we ought to be glad we don't have to go like she did. She said she was teased relentlessly and called names. She said her sister Carla hated going to school in a dress so much she would wait until she was out of sight of her house and then she would change into a pair of bell-bottoms or a miniskirt before walking to school. She would take the bun out of her hair and leave her hair hanging down her back. Mother Kay showed me some pictures of her and her sisters before the dress code. Mother Kay was a little girl, sitting on her front porch, smiling, surrounded by other family members. Everyone was wearing short sleeves and the women were in pants with fashionable hairstyles. It seemed like I was looking at pictures in a book and not of people I knew.

Mother Kay said it was a dangerous time for her family. The police were constantly on the lookout for suspicious activity. Her mother had to live in a separate house because she was the second wife. That's why they all had to have fake last names, just like I have a fake last name. She told us how she let her feelings out to a Gentile boy and had to quit school. Her father didn't want her getting involved with a Gentile. I guess it would bring the world and the police closer to their door. She told us how she had prayed and prayed and found out that she belonged to Father. Mother Kay then told us how we need to find out who we belong to. Each one of us girls made a covenant in heaven to marry a certain man. She says we belong to that man even if we marry someone else. She said it's of dire importance that we marry the right person, the person we belong to. She used that word, "dire." She said we shouldn't let our feelings out for anyone until we get an answer from the Lord about who we are supposed to marry. She said letting our feelings out could muddy the waters. I guess the waters are like a crystal ball and if you stare into it and have no feelings for anyone else a picture of your husband-to-be will appear and you will know for sure. She said if you marry the wrong person you are damned. You can never ever go to the celestial kingdom. She said we are so blessed to be in the Work and get to have home school and we aren't tempted to do wicked things and lose our salvation .

Amanda knocks on the schoolroom door.

"You guys, the parents bought everyone presents!" she says through the door. "Mother Kay says you can come out when it's your turn." She unlocks the door and leaves it slightly ajar. Lillian comes to get us. My present is wrapped in tinfoil-shiny blue paper and is sitting by itself in front of the couch in the playroom. Father and Mother Kay are sitting on the couch and Mother is taking pictures. There is a huge pile of unopened presents behind me and an equally large pile of torn wrapping paper to my left. It's heavier than I expect and I give it a little test.

"It feels like my brain is in here." Father reacts with an uproarious laugh. I tear the paper to find a pair of blue and red roller skates. I give them the reaction they want because I have no idea how to feel. Tom gets a pair just like mine only a half-size larger, and Danny gets a game. Ruby gets a new purple robe with matching slippers and Emily gets a pair of socks and some art paper. Amanda gets a new watch. I put my roller skates in my bedroom and go back to my desk to finish an assignment on Lewis Carroll, but I can't stop thinking about how it will feel to learn to ride them, to sail through the lean-to and out the front gates, to feel the wind whistle in my ears as I twirl and speed Olympic-style past the 7–11 on the corner, the school, the auto parts store, the high school and all things familiar, the whole world watching me. I imagine what it would feel like to skate right out of my life, like walking off a stage through heavy red curtains, leaving the props, the costumes, the bright lights, and the loud voices behind me.

XVI

Mother Kay hates cats, which is a problem for her because we live in an inner-city cat zone. There are more strays in the area than kids who walk to and from school every day. I, on the other hand, love them, which is a problem for me because I am the kid and Mother Kay is the mother. No cats allowed. I close my eyes and will every cat in the area, with my animal telepathy, to my house. Strangely enough, cats of all sizes and colors find their way to me.

There was one cat, a large shiny black cat that liked to hang out under our porch. I was the only one who knew she was there. I would feed her bits of corn-bread that I had sneaked away from the table. I risked stealing cans of tuna fish from the pantry for her.

It was one of the first warm Saturdays of spring and the curtains in the dining room were pulled down and washed and the windows were wide open. An unusual brightness filled the room. Mother Kay walked over to the window and sniffed the air, closing her eyes to the sunshine. I stood a few feet behind her, oddly interested in her behavior. She leaned her hands heavily on the sill and stood there without moving. It was about then that my cat sashayed out from under the porch. There was a deafening scream, the kind of surreal sound you hear in horror movies and not in real life. I had never heard Mother Kay scream like that before. She nearly fainted from fright. The cat, equally terrified, scrambled back under the porch, no doubt trembling, with her soft coat standing on alert at the back of her neck.

Once Mother Kay had regained enough color in her face, she made her way, shakily, to the kitchen. She grabbed the teakettle, which was heating up and close to boiling for her morning raspberry leaf tea. Potholder in one hand and kettle in the other she headed straight toward the window. I heard the water hitting the pavement and another screech, this one from the cat. Mother Kay filled the kettle back up with water and stood over it until it boiled again.

"That's the last we'll see of that cat," Mother Kay said, more to herself than to me.

"What happened?" I asked.

"What do ya mean what happened? I poured boiling water on the damn thing. I got it square in the face; it took off like crazy." Mother Kay stood at the counter, straining the leaves from her blue plastic mug in a small cloth. She pressed the little sack of boiled leaves until they released their dark juices. She tossed it casually in the sink. The mug steamed as she held it in both hands and sat on the step stool under the kitchen telephone. I realized I was alone with her in the kitchen.

I couldn't stop thinking of my cat, confused and wandering around the unfriendly city, with third degree burns on her body. I wondered if the hot water had made her blind. I looked at Mother Kay, sitting serenely on her stool, her loosened bathrobe hanging over her bare feet.

"Why did you do that?" I finally asked. She looked up from her tea, realizing I was still standing there in front of the dishwasher.

"I don't like cats. I'm scared of them." She looked deep into the mug, and I could tell she was remembering. "My mother is scared of cats and her mother too. Especially black ones." There was a pause and she took another sip. I fidgeted with the end of my braid that rested over my shoulder. "I was attacked by one you know," she said without looking up. "It was when I was working at the rest home.

"I was in the basement; there weren't lights, only one of those really small windows that sits above your head. It was startin' to get dark outside. Let me tell ya, that basement was really creepy. There were mice and rats as big as a barn down there and they were mean too. Susan was chased by one and it nearly bit her foot.

"None of us liked goin' down the basement. I went most of the time because the other girls were too afraid. They knew I was afraid of cats. Marge and Ada weren't so much. Of course, they didn't like 'em either but they weren't afraid. It was those rats that scared the other girls. I was the oldest and more responsible, so I went down there most of the time." She sighed and took a long sip of her tea, and just when I thought maybe that was it, she continued.

"I'd finished gathering supplies for the next day and was ready to go back upstairs when I saw a black shadow move over the window." She paused letting the image form in my mind. "I didn't have time to think when it jumped right on my head. It was scratchin' and bitin'. It was terrible. I fell on the floor screamin'. Marge and Ada came runnin' down and it took both of them to get the cat off of me. It was a huge black tomcat. It coulda killed me if the girls hadn't come down and scared it away. Same thing happened to Mother, attacked by a black cat. Grandma too." She finished her tea and set the mug on the highchair that sat next to her. "We are all first daughters, ya know. My mother is Grandma's oldest daughter and I'm my mother's oldest daughter and Grandma is her mother's oldest daughter." She sat there thinking and I wondered if I had been there too long for my own good. "That cat was possessed by an evil spirit."

She sat quietly for a few minutes, not once looking up at me. Finally as if broken from a trance she looked straight into my eyes and said, "Don't you have work to do or somthin'?" The old Mother Kay appeared out of her eyes and I left her sitting on the stool in the kitchen.

There is a faint meowing behind the metal garbage cans on the North Side. It's a skinny, orange-striped cat. Large chunks of fur are missing, exposing her pink skin. She has scratches on her face. I sit down next to the garbage cans and hold her in my lap. She doesn't try to get away. I pull out a piece of cornbread from my apron pocket and feed it to her.

XVII

Charlotte's getting married today. Mother won't tell me who she is marrying; she says it's a secret. She said the same thing when Maria and Ella got married too. When a girl is ready to get married, Father goes to one of the brethren and he prays to the Lord to find out who she belongs to. I don't know if it works the same way with the boys because none of them are married yet.

Father and the mothers just drove out of the driveway with Charlotte. I stood at the top of the playroom stairs before she left to say good-bye. Everyone was crowded around her. She was wearing a borrowed pink dress with a high lace collar and a ruffle at mid-calf. I wonder why she doesn't get to wear a white dress like Maria. Maria wore an ultra shiny white satin dress and was smiling from ear to ear. Charlotte is crying. I can't tell if it's because she's so happy or if she's sad she's leaving. Last week I found her crying in the kitchen over a pan of pudding. I rarely see any of the Big Girls crying. I hugged her and kept asking her what was wrong. She just said, "It's nothing. I'm okay." Then she forced herself to smile so I would believe her.

I don't want Charlotte to go. I felt bad when Maria and Ella got married but Charlotte's different. Charlotte is the best Big Girl. She made everything fun and made me feel like I belonged to something. She taught me to sing and showed me the difference between singing and singing with feeling. She loved art and was encouraging all of us to stretch our imaginations. She used to take us on tours of our own house. We would line up behind her and she would guide us through the house as if it was an ancient manor owned by a famous duke. She made us forget that we lived there and brought attention to details we never noticed before. She was the storyteller.

She put on a play for the parents once. It was in the basement. Ruby was the fairy, Emily was the queen, I was the princess, and Tom was the handsome knight that saves the day. Danny was the king and Glenn was the evil wizard. She hung a red blanket from the ceiling and put a lamp behind it for a silhouette of the evil wizard stirring his dangerous potion in a big pot and laughing ominously. She had a tape recorder playing appropriate music for each scene. When we needed to change our set she had Amanda do commercials memorized from TV in front of the curtain while we changed our clothes and moved things around.

The first year we had home school, each of the Big Girls taught a class. Charlotte taught us history and geography. Well, sort of. She would sit on top of the teacher's desk and read *Johnny Tremain* out loud. If she heard someone coming down the stairs she would jump off the desk, hide her book, and pretend she was correcting papers. Sometimes she would turn on music and have us draw pictures of what the music made us feel like. She took us to the library to find books on famous explorers and then she would read the books and improvise them with dialogue and a little acting. She made Sir Frances Drake and Ferdinand Magellan into real-life characters with real-life problems. She showed us humanity in Hernando Cortez and Francisco Pizarro. She made history real.

I begged Emily to tell me if she knew who Charlotte was going to marry. She said she did but she wasn't going to tell me. I know Mother will tell me in the morning after Charlotte is married but I need to know tonight. Mother says Charlotte is a daydreamer and marriage will give her a dose of reality. She isn't a very good cook and Mother says she's too slow and disorganized at housework in spite of the fact that she does it well. I don't care if Charlotte is good at those things because she's a writer, a poet, a musician, and an artist. She knows how to do things no one else does. She and Camille spend hours on the typewriter writing their own poetry or songs. Mark and Bryan write the music and Mark plays the guitar. Then the four of them sing the songs they've created. Sometimes Charlotte plays the piano for them too. Now, the band is broke up.

I ask Ruby if she will tell me who Charlotte is marrying. She says she is marrying Mother Kay's father. I don't believe her. I don't want to believe her.

I probably won't see Charlotte anymore, at least not as my sister. She will be a wife to Mother Kay's father. Mother Kay says that when someone gets married it's the same as dying. You will belong to your husband and not to your father anymore. I don't want to belong to anybody. She said that some men make their wives change their first names when they get married and the husband sends all her stuff back to her parents, even down to the pins in her hair. I guess they don't want them remembering anything from their family. Mother Kay said Father didn't do that to her but there are a lot of men who do and there is nothing the woman can do but obey her husband. She says it's in the Bible: "A woman's desires shall be to her husband and he shall rule over her." She says a woman is saved in childbirth, and that the husband is responsible for the woman. She talks about it a lot, women being subject to men. She says the woman is the glory of the man. The man is not of the woman but the woman *is* of the man, so a woman should submit herself to her husband. She says a woman cannot get into the celestial kingdom without the man and a woman can't hold the priesthood. I don't want to hold the priesthood and when I get married I won't obey my husband; I don't care what the Bible says. The Bible is wrong.

XVIII

Danny is hanging his head out the window, looking skeptically at a narrow strip of dirt below. He is sitting with one leg on the sill and the other on a chair.

"What do you think?" Ruby asks. "Do you think we can do it?"

"Anything's possible," says Danny in his all-wise voice. Tom is at his desk, memorizing the Declaration of Independence.

"When in the course of human events it becomes necessary for one people to dissolve the political bands which have connected them with another …"

"Blah, blah, blah, I hate that stupid declaration." Ruby throws her history book to the floor. "So there."

It's lunch so we have some time to ourselves. It's warm outside, almost summer.

"So when do we start digging?" asks Ruby.

"We have to make plans first so everything goes without a hitch. Then we could start as soon as we get out of school for the summer."

"You mean, *if* we get out of school for the summer," says Tom.

"I'll help; what are we doing?" I am anxious to take a break from my studies.

"We're building an underground room right below the window, somewhere where we can escape where no one can find us." Ruby makes everything sound possible.

"How are we going to hide it from the parents?"

"We'll put a board over the top and make a rope ladder so we can get down there," she says, always with an answer. Danny and Ruby sit back in their desks.

"We're going to need to vote for a president and counsel." Danny tears the corner off of a piece of paper and shoves it in his mouth. He passes the torn paper to me. I like the way it dissolves so quickly in my mouth, into a small wad.

"Okay," says Emily, "there are five of us. Who's gonna be who?" She uses what's left of the paper to write down positions.

"We need a president," says Ruby "and a vice president and … a secretary of defense and a clerk." I don't have any idea what a secretary of defense or a clerk is, but they sound real, like something we studied last month in history about the legislative and judicial branches of government.

"That's only four."

Ruby pays no attention to me and stuffs a large piece of paper in her mouth, muffling her voice as she shouts, "Let's vote! I vote Danny for president."

"I vote for Ruby to be vice president," says Danny who is finished chewing his paper and is under the cupboard, getting a new piece.

"I'll be the clerk," says Emily. "I'll be in charge of keeping track of everything."

"Tom can be the secretary of defense," says Ruby.

"I'm not bein' no secretary!"

"It's not that kind of secretary, it's just a title. It means you're in charge of taking care of weapons and doin' the other war stuff."

"Oh … okay. Just call me general then."

"Hey, what about me? Who am I going to be?" I get tired of being last.

Ruby presses her fingers to her temples.

"I know, you can be the first lady."

"What does the first lady do?"

"Nothin', you're just the president's wife."

"Duh, I already knew that. What does she do?"

"Nothin'. She just sits around the Oval Office lookin' decorative."

"Okay, whatever."

We draw a map. We could connect to the electricity through the basement and keep a stash of blankets and food down there. I imagine lamps on clay end tables next to clay couches, and me sweeping a dirt floor. I imagine uncensored laughter; the kind Mother says is a false and delusive spirit. She calls them laughing spirits. I want to have a laughing spirit. I want to laugh so I hard I can't breathe.

"Pass the paper," Tom says in a singsong voice. During the summer when there isn't snow on the roof to eat and take the sharp edge of hunger away, we eat paper. Ruby hands Tom the paper after popping another piece in her mouth. She tears him a piece and he crumples it before putting it in his mouth. It becomes quiet except the sound of chewing. I can hear our thoughts mingling in midair, like the clanking of silverware.

"Guys, we're gonna be in big trouble if we don't memorize this declaration," says Emily, swallowing her paper and tearing another piece.

We clap in time to the rhythm of Emily's chant and after a minute or two we chime in: "When in the course of human events …"

We repeat the words from the document over and over. I don't know what it means. Not really. I only know that it is a declaration for freedom. I don't understand the many big words and Thomas Jefferson wrote in a very complicated manner, but some of the words I do understand and they feel good to my ears. Words like abolish, unalienable rights, life, liberty, and the pursuit of happiness. Although there are many words that I like it is the last paragraph that reverberates inside me.

"But when a long train of abuses and usurpations, pursuing invariably the same Object evinces a design to reduce them under absolute Despotism, it is their right, it is their duty, to throw off such Government, and to provide new Guards for their future security …"

The irony of being forced to memorize a document about freedom is not lost on me.

XIX

Camille appears in the doorway of the schoolroom with her new husband. Bobby is tall with nicely cut blonde hair. We've known Bobby for years; another one of the eligible young men in the Work. He helped Father remodel the kitchen last year. That's when Emily fell in love with him. I think she liked him for a while but it was when he started coming over every day, tearing out old walls with a huge sledgehammer, that Emily's heart was lost. He was handsome and burly, and it didn't help that he was such a genuinely nice person, the kind of guy to smile at the babies in their highchairs when he passed by with a load of two-by-fours balanced on his shoulder, or help one of the little kids tie their shoe. Bobby could make anyone believe in romanticism, knights in shining armor, and the like. A man capable of rescue.

Emily looks ill. Her face is white and she tries to hide the shock and disappointment of the arrangement. She won't be able to daydream about him anymore without thoughts of Camille interrupting. Bobby has his arm around Camille's shoulder. She is wearing a cream-colored sweater I have never seen before. None of us know what to say. I didn't know she was getting married. There was no family crowding around her before she left for the ceremony. I didn't see a white dress or the camera flashing pictures of the last moments of a daughter, a death, a good-bye. Nothing.

There's a picture that hangs on the wall in the bedroom where Camille sleeps. It's a woman standing in a field of daffodils, looking at her future in front of her, and the words inscribed beneath say "This is the first day of the rest of your life." The rest of Camille's life is just a mystery. I don't know what happens when someone gets married and begins the rest of their life. The rest of your life just feels like good-bye. The end.

"I just thought you guys would want to know," she says, still smiling.

"How long are you going to stay?" Ruby breaks the silence.

"Just for a few minutes; we'll be leaving soon." Her words are like rocks thrown at my stomach. Camille is dead. Camille the mysterious, sometimes unpredictable, and the epitome of strong—as an ox, Mother Kay would say. Camille is not an open book. There are lines in her young face, like traces of her own secrets that no one recognizes, like faded spots of grease on an apron.

It feels like the family is shrinking. People are leaving faster than babies are born. Mother and Mother Helen are done having babies. Annie is Mother's last, a pleasant surprise at forty-three, she says. Thirteen is a good number. Mother Helen's baby is Lucy, number sixteen. Mother Kay is going to have a baby right now. It's her sixth. I hope she doesn't catch up to Mother.

Whenever Mother Kay is pregnant, she only comes in the schoolroom when she has to correct papers or give assignments. She writes everything on the chalkboard and disappears upstairs to lie down. If we have questions, we have to go upstairs and knock on Father's bedroom door and risk disturbing one of her migraine naps. She is always lying around. Though she says she's too tired to do anything she always has enough strength to give us plenty of spankings. It's worse when she is going to have a baby—at least once or twice a day.

She doesn't spank everyone that much, just me, Tom, and Ruby, and some of the little kids, like Carl. He's six. I know she doesn't like him; I can see it when she looks at him, the same way she looks at Albert and Ruby and sometimes me. She used to make Albert sit Albert on a chair and fold his arms for hours at a time. He's too big for her to do anything like that anymore. She can't hit him with the stick anymore either. I think she's really afraid of him. I heard him once on the north side of the house, on his knees praying to Satan to take her life away. It was kinda scary. He's usually gone during the summer though. He works at Aunt Liesel's, in the garden. Glenn works too, at the egg factory. He comes home smelling horrible. Chicken manure. He says he'll give me a dollar if I wash his coveralls but he never does. Keith, Mark, Bryan, and Gerald all go to work early in the morning. I'm not sure what they do, all I know is they give their checks to Father on Fridays.

Now with Camille leaving, all the Big Girls are gone. Amanda is the oldest daughter in the house. Mother says she'll have to step up to the plate. Amanda is only fourteen and she is the oldest unmarried girl in the house. It feels wrong and backward and scary, no longer surrounded by older, wiser sisters: the ones that bathed me when I was young, brushed my teeth, combed my hair in tight braids, and washed it every Saturday morning. They are like my mothers.

Ella taught me how to tie my shoes and Maria showed me how to sweep the kitchen floor. Renee carried me to bed when I was sick, and Charlotte showed me how to make beds like they do in the army, and Camille taught me how to braid my own hair and to answer the phone politely.

I don't want to be a Big Girl. I don't want to get married or grow up or have Father tell me I'm practically a mother. I don't want to be called on to talk in

Meeting and say how thankful I am for everything. I don't want to cook, tend kids, change diapers, or sew. I want to be different.

I don't want to be invisible.

XX

I didn't think I was going to feel bad about what happened today. I knew it was wrong but I do a lot of things I know are wrong and it doesn't feel like this. Tom and I have been locked up for the last two days and nights together. It's definitely better than being locked up alone but I feel so much shame.

I should have known something was up. Tom has been acting strange lately. He talks about gross things and has this goofy smile on his face the whole time. Last Saturday I saw one of his magazines that I know he hides in his closet. I was folding laundry in the basement, alone. Tom burst through the outside door. His face was red from the cold and he was breathing hard. He didn't expect to see me there.

"Oh, what are you doing?" he said. I could hear the rustle of paper under his black coat. I knew what it was but he didn't know that I knew.

"Wash. What else would I be doing down here?"

"I dunno." He disappeared into his closet. It was quiet for only a moment. I could feel the hairs on my skin come alive and I knew he was standing behind me but I kept my back toward him.

"Check this out." His voice was strangely low and deep. I realized that Tom was a stranger to me. He had been different the last few months but I had told myself it wasn't happening, that he was still the same old Tom he had always been. Something in his voice or rather something that was no longer in his voice made me realize I did not know this person, I was afraid of him.

I turned around and was assaulted by a centerfold of a woman completely nude, her tan skin glistening. She was straddling a chair, her legs spread wide. Her arms were crossed over and behind her head so that only her elbows were showing above her fake blonde hair, her breasts pushed forward. Her eyes were half-closed, exposing the deep purple eye shadow that extended out toward her temples in points.

"Ahhh!" I backed up into the laundry basket, spilling towels onto the floor.

"Shhhhh! You're not supposed to let the whole world know about it."

"That's sick, Tom, that's just sick! Don't ever do that to me again."

"Oh, I'm sorry. That was mean, wasn't it? Just look at one more. It's not a bad one, I promise." He started flipping through the pages. I didn't stop Tom. I wanted to be disgusted but when he offered another picture I looked again.

This time it was a white beach, with the sun just beginning to set. It was a different woman. She was walking serenely near the shore, wearing only a sarong around her waist. She was posed as if she were covered. I couldn't take my eyes off her. It was the strangest thing, seeing someone bare like that. I wanted to look at some more but I didn't want Tom to know.

"See, I told you. It's nice, isn't it?"

"Put it away! I don't want to see anymore." I was fighting guilt that had crept up and was choking me.

"Don't tell anyone, okay?" He hung his coat in the closet and ran up the stairs in three leaps. Though I tried to resist the temptation for the rest of the day I kept going back to the closet to see more of the strange and tantalizing photos. The forbidden nature of the photos was an unstoppable force. The physical reactions I was having left me reeling. I'd never felt that way before.

When Tom showed me the pictures it made me uncomfortable but nothing like what happened today.

We were both so hungry. Neither one of us had eaten for a couple days. I wanted Tom to like me. That's why I let him touch me. I let him do things to me that I had never done to myself. I just closed my eyes and held my breath. He talked about it the rest of the time we were locked up together. When we finally came out of the schoolroom I stayed as far away from Tom as I could. Just looking at Tom from across the room made me feel guilty and dirty. I want to forget what happened today, I want to forget about the pictures and the magazines and make this awful feeling go away. I want to take back what Tom did to me today, what I let him do to me. But I can't make it go away—I can't even forget about it. It's my secret and I'm not telling anyone.

When Emily told me her secret behind the furnace, she didn't say it made her feel like wickedness itself. She didn't say it made her feel like a dirty old toilet. She didn't tell me she cried in the bathroom for an hour when the realization of what had happened finally hit her. It seemed almost normal to me at the time; I mean, she came and told me about it. Maybe she doesn't tell me everything that has happened to her, just like I won't be telling her what happened today. The weight of this secret makes it hard for me to look at myself in the mirror or hug Mother in the mornings.

Whatever it takes, I will never let it happen again.

Part II
Endings

XXI

School's over.

Just like that. We are never going back. I'm not even finished with the fifth grade. It's been a grueling four years since Mother Kay started teaching school. The countless Fs that resulted in beatings and doing dishes by myself; the hours and hours, days stacked upon days, hunched over my desk, writing, worrying, always aware of the hand wrapped around my throat, ready to squeeze the breath out of me.

The shame of being bad—irreparably, despicably bad—stings worse than the welts and bruises of all the whippings of yesterday, and the blunt mark of it is seared deeper into me than the discolorations on my legs. But of all I am thinking of today, on this first day of liberation, is food. In all four years, there haven't been many days where I had three meals. Especially in the last two years, our meals have been rationed down to one. And there have been so many days when I did not eat at all. Today I will eat.

Father came into the schoolroom this afternoon while we were trying to finish our history books. It was a long stretch this time, two weeks with nothing but a bowl of oatmeal in the mornings. Mother Kay was right behind him, wearing a green duster under a white cable-knit sweater, her arms folded; she was looking straight ahead. Father, who usually took the time to bore a hole through you before speaking, immediately said, "It's over. You're done with school." He was visibly irritated. Mother Kay stayed in the corner, her face clean of an expression; she didn't say a word.

We remained in our chairs, our pencils poised in our hands, the textbooks suddenly useless. Frustration roiled Father's face. He grabbed the stack of papers marked "DO OVER" and tossed it in the garbage can next to Mother Kay's desk.

"You're done!" he said, shaking the contents out of the metal bins on her desk all over the floor. None of us looked at each other, uncomfortable by Father's new and unpredictable behavior.

"Put away your books! You guys are finished with school," his back was toward us as he was leaving, "forever!"

Mother Kay looked a little startled by the announcement and gave us the eye before she followed him out of the room, leaving the door wide open.

There was a long silence.

"What do ya think he meant?" Emily asked when they were completely gone.

"I guess we can leave." Ruby stood up and ceremoniously closed her history book. "I guess we're done with school."

"What are we gonna do? Do ya think he's mad at us?" This wasn't exactly what I had pictured for a graduation.

"Who cares? We're outta school," Ruby said.

Out of school.

We hesitated at the offer of freedom. Crowding around the doorway, we stood before the threshold, looking at each other. Ruby took the lead and walked out of the schoolroom. We followed her through the kitchen, single file, deciding whether or not to disperse. Everyone was looking at us, wondering what was going on, and their thoughts like ticker tape across their foreheads. No smiles or cheering, or hip hip hurrays, just grim faces and "what have you done now" looks.

I remembered seeing pictures of Ted Bundy in a bright orange jumpsuit, chains around his ankles, after he'd been caught in Florida. He was walking with his head bowed while the staring public looked on in disgust, but his face was still defiant. He had been plucked from among them, a marked defect.

No one spoke to me or told me what to do. The afternoon, as strange to me as the cold stare of fluorescent lights, was familiar. I had been freed and I was walking in broad daylight, though I felt distinctly that one prison was being substituted for another. This new prison had no visible walls, no door to lock and unlock, no way in and no way out. Suddenly I had the strongest urge to run back to the schoolroom, to accept my punishments, to dream of escape again—anything in exchange for this bitter realization.

Last year our house and front yard was toilet-papered and our front gates had the word "Alcatraz" spray-painted all over it. Everyone had suspected it was Bryan, and at the time I couldn't imagine why a family member would toilet paper their own home and what Alcatraz had to do with anything. Mother was very upset about it, especially when Bryan was blamed.

I understand it today, like a puzzle being put together that finally takes obvious shape.

I only have to wait a few hours until dinner. Dinner! The sound of the word is like rich gravy slathered all over my imagination. I will never go hungry again. I hope.

I don't know what to do. I rove around the house shifty and uneasy, constantly checking over my shoulder, my heart in my throat and a terrible thick knot in my stomach. I remember my roller skates, under the bed, the tags still attached. Do I dare to try them out today? Would anyone notice?

It isn't that easy. I hold onto the side of the house and ease my feet forward. I feel taller, like I am on stilts. The yard is terribly quiet and I feel like an actor waiting for a cut. The vacuum created by my freedom is distracting, like a fly buzzing around my ear. I make my way twice around the house and I am beginning to synchronize my body with the skates when the upstairs window screeches open and Mother Kay's head appears through the curtains.

"What do ya think you're doin'?"

I look at my roller skates and back up at the window. "Skating?"

"Don't you get smart with me, young lady! Just because you're not in school anymore doesn't mean ya get ta play. What's the matter with ya?!"

I hold myself steady at the sandbox but my feet are moving a little without me.

"Huh? Answer me!" She leans out across the sill.

"I dunno."

"Get in this house right now. You've got work to do and I don't want to catch you outside playing again without permission. Do you understand me?"

"Yeah."

"Besides, you're too old to be playing anyway. You're gonna need to grow up and start acting like a Big Girl from now on." The window slams shut.

I have work to do! The words are like music to my ears.

XXII

Everyone said thirteen was a hard age but they didn't say it was liver and onions hard, balancing each day on the end of a fork with a glass of water nearby to wash it down.

We started a new work schedule after we quit school. I have been doing the laundry. It usually takes me all day. I drag tall barrels of clothes from the bathrooms, down the stairs to the basement, and start the wash at about six thirty in the morning. It takes me all day. On a good day I can be done by five or six in the evening. On a bad day, well, it's really late, ten or eleven o'clock at night. That's mostly on Monday when there are twenty batches. Tuesday is better, twelve or so, and Wednesday is the best day of the week and I have about eight or nine, then it's back to ten or eleven batches on Thursday and Friday. Saturday is usually a small one, nine or so. Then there's no wash on Sunday which is only good for Sunday because it makes Monday particularly awful.

I don't mind putting the wash through the washers and dryers. I don't like to fold. There is a pile of clothes for every person, starting with Father, whose pile comes first, and ending with the baby, whose pile is at the very end of the folding table. It's hard to keep track of everyone's clothes. Mother marks the tags with an initial or some other identifying mark with a permanent marker. Still, there are rags to fold, whole batches of rags. Towels make up three batches and the diapers have to be washed twice, once in bleach water and once in a regular cycle. But the worst of all is the hanging ups. The pile rises with each batch, filled with dresses and skirts and shirts and slacks and blouses. I put off this job until last. There is a tangle of wire hangers to be sorted out like a rat's nest. Sometimes I get so mad trying to get a hanger loosened from the grip of the cluster that I shake the whole pile until wire hangers go flying around the basement in a tantrum.

If I do the wash good for a week I can the clean house for a week, otherwise I do wash for another week. I've had to do wash for four weeks in a row now. That's because in addition to wash I have to clean the basement—that's what takes me so long. That and a copy of *Old Yeller* I found under the dryer.

Danny and Tom have been going to the garden every day to weed or help Father at the shop. Ruby and Emily take turns with Amanda on kitchen duty and house duty. Mother tends to the little kids. Things are so different now. Mother says change is good and I had better get used to it because life is full of changes. She said that sentimentality will just cause me problems but I like being sentimental and I'm not going to change.

What really bothers me is the way my body is changing and the way other people are noticing. Yesterday I had my hands resting in the bib of my jumper and Mother Helen got mad at me. She said to quit touching myself. She didn't know I wasn't touching myself; I only do that in the bathroom when I measure them. Mother wants me to wear one of those stupid training bras. It's so uncomfortable. I just pick at the straps all day. Most of the time I just wear a T-shirt under my dress. If Mother notices, she calls me to her room and tells me I need to be more modest and I am too old to wear T-shirts. If Mother Kay notices, she embarrasses me in front of whoever might be standing there, saying everyone can see right through my dress and to go get a bra on. Lately I've been wearing a belt around my chest, hoping to stunt the growth. I saw an old Western movie where the woman was pretending to be a man and she cinched a belt around her chest before she put on her shirt.

I read about women who pretended to be men and went to war, like Deborah Sampson. She dressed up in a man's uniform and fought for years during the Revolutionary War. I wanted to include her in my report but Mother Kay wouldn't let me.

The belt doesn't seem to help much; everything is just growing around it and bulging out the sides. Ruby says if I don't wear a bra my breasts will travel all the way around until they are under my arms. I certainly don't want bulges under my arms any more than I want them in front but it doesn't make a bra any more enjoyable to wear.

Mother Kay says I'm a late-bloomer and that most girls start growing on top at eleven or twelve. I don't mind being different from other girls. When I was nine Mother Kay took me to Father's bedroom and brought out homemade drawings of a female body and told me strange things would start happening to me. She said it was the sign of womanhood and I should feel very grown up when it happened. She explained about the uterus and how it cleanses itself and she showed me what a sanitary napkin looked like. She said when I was a little older she would tell me where babies came from but she never did. I was terrifically bored with the whole thing and couldn't have cared less. When she finished, she told me to send Lillian upstairs. Lillian came back looking a little embarrassed but said she couldn't wait until she started on her period, (that's what Mother Kay called it, a period) but that's just Lillian—she's always wanted to be grown up. She'll probably love wearing a bra and those other things. I hope I don't start that business 'til I'm twenty.

I hate being a girl. I hate periods. I hate long hair that has to be combed in braids. And dresses that get in the way of everything, and tights, especially when they get big holes in the crotch. Boys get everything good: short hair, comfortable clothes, and most of all freedom to leave the house where Mother Kay can't make them do things they don't want to do. I guess I hate boys too. I hate them for being different from me. They aren't smarter or faster or better than girls. But I'm the only one who knows that. I hate that I'm a girl; that I am supposed to be weak and worthless. I hate bras and breasts and not holding the priesthood. I hate pink and feminine and flowers. I am going to be different from all the other girls in the world; I'm going to be lumberjack strong and Einstein smart. I'm going to marry who I want and no one is going to rule over me. I will always be one step ahead of them, one move ahead, so that I will never be behind, never be walking in the dust of a boy.

XXIII

It's been a week since I came home and I'm still sick. Mother says it's probably food poisoning.

I was so excited when Father told me I was going Down South to help Heidi, who had just had a baby. I barely knew Heidi. The night before we left I packed a suitcase and dreamed all night about my abilities and why I was chosen to go. Mother woke me early Sunday morning and we left with Mother Helen at the wheel. It took six hours because we stopped at a restaurant for dinner. It was my first time at a restaurant and I ordered a club sandwich and root beer.

When we arrived at Heidi's house I got out of the blue station wagon, holding the ancient green suitcase in my hand. I was having second thoughts about it. There was almost no grass in the front yard, just red southern dirt and a big cottonwood tree with a rope swing swaying in the hot wind. There were a couple of old sun-baked tires nearby, home to several cats. The front porch was two-by-fours nailed together and filled with more red dirt that was compacted from years of use. The front door, once painted white, was a dirty with a collage of hand prints concentrated near the knob.

Ernest came out to greet us. I remembered immediately how much I didn't like him. He was tall and gangly, balding and rail thin. He was wearing dirty tennis shoes and a brown plaid shirt with big pearl snaps up the front and on the cuffs. The sleeves were so threadbare I could see his elbows. His fingernails were black like he'd been playing in the dirt and his face seemed to ooze grease. Mother told me he was a mechanic. He looked more like an overgrown teenager and not the husband of my oldest sister and father to fourteen children.

Ernest's eyes darted between the ground and everything else.

"Do you want to come in?" he mumbled. "See the baby?"

Mother Helen's enthusiasm made up for the overall lack of it. "Absolutely! How many grandkids does this make for us, Mary?"

Mother bit her forefinger. "Let me see, there's gotta be at least twenty now. Charlotte's about due with her first." Mother seemed happy to be distracted with details. We followed Ernest into the house. It smelled of warm urine and dirty socks, and mold. It was so pungent it assaulted me like a physical force. I wrapped my arms around myself as though the smell was being absorbed into my body through the pores. We walked past the kitchen full of dirty dishes. Breadcrumbs trailed all the way down the hallway to Heidi's bedroom. It was very dim and I could see, once my eyes adjusted, that she was lying in bed with a sleeping baby at her side. The smell in her room was entirely different than the smell of urine and mold, but it was no less distasteful. There was a pool of dried blood on the dark blue carpet and we walked around it to get to the bed. Heidi told us she had given birth to the baby on the floor and there hadn't been anyone to clean it up. Her face was gray and her long black hair was tousled and sweaty. She didn't seem embarrassed, which surprised me.

Mother and Mother Helen were ready to leave.

"We'd better get over to Grandma's," Mother Helen said. "We'll be back to pick up Susanna in a week."

"You be good and help Heidi, okay?" Mother hugged me and the two of them walked out and climbed in the station wagon and drove away. I felt two cinder blocks sinking me like quicksand into a strange choking darkness.

There were kids everywhere. I walked down the hall and asked Heidi what she needed me to do.

"Can you cook?"

"Sure, of course." I wasn't nearly as confident as I pretended to be. I had cooked a little at home but there was always a Big Girl around to answer questions or help me if I needed. Here there was nobody besides; I was trying to impress her with my competency. As for Ernest, I wasn't going to be volunteering any conversation with him. There was Rebecca, though. She was Claire and Lillian's age and she seemed willing enough when I asked her to help me with dinner. The kitchen seemed ridiculously small for the size of their family and I decided I couldn't think about cooking until I cleaned up the place. I rolled up my sleeves and flipped on the light, which seemed to be about twenty watts. The sink, when I removed the dirty dishes, revealed a family of cockroaches that scrambled around the slippery sink in a hasty attempt for darkness. I stepped away.

"Rebecca, there's cockroaches in the sink."

"It's okay. They can't come up through the plug. Just shoo 'em down the drain." She came over and literally shoved them down the drain with her bare hands. I winced and felt a slight gag in the back of my throat.

"There, plug it up real fast and you should be fine."

I filled the sink with water and washed the dishes. I couldn't stop thinking about the cockroaches and several times when I was sure I could feel one of them running up my arm I did the panicky "get the bug off me" dance. Rebecca laughed.

"You scared of cockroaches?"

"Aren't you?"

"Nah, there's tons of 'em down here. I get used to it."

When we had finished the dishes I wiped everything down except the stove, which had a wilted tomato sitting on the main burner, black and green mold growing out of its insides. Rebecca swept the floor but she didn't do a very good job so I swept it again.

I made hamburgers for dinner. A no-brainer. I was used to cooking for larger crowds than this so I was feeling pretty good about myself. Heidi came in and sat at the table holding the baby in one arm. She seemed very grateful to have someone take care of her family. I stood at the stove, cooking the patties, while Rebecca made them up and served them. Ernest came and stood right next to me, holding his plate with a ketchup-smeared bun in front of him. I felt his eyes observe me, my hair, my back, my hands; I never dreamed meat could take so long to cook.

It was late when I finished the dishes and Heidi told me I could sleep in the girls' room on the floor. She apologized that she didn't have an extra bed for me.

"Good night," she said before she disappeared back in the bedroom with Ernest right behind her.

"C'mon," Rebecca said, "get in yer nightgown and come to bed."

The room was full of dirty clothes and blankets and smelled like the localized source of all the stink in the house. A mattress had been pulled off one of the bunk beds and laid haphazardly on the floor. I went to the bathroom and changed into my nightgown. I kept my socks on; the floor seemed alive with dirt and smell. Rebecca was in bed when I arrived.

"I can't sleep in here."

"Why not?" she said, not understanding my trepidation.

"I'll just sleep on the couch. Really, I don't mind."

"Okay, if you want to, but there's room right here," she said, pointing to the floor.

"No thanks. I'd rather be in the living room. That way if Heidi—I mean, yer mother—needs me, I'll be close by. Good night." The couch was filthy, with threadbare and matted cushions. I decided to sleep in the chair instead.

The next morning I woke to hear Ernest making himself a lunch in the kitchen. I pretended to be asleep. I held my position, eyes closed, until the house became quiet. Too quiet. I realized Ernest hadn't left for work but was standing in front of the chair, his shadow hovering over me like bad breath. I hoped he wouldn't try and wake me and I prepared to be a *very* deep sleeper. I was glad my robe was still on me. *Go to work, you dummy*, I thought. He didn't move but stood there until I felt the first warm light of sunshine on my skin. The door opened and closed, a car engine revved, and he was gone.

Each day was pretty much the same. I woke up to Ernest's shadow and tried not to hold my breath, pretending to be peacefully asleep. He would leave as soon as the sun rose and I would get up and try to take care of everything. The first day I tried to do the laundry, I dug through the piles of dirty clothes to find the washer and dryer, only to discover that the dryer was broken and Ernest would fix it when he came home. There were hours spent each day hanging clothing on the line outside, behind the compost pile that looked more like a city landfill. The flies that swarmed the house were fat and healthy, reproducing by the thousands until eating at the table became an exercise in swatting. The house seemed to produce dirt on its own when I wasn't looking. I vacuumed the living room five times a day, tried to clean marker off the walls and get the smell out of sheets, but to no avail. My enthusiasm drained out of me like raw eggs in my shoes. The highlight of the week was when the two-year-old, who had fallen asleep under the cottonwood tree, was pecked on his bare feet by the pet crow that was more wild than pet. I wrapped his feet in bandages and took him to Heidi.

"I told you not to let him out by the crow. He's kinda ornery." I was devastated and couldn't stop apologizing. The next day he stayed in the house with me and Rebecca, begging to be carried so he wouldn't have to walk. When Rebecca sat him up on the table while she made bread, he sat in the batter with a dirty diaper still on him. She refused to throw out the bread and start over, and instead made the dough into round brown loaves that I refused to eat.

By Saturday I was despondent. I had completely lost my appetite and was running a low fever. After preparing Saturday's dinner I walked outside to compose myself. Heidi, who was up on her feet, opened the door.

"Susanna, are you okay?"

"I'm fine," I said without turning around.

"Are ya sure? Why don't ya come in and eat." My stomach churned at the thought.

"No thanks. I'm not hungry." The tears I couldn't hold back were squeaking my voice. She came out and put her arm around me.

"You miss everyone, don't you?"

I nodded.

"Mother's gonna be here tomorrow to pick ya up. I'm sure glad ya came down to help me."

"I'm glad to do it," I said, but I didn't mean a word of it. She let me go and walked back to the house.

"If a change yer mind I'll be in the house. I'll save ya some."

"Okay, thanks."

Mother and Mother Helen came to pick me up at noon the next day. I had been packed since early in the morning and was waiting outside for them. I was grateful for Mother's punctuality and brevity as we said good-bye. Once we were on the road home with Mother Helen at the wheel, Mother turned around.

"Are you feeling all right?

"No, I'm not. I think I'm gonna throw up."

"Well, don't do it in here."

"I won't."

I lay down on the clean warm seat and fell asleep.

XXIV

"Ooooouch!!" Mother has both hands on the hairbrush, pulling at the huge tangle in the back.

"Good gravy, girl, how on earth did yer hair get so snarly?"

"I dunno," I wail. Mother has been working on my hair for a good fifteen minutes. I can't stand it anymore. "Please, let me do it!"

Mother hands me the brush.

"I don't know how yer gonna get that out, but you know what Mother Kay said."

"I know."

She leaves me standing in front of the living room mirror, my hair looking like something out of a horror film. I can hear the TV on in the playroom; the rest of the family is watching *The Cosby Show*. I reach my hand to feel the back of my head and seriously consider cutting the matted tangle of hair out of my head. I'm unsuccessful at getting the brush through it.

"Watcha doin'?" Danny comes up behind me, looking at my dilemma. "Oh boy, that's a big one."

"I know."

"Here, give me the brush and I'll try it."

"Not unless you promise that if I say stop, you'll stop."

"I promise."

I can tell he means it. He runs his hand over the surface of my hair, assessing the situation.

"Okay, here's what we're gonna do. I'm gonna take little tiny sections of yer hair and see if we can get the snarl out of a small piece. We'll keep doin' it until it's gone."

"Okay, that sounds smart."

Danny gently separates a small section from the rest of my hair and begins brushing. I hold both hands to my scalp and squeeze my eyes shut.

"So, are ya on a punishment?" Danny glances in the mirror at me.

"No. Well, kinda," I still hold tightly to my scalp. "Mother Kay says I can't go to bed until my hair is combed out."

"That's not so bad."

"Why don't *you* try it, if you think that."

"I didn't mean that; I just meant we're gonna have yer hair smooth and combed out *long* before bedtime. That's how you get out of the punishment. I'll get it done before it turns into something."

"Danny, it's already my bedtime."

"It is? What time do ya go to bed?"

"Eight."

"Well, that's stupid. We went to bed at nine while we were in school."

"I know. Mother Kay changed it back to eight so I would have to go to bed at the same time as Claire and Lillian."

"Feel this." Danny is pleased with himself. I pick up the section and run my fingers through it. It feels as soft as cat's fur.

"Wow, that was fast."

"Okay, I'm gonna do the next part."

I can't believe how good it feels to have Danny helping me. It's just like he's thrown me a life preserver when everyone else is walking by, pointing their fingers at my flailing arms.

"Danny?"

"Yeah."

"Thanks for helpin' me."

"No problemo."

Danny is different than Tom. He isn't like Glenn and Albert or any of the other brothers. It's like he is part girl. He likes being with me, playing two square in the backyard or teaching me how to shoot hoops, while he tells me all about his latest idea for an invention. He has already invented in his mind a machine to replace setting the table and doing the dishes. He explains that there would be a conveyor belt inside a box that runs the length of both sides of the table. Everything Danny invents has a conveyor belt. Each person puts their dirty dishes on the conveyor belt, where the dishes go through a sort of car wash underneath the table. By the time the cycle is finished the dishes are dry, and when you sit at the next meal you just open the box, retrieve the clean dishes, and *voila*. Danny likes to say that at the end of his imaginary demonstration. "Two birds with one stone."

I think Danny is really smart. Mother Kay doesn't think so because he doesn't do real well in school, except for history. He loves history. Writing and spelling he's not so good at. Last year Mother Kay made him spell "beginning" five thousand times. No food or sleep until he did it. It took him the entire weekend. By Sunday afternoon, Ruby and me were sitting next to him counting the last row—4,988, 4,989, 4,990. He had a stack of papers separated into three columns, each filled with the word "beginning" written one on top of another in Danny's famously dark handwriting. His hand was shaking so hard his writing looked like a first grader's. Ruby tried to do it for him but her writing didn't look anything like Danny's so he erased them and rewrote them. Mother Kay did the same thing to Tom. "Vanquish" five thousand times. She is a bear about spelling. And handwriting. She refused to teach Danny cursive because she never thought his handwriting was up to par. That's what she would say, "up to par." She says lots of weird things. We don't listen to her much.

    I am going to save the snarl that Danny brushed from my hair. I am going to put it in a sandwich bag in my junk drawer. Mother says I'm ridiculously sentimental. I don't care what Mother thinks. She's not the one who stayed and helped me. She doesn't understand.

XXV

Everyone gets to take piano lessons except for me. Big surprise. Mother Kay's Aunt Lucille comes once a week and teaches all of the kids piano. Except for me. I stay in the kitchen helping Amanda cook lunch or stay in the basement folding the laundry. Mother Kay says I can have piano lessons if I will apologize and finish my sewing class. I guess I will never take piano lessons because I am never going to apologize to her. She should be apologizing to me for making me take her stupid sewing class in the first place. She dragged us all in the living room and announced that every Wednesday was sewing class. We brought out notebooks and pencils, which felt alarmingly familiar, and sat us around the table—Ruby, Emily, Amanda, and me. (Claire and Lillian weren't quite old enough.) She had a fat book with a picture of a piece of fabric and a measuring tape snaked across it on the front cover. Inside was a list of sewing terms. Our first order of business was to memorize the sewing terms, the names of everything, etc. It was like memorizing the dictionary. We copied them down in our notebooks, which ended up taking the first whole hour. She said we would have until next Wednesday to memorize it. I couldn't believe I'd gotten roped into doing another form of school.

Next week I could only do half of the rules while the other girls advanced to learning how to iron handkerchiefs. I stayed one lesson behind everyone else. While I was mastering the art of ironing hankies, Ruby and Emily were sewing on buttons. Amanda, who took to sewing like a second language, was already at the machine, sewing mazes on pieces of paper. Mother Kay supervised all my ironing, checking to see if I folded each one just right. She told me her mother took in ironing for rich people when she was a little girl. She said her mother taught her the proper way to do it and now she was passing such nuggets of wisdom to me.

Once I mastered the hankie, we were onto tablecloths, then pants and shirts. Last of all she taught me to iron permanent pleats into dark brown skirts with a dishtowel and vinegar. I had finally advanced to sewing buttons. Week after week I presented my button sewing talent only to have her scoff at the sloppiness.

"You'll never pass off buttons until you can get it perfect. Practice makes perfect. Go do it again." She always smiled when she sent me away with last week's buttons torn off the old shirt and I had to start over again. I never could get it right so I quit. I didn't show up to Wednesday's classes and everyone advanced to higher sewing projects, like hand hemming. I was glad to be done with it all and thought I had really gotten away with something until Aunt Lucille came into the picture. When Mother Kay announced to us that all of us would be receiving piano lessons from Aunt Lucille, who performed her talents on our old piano like Van Cliburn, I was elated—not only to learn the piano but to have a half of an hour all to myself with someone that wasn't in the family. My social appetite is fierce.

My excitement was dashed a week later when Mother Kay called me into the living room during sewing class and told me I wouldn't be receiving lessons until I finished the class. I was prepared to finish learning to sew until she said I had to apologize for leaving and being so disrespectful. She wanted me to say that I was wrong and she was right. I knew then I would be excluded. I would have to tolerate everyone else getting something I could not have.

Every Friday at ten o'clock in the morning when Aunt Lucille arrives in her yellow and white suburban, Mother Kay asks me if I am ready to apologize. I always answer the same way. "No."

"Okay," she says. "If you want to punish yourself, that's fine by me." Then she whispers to Aunt Lucille. I don't have to try very hard to imagine all the things she is saying. She thinks someday the pressure is going to get to me and I'll cave. She's in for a surprise. I couldn't care less about piano lessons or sewing or anything else that has Mother Kay's handprint on it. Although I do care that Lillian can do something that I can't. Her and Jacob are doing the best and are getting a lot of attention for it. I am going to learn to play the piano someday. I'll teach myself.

XXVI

We've been selling bread to earn money for the new school that's being built Down South. All the other people who are in the Work live Down South. Some people call it Colorado City but we just call it Down South. I would love to go to a school like that with kids my own age. I doubt I will ever go to school again. Mother Kay says Brother Coleman asked everyone for money to donate to the building and support of the school. So far we've done pretty well, at least according to Mother Kay. She keeps the money in a box in Father's closet. After we donate to the school Down South, we will use the money to buy a new piano.

We sell bread on Fridays. At first we just made signs on white poster board saying:

Delicious Homemade Bread
$1.00 per loaf

Me, Lillian, and Claire would stand outside on the street holding the signs over our heads. Sometimes cars would stop and we would sell big soft loaves of white bread to them. Tom and Danny would load bread in boxes and sell them door to door. The first day we made fifty dollars. Tom sold the last loaf to the ice cream truck driver. Mother Kay gave us all popsicles for our hard work. Each Friday we made a few extra loaves and tried to sell even more. Now we make about a hundred to a hundred and fifty loaves each Friday. Mother makes chocolate chip cookies and brownies too. They sell real well. Now we have a big wooden sign made from plywood and an old construction barricade we found on the road. Mother Kay painted "Bake Sale" in big red letters on both sides. Lillian and I set up the table out near the road and load the baked goods on it until it's full. Mother Kay sits at the front window and waits for the money. Whenever someone buys something we run the money over to her at the window and she counts it and puts it in the box. Sometimes she gets mad at us if we don't sell enough bread. On the good days, though, she's real sweet. I try and sell as much as possible. After Mother finishes baking the cookies and brownies she takes Annie, Benji, and Jonathon in the car and they go door to door too.

I think selling bread is fun and I like talking to the people who come to buy. But if Mother Kay sees me getting too friendly with someone she calls me over to the window and tells me that the customers don't like it and to quit being such a blabbermouth. I think the customers like me and I like talking to them. Sometimes I will stand in front of the cypress trees so she can't see me.

Lillian doesn't like selling bread very much. She's more shy, especially when the teenagers come by on their way home from school. She hides in the bushes when she sees them coming. I don't admit to Lillian that they scare me a little too. I want her to think I'm really outgoing, and even a risk taker. I say hi even when they spit on my dress. Last week a group of teenage boys kept driving around the block and giving us the bird and screaming obscenities when they drove past us. I just waved at them and flashed a big smile. I pretended they were being nice to us. They made round after round and I eventually started shouting back, "Same to you too!" Finally they gave up and smiled and waved back at me.

I wonder why all the people, all the Gentiles who buy our bread, I wonder why they are on the earth if they're no good. Mother says we should be nice to everyone no matter what their race or religion but to remember that we should always represent the priesthood and the kingdom of God in everything we do.

"Why are all those other people on the earth if only a few of us are going to make it back to heaven?"

"They have to be given a chance to accept the truth." Mother speaks with such confidence.

"Well, how do you know, we have the truth? I mean, how do you know for sure?

"Because, I just know."

"How, Mother? How do ya know fer sure?"

"Because, we're right."

"But, Mother, they think they're right and we're wrong. How do ya know fer sure?"

"I just know."

"What if we get to heaven and find out that we aren't the true church and all the Catholics are going the celestial kingdom instead?"

"What do you know about Catholics?"

"I read about 'em in the encyclopedia. I read about Jews too. They don't believe that Christ has come."

"Why don't you go talk to Father about all of this? He can explain it much better than I can." Mother turned back to the stove.

I have tried talking to Father before. It feels like I am bothering him with my silly questions. I know that he believes that we are the true church of God and that we should wear long sleeves and dresses. He says we should read the Book of Mormon too. But most of the time Father doesn't say anything. He doesn't reveal himself and what he thinks. He lets Mother Kay preach whatever she wants and he doesn't correct her or stop her. It makes it seem as though he agrees with everything. I would like to ask him so many things, but I can't talk to Father the way I talk to Mother. I guess I won't know until I am grown up myself.

XXVII

I don't know what I did to deserve this. I know I'm bad sometimes: I don't do the dishes, I lose peoples clothes, I sweep the dirt from the kitchen floor down the basement stairs. But I have been doing those bad things for a long time. Mother Kay says I'm a smart aleck. Mother Kay says a lot of things that aren't necessarily true. Father believes her though—every word out of her mouth.

Father came out of his bedroom last week with Mother Kay inches behind him. She was looking rather pleased with herself. Like a cat, she sashayed down the stairs, looked around the room at her subjects, and then gingerly walked around us to avoid contact before cushioning herself on the couch. Father then announced to the family that no one was allowed to talk to me or have anything to do with me. I was being punished. I asked him what it was for, and he looked at me like I was being a smart aleck to *him*, which I would never do. He said, "I think you know," and then walked out the door leaving me with the vindictive cat, her unclipped claws on display.

Now that I think about it, I'm sure Father only meant for me to be ignored for one day, which is bad enough, but Mother Kay has taken it upon herself to extend my punishment for an intentionally undisclosed period of time. Father doesn't really know what's going on; he goes to work at the water softener company and I don't see him until night. He put Mother Kay in charge, at least I think he did. If Father was home more he would see what Mother Kay does and how mean she is and I think he would stop her. But he isn't here and if he isn't at work he is gone to a meeting somewhere or up in his room doing bills. She is always with him and I know she lies to him. She probably convinced him that I deserved to be ignored for a long long time.

I am at her mercy. But then, she doesn't have any mercy, so here I am. It's been a week. I have been nobody, for a week.

Mornings are bad. I pretend to wake up when the other girls get up; I pretend that everything is normal. We dress silently and in the dark. I can hear the rustling of their clothes but no one speaks. Claire and Lillian leave the room to go start breakfast and I stay behind. I understand their predicament. They are pretending as much as I am. I close the door and crawl back under the covers and pretend that it is the middle of the night.

I slept in late today. The sun cutting through the window like a blade—not morning sun, time to get up sun, everything is right with the world sun; but middle of the day sun, you're gonna be in trouble sun. A sickly silence permeates the room; it is far too quiet to hide from the shame. I slide off the bunk to get dressed and comb my hair as quickly as possible, hoping to alleviate the weight of this feeling. I open my door quietly and peek out into the hall. I can hear Amanda downstairs in the kitchen cleaning out the fridge. She is humming a song, *There is work enough to do, 'ere the sun goes down, for myself and kindred too, ere the sun goes down, every idle whisper stilling, with a firm and purpose willing, all my daily tasks fulfilling ere the sun goes down.* I must have missed breakfast again. From the hall I can see Mother vacuuming the house. That's *my work.* Mother is doing my work. I back up into my bedroom and close the door.

The first day of my punishment I missed breakfast and when I came to the table for lunch Mother Kay had moved my bowl and spoon to the counter and removed my chair from the table.

"Here, Danny," she said "take this chair to the playroom. We won't be needing it for a while." She said it all without looking at me but I was undeterred and filled up my bowl with the lentil soup boiling on the stove and took it to my room. I wasn't going to let her get to me so easily. I had to pace myself for whatever she had in store for me.

I wish someone would stand up against Mother Kay. Why does everyone do what she says? And for goodness sake, why does Father believe her lying tongue? But I'm afraid of her power too, the limitless power she has to hurt me. She can hurt someone else in order to hurt me too. Like Mother. She talks to Mother like she is a child. "Mary! Why didn't you change my sheets? Mary, I have a doctor's appointment today. I hope you aren't planning on using the car." That's how it goes.

I stay in my room mostly, because it's easier that way. I found a history book under the bed. I decided to memorize the whole thing. So far I have memorized two pages about Mesopotamia and the Cradle of Civilization. It's not much yet, but it's a beginning. I am not allowed to read novels except the ones Mother Kay has read first, which is pitifully few. I can't read the newspaper because Mother has been hiding it from me now that she gets to it first.

I close the history book. I can hear Mother coming up the stairs. She's putting laundry away. The laundry I was supposed to be doing.

"Mother?"

She flinches ever so slightly at the sound of my voice and I can tell she wants to turn around and say, "Why do you do this to yourself? Why in the world do you put yourself through all this misery?" But she doesn't say a word and all of the disregarded emotions inside of me press at their boundaries. She really believes that I am doing this to myself! She thinks I am a bad and wicked human being. I will never be able to convince her otherwise even if I live to be one hundred. When I had to stay home from Disneyland she said it was my fault. I tried to tell her that I had too much schoolwork and that I would never have finished it in time, but she refused to accept that.

"Mother?" I say again, I want so badly for her to turn around and look me in the eye. I know if she looks into my eyes she will be compelled to speak to me. But this time she is more stoic. She walks past where I am sitting on the bottom bunk. As she walks past me, her skirt brushes my leg, her white apron just within reach, and out of sheer desperation I grab at the hem.

"Mother," I plead, my voice wobbling. "Please!" She pulls away from me indifferently and hangs clothes in the closet. I fall to me knees behind her, begging.

"Don't do this to me, Mother. Please tell me what I did wrong so I can fix it. I don't know what to do." The tears were run unchecked down my face. I think that in any moment she will turn around angrily and say, "You know very well what you did," but she only looks directly over my head, retrieves the empty laundry basket and walks out the door. I climb to my bed and in the nearest corner I curl myself in a ball and cry—not the fresh tears of frustration but moldy tears of deficiency.

I have a rebellious streak. Mother says it's a wide rebellious streak, almost as wide as the stubborn one that I have. It is this rebellious and stubborn nature that assures me I will never cave, that nothing Mother Kay does to me will rock the core of what I believe about myself. Until today. Today I am breaking. I can hear the groans and creaking of my spirit giving way to the terrible pressure. I am Black Beauty, my body used up long before its prime, head bowed low to the ground, and the light inside snuffed out. The scars will not heal. I am pulling a cart in the streets of London awaiting a fate I have no control over.

I have a knife. I snuck it into my room yesterday, wrapped in a dishtowel. It is a new knife, very sharp. It has a shiny serrated edge. I cut the dresser with it. I don't know why I did that; I just sawed a notch right into the side of it, revealing the white pine beneath the stain. I guess I wanted to see how sharp the knife was. I wanted to destroy something. I have been hiding it under the bed. I retrieve it, still wrapped in the dishtowel, open it up, and look at my reflection in the shining stainless steel. I fold my hand around the blade and hold it tight until it is warm. I hold it while I sit at the window counting one hundred red cars that drive past the house. I hold it while I sit in the closet with the curtains drawn. I hold it simply to feel it, poised and waiting. I don't know why I want to hurt myself, except the very idea of it makes me feel supremely powerful. I wonder if a wound I inflict upon myself will heal. Maybe it will simply hurt, throbbing every time I touch it, forever and ever … throbbing. But still, I wonder what it would feel like to have that blade cut through my flesh. I wonder how it would look seeing the jagged skin hanging loose off my hand. I wonder …

I yank the knife down through my closed fist in one stroke. It hurts, but I keep my fist closed. I let the knife fall to the floor. I look at my clasped hand as if it belongs to someone else. I watch it until blood seeps through white knuckles and down my wrist.

XXVIII

Amanda got married. She just turned seventeen. I knew it was coming when she started acting different. She changed overnight. She stopped wearing her favorite western shirt and black skirt and started wearing clothes that the parents liked. She carried a mini hymnbook in her pocket and sang her favorite hymns while she worked. The parents treated her different too. Mother Kay talked to her like she was one of the mothers.

She married one of Uncle Heber's boys. He's not really our uncle. Mother told us to call him that out of respect. Uncle Heber used to be in the Work, then he left to marry a Gentile lady. They divorced and Uncle Heber came back into the Work with his three sons. Now he's married to two of Mother Kay's sisters, Aunt Marge and Aunt Ada. Amanda married Uncle Heber's oldest son, Greg. I begged her on her wedding day to tell me who she was going to marry but she kept her secret hidden right behind the smile she couldn't wipe away. I followed her through the house, promising not to tell a soul. She didn't budge but said, "You'll see." I had an idea it was Greg because of how she acted when he was around, but I didn't know for sure.

Since Amanda left, things have been changing again. Ruby's the oldest Big Girl and isn't doing too well in the parents' eyes and Albert ran away from home. I haven't seen or heard from him in weeks. A few days before he left, I went to his room to put away clothes and I found a half-empty bottle of vodka by the dresser. I hurried out, hoping he wouldn't notice. Maybe the parents found it and kicked him out. I don't know. What I do know is that Mother Kay hated Albert. She was always telling Father how Albert wouldn't wear his sleeves rolled down and when he walked into a room Mother Kay bristled like he smelled really bad.

I didn't want Albert to leave. I don't want any of my brothers and sisters to leave but that doesn't change the fact that they all leave. Sometimes they just disappear and I rarely see them again. Other times they get married and then they disappear just the same. Albert made dinner rolls sometimes for Sunday dinner. He liked to flip us with a wet dishtowel when we did the dishes together. He has the most wonderful laugh I have ever heard. Aunt Liesel loves him like no other. I wonder if Albert will ever come home.

We've been to Uncle Heber's for a few summer holidays since Amanda has been married. They have a big yard and we can play games and eat good food. Last time we were there Uncle Heber gave us a hayride and we raced in the backyard. Emily raced Uncle Heber's son, Aaron. They're the same age and Emily won. I was rooting for her. Aaron didn't seem bothered that a girl beat him but came and sat down on the grass while we ate.

"I heard Albert ran away," he said nonchalantly. I couldn't believe he would bring up such a sensitive subject.

"Yeah." Emily didn't offer more.

"So, I guess that means he's a Gentile now."

"He is not a Gentile!" I wasn't prepared for the anger that rippled up through me. "He'll always be our brother!"

Aaron looked a little startled.

"Oh, I know, I didn't mean …" he didn't finish. He might have had the chance if I hadn't stood up and walked away. I avoided him the rest of the day and told Claire and Lillian an embellished version of what he had said. I want to hate someone for what had happened to Albert; I want to hate Aaron for not understanding. He had pushed a button that released an anger that wouldn't fit back inside of me again. I can try folding it a million ways but once it has been inflated, it seems larger than before. I want to let it loose, like a hurricane dismantling and destroying everything in its path, this wild and unpredictable force that begs for regurgitation. I don't let it loose; I simply rearrange it inside of me.

XXIX

We've been going to the garden in the evenings and on Saturdays since Albert left. I can't believe how much work he had been doing. Even Mother Kay said the garden still doesn't look the way it did while Albert was taking care of it. Aunt Liesel really liked Albert. The garden is really Aunt Liesel's place. We take care of her property in exchange for all the vegetables and fruit we can use. I don't mind going to the garden on weeknights because Mother Kay isn't with us, but on Saturday she comes and I would much rather be home. She makes me pick the dead flowers all day long on Saturday. It's not too bad if Claire or Lillian comes with me. Usually one of us goes and the other two stay home to help with kitchen duty or wash duty.

Mother Kay tries to keep me away from Claire and Lillian as much as possible. She says I'm a bad influence on them. She's gotten worse since Emily caught me and Lillian mooning the cars out front one day when we were supposed to be doing the wash. I tried to get Emily to keep her mouth shut but she had to tell Father and he made a big deal out of it, threatening to make us moon the family. It was my fault. I had to talk pretty hard to get Lillian to do it. I had seen the next door neighbor do it to me and was quite amused. From that day on we called the neighbor boy White-Butt.

I don't know what possessed me to do it except it felt really bad and exciting. Lillian swore up and down that she was never going to do anything I said ever again. Lillian just isn't used to getting in trouble like I am. Last Saturday when Claire came with me to the garden, we went to see the horses that are in a field across the road from Aunt Liesel's place. We went while Father and Mother Kay were home picking up lunch. It took two carrots to get one of the horses near enough to the fence for me to hop on its bare back. I guess it hadn't been ridden much because it took off around the pasture like a bullet and I bounced around for a second before I flipped off its back and landed hard in the weeds. The horse that looked harmless seconds before seemed to transform into a wild beast. It neighed loudly and started charging before I had a chance to jump up. Claire was screaming as I scrambled toward the fence and squeezed through the beams. It was the most exciting thing that ever happened to me. I couldn't wait to try it again but Claire said if I did it, she would tell on me. I guess maybe I am a bad influence on Claire and Lillian and I deserve to pick dead petunias 'til the cows come home. So I was surprised when Father let me spend a week at Aunt Liesel's with Claire and Lillian.

Aunt Liesel brought us into her tiny old-fashioned house. It seemed as quaint and foreign to me as the German language that she loved so much. To be allowed in Aunt Liesel's house was being allowed into her inner world. Everything about her past interested me. She was born and raised in Germany during the First World War. She came over to America when she was forty, during the Second World War, to marry a man she'd never met. She remained childless, which seemed to be a source of great suffering to her. Her husband died before they could live out their lives together and it was her widowhood that brought her into our lives. She talked about Erik like he was still there, his picture hanging above her chair on her living room wall for consultation. She told me how he had made her into the person she was and that even after twenty years she missed him every day. It was because of loneliness that she had asked Father if we could come and stay at her house.

I went out with her in the early mornings to pick currants. She wore simple clothes and an apron made out of the same fabric as her dress. We worked without a word exchanged but her presence filled the silence with adequate substance. I felt safe and warm when I was near her and I wanted to stay with her forever.

It was like no other week in my life. We played whenever we wanted, and when people from home came to weed the garden I felt encroached upon. Aunt Liesel let us watch TV during the day and we relaxed on her porch with Mooney, the cat, in the evening while she knitted socks for her relative's children. In the evening she came alive, telling stories and listening to music. She taught me how to read German from *Brothers Grimm Book of Fairy Tales*. She let Claire and Lillian take turns with me. She said the greatest fairy tales ever written were from Germany. I thought she should love America, but she remained strangely loyal to all that Germany stood for. She believed that even the Bible was more beautiful when translated in German. She loved to listen to me read to her in my choppy attempts before we went to bed at night. I loved her listening and telling me I was a natural.

The night before we had to go home she brought out her photo albums and showed me pictures of her childhood: her loving father and strict mother, her two sisters and one brother. She said she was the mischievous child.

"Look, you see my face, you see mischief there?" She laughed abundantly. "Oh, Susieline, you should have seen me; I was full of life!" She squealed at the memory, her delight at herself a wonderment to me.

"Look, see this one here? Ahhh, I was beautiful then. I was beautiful, no?"

"You were very pretty. I bet all the guys were after you," I said.

"Many men wanted me to marry. I say no to all of them. They not be the right one," she said, holding her forefinger in midair. "I only marry the right man if it takes forever. I tell my father I will never marry until I know he is right for me. My father was very sad about it. He only wanted me happy."

"Can I see the picture of you and your friends swimming?"

She laughed again. "Oh yes, Susieline, you did not forget." She seemed pleased. She had to go back to the closet to get another album before we found it. She was naked and poised to dive while her friends were in repose on the rocks. It looked like a renaissance painting—people in the nude, like it was no big deal.

"In Germany, being naked is not to be a problem." She gazed for a long time at her younger self. "I didn't know better then." She closed the album. "Come girls, help me make dinner. You too, Little One." That's what she called Claire: Little One. Lillian was Barbara and I was Susieline.

That night at bedtime I asked Aunt Liesel how she got out of Germany. She went to the tiny closet under the stairs and brought out a small box. She showed me the passport dated 1944.

"I sailed."

"You look mad." Her face in the picture was like stone.

"I was angry. The officer thought I was a Jew and wouldn't let me on board. I am not a Jew! Look at my shiny hair." Her voice was rising in pitch. "Jews do not have shiny hair!"

I didn't mean to get her angry. She put the passport back in the box and rested her head against the back of the black leather chair. "That Hitler was a bad man. He make a dirty mark on Germany. He was very bad. All Germans are not like Hitler." She paused and I could almost see the history passing through her gray eyes. "He made a road out of dead Jews and covered it with rocks. It smelled very bad. Susieline, do you understand?!" her voice quivered. "It was very, very bad. None of us used that road again but the smell …" she closed her eyes and breathed in deeply. "It was a long, long time ago. I don't want to remember anymore. Guten nacht." She turned out the lamp and went upstairs to bed.

The next morning I asked Aunt Liesel if she would put the passport in her will so I could have it some day.

"You like it?" she said, surprised.

"It's my favorite one."

"You take it now." She was already fishing in the cupboard under the stairs. "Here, you like it? It be yours." I didn't know what to say, and before I had a chance to think about it I heard the car in the driveway coming to pick us up.

"Danke."

She smiled and hugged me tight.

"Ich liebe dich!" I hollered on my way down her porch steps`.

"Ich liebe dich auch," she called craning her head to see my face as we backed out of the long driveway. *I love you too.*

XXX

Football is my passion. I can't decide if I like it because no one wants me to like it or if it's something else. I love it. I love watching it, I love playing it—the sheer strength of motion, the line of scrimmage, a boundary guarded by black-and-white judges, the light reflecting off of round helmets in the Saturday afternoon sun. I also like it because it's active, masculine—male. Football is the opposite of everything female. There is nothing feminine about football, and I don't want anything that is feminine.

I don't get to watch football as much as I would like because I'm always doing the wash. It doesn't seem to matter how hard I try, I can't get it done by five thirty like I'm supposed to. Mother Kay says she's going to start whipping me every day I don't get done. I try, oh so many days I try. But trying doesn't count; effort is only evidence to me. I cannot find words for this kind of prison. So I wake each morning, peeking out of blurry sleep with one eye to see if the world has changed, if life became something else. But there is football. Another world altogether where there is a winner and a loser and a fair game played. There is hope; there is glory and reward. I wish they would change Monday Night Football to Friday Night Football. It starts at seven and I can only watch it if the wash is done. I can never finish the huge Monday wash so I watch football when I put the clothes away by crossing the playroom as many times as possible and standing at the base of the stairs until I hear Mother Kay's distinct footsteps heading in my direction.

Sometimes Mother lets us go to the park in the evening and play on the long stretches of green grass. We don't have grass in our yard, just a big slab of cement—unless you go out front, but no one is allowed out there. Mother Kay made a rule about no one going to the front yard. I guess it would draw further attention. She says we need to be discreet. Sometimes I sneak into the front yard and sit directly beneath the window so even if Mother Kay looks out she won't see me.

I dream about playing professional football. I decided I'll play for the Miami Dolphins, mostly because Dan Marino is so handsome. Gerald asked me one day what I wanted to do when I grew up. I told him I was going to be linebacker. He laughed so hard. He took me straight to Father and had me tell Father what I was going to do when I was older. Father was greatly amused and asked me what I would do about my husband. I told Father not to worry because I was going to marry a wimp so I could punch his lights out. This was obviously the right thing to say because Father laughed so hard his face was red and the chair he was sitting in was rocking back and forth. He sat up and wiped his eyes and said, "Remind me to tell your husband what you just said on your wedding day." I made Father laugh. It feels good. Football is good.

I have a scrapbook about football: newspaper clippings of my favorite games, statistics, and a few autographs given to me by one of the Cook girls that live down our street. They go to Meeting so Father lets us invite them over to our house once in a while. They all like football so we get along. We trade pictures taken from the sports section of our two different newspapers. I found a copy of an old *Sports Illustrated* at the thrift store when Mother took me to buy clothes. It cost ten cents. I paid for it myself.

On Saturdays when I am tending the kids in the playroom and Father is watching college football I sit on the couch and talk to him. It is the neatest feeling talking to him and seeing his smile. It doesn't matter that we are talking sports. It is the only time I feel connected. But it isn't real and I know that. I know that I am pretending. Sometimes after the family has gone to bed I sit quietly in front of my drawer and look at the pictures I have collected. I am hiding under a stack of them, wearing them like an uncomfortable mask. A great swell of sadness comes over me. I cry awhile; it feels so good. I feel sorry for myself for a moment or two even though I know I shouldn't. Mother says I should never feel sorry for myself because there are so many others who have it worse than I do. I don't want to think about other people's problems. I just want to feel bad about myself for a minute.

I know that the only reason I like football is it helps me to be noticed. I also like it because I want to be good at something. I can throw a football pretty far and I can knock down anyone who gets in my way. Football feels so powerful and I feel utterly invincible just imagining myself playing it. For that I will keep pretending.

XXXI

I've been doing wash duty for nine months. Six days a week without a break. I have to do the wash good for one week before Mother Kay will let me change jobs. She says I don't care about anything but myself.

I care. I do. I care about the way Mother looks at me when she sees I am far behind or catches me reading a book. The disappointment in her face and the silence that she carries as she walks back up the basement stairs leaves me feeling sick to my stomach.

Do I care about the wash? She is right, I don't care about that. I don't care if I make Mother Kay mad. I wouldn't care if she disappeared into thin air like a plane that mysteriously vanishes in the Bermuda Triangle. In fact, I wish she would vanish and never return.

Sometimes when I get mad I tell Mother I hope everyone's clothes get permanently wrinkled, the dryer will make a tear in a favorite blouse, or one of the kids would leave a bright red crayon in their pocket and it would melt all over the dark batch. She gets really upset when I talk that way, and leaves the room.

I admit to getting desperate and throwing the towels in the dryer before they were washed. The smell of warm dirty towels filled the basement with a mildewy scent. I poured a capful of fabric softener, undiluted, into the dryer with the towels. The smell got worse. The yellow towels came out of the dryer looking awful and smelling worse than before. I folded them and put them in the bathrooms anyway. Mother Kay found them and I could hear her yelling my name long before I found her standing at the top of the stairs with her hand on her hip. When I got near her she pulled me all the way upstairs by my braid and shook my face into the dirty towels. It didn't turn out very well.

Glenn tried to help me one day by telling me how I could do the wash better. "Do it this way," he said. He doesn't understand. After he left, I cried a little and then did twenty chin-ups on the copper pipes in the ceiling.

I crammed an entire batch of permanent press clothes up the dryer vent. Mother found the clothes the next morning, a shirt dangling out of the dryer vent outside, over the coal bin. I guess I pushed them up too far up. She was not happy and I had very wrinkly clothes and had to rewash them and do the batch all over. Other times I hide baskets of clean clothes in people's closets. I throw piles of clothes behind the dryer and washers. I slide baskets of rags under the beds. On really bad days I just throw clothes right in the outside garbage can.

I don't want to do it anymore. I can't seem to bring myself to do the work when there isn't a single reward. Mother says that a job well done should be reward enough. I don't feel any reward when I do my job right. It only feels like Mother Kay won. She made me do things the right way with her beating and slapping. I can't let her do that. I can't let her take that away from me. I want to win.

Sometimes I lose people's clothes. I suppose that is to be expected because I don't try very hard not to lose them. The problem is I lose important clothes, like Mother Helen's pantyhose. She checks the night before to see if they are in her drawer and then hunts me down and makes me find them. Sometimes I lose Mother Kay's pantyhose too. She hollers down to the basement and when I come up the stairs she grabs me by the hair and drags me through the house making me look for them. Sometimes I know where they are; most times I have no idea. It might be because I throw the clean clothes back in the hamper. Or I pretend to forget to get the clothes in Father's bathroom when I sort the laundry. Sometimes I just get so lost in my daydreams while folding that I forget where I put things.

Danny helps me sometimes. He folds clothes and races up the stairs to put them away for me. But he has to work in the garden at Aunt Liesel's in the afternoon so he leaves me after lunch, riding down the street on his ten-speed bike. I cry unashamed until he pedals out of sight.

Yesterday when Ruby, Emily, Danny, and Tom went sledding on the hill at the park, I had to stay home and finish the wash. Tom and Danny bought a new inner tube with their own money. We've been getting an allowance. I'm not sure why Mother Kay is giving us money. I've never had money before so this is really new to me. I get about two dollars a week. I could get more but it would be risky. Mother Kay pays us. She takes us up in Father's room one at a time and asks us what we think we deserve to have for our labor. The most we can get is five dollars but she makes it clear that we will never deserve that much. She says that's a mother's salary. I usually say I deserve two dollars. It keeps me right about where she thinks I ought to be and makes our weekly visits less dreadful. She tries to get me to talk too. She asks me things like "How are things going?" and "Is there anything you want to tell me?" I always play like I'm doing great and I couldn't think of anything if I tried. She asked me one day why I wasn't friends with her. I was muted by the question. Finally I just told her I didn't know. Claire, on the other hand, pokes her head in the doorway and says, "Fifty cents." Then Mother

Kay wants to know why she thinks she only deserves fifty cents and then Claire says, "Okay, one dollar." She keeps upping it until Mother Kay lets her go.

Ruby makes it a little harder. She asks for five dollars all the time and then ends up in Father's room getting in trouble for an hour. She always comes out saying, "I deserve five dollars. I work harder than the mothers." Mother Kay does not like Ruby.

Now that we're getting money Mother Kay told us we have to buy our own clothes and everything we need. My eight dollars a month doesn't go very far but I like to choose how I will spend my money. I'm saving to buy a *Sports Illustrated* subscription. Sometimes I pretend that a witch turns me into a football. Mother will come downstairs to check on me and I'll be rolling around the floor. She won't be able to find me and I will get thrown out or left on the grass at the park and found by a wonderful man that plays football at which point I will turn back into a girl and he will fall in love with me and we'll live happily ever after. Sometimes I pretend while I am throwing the ball to Jacob that there is an agent sitting on the park bench. He doesn't care that I am a girl. He'll take me away to play for the Cincinnati Bengals or the Seattle Seahawks. I'll be the star player and amaze the world with my unbelievable strength. Of course I'll get hurt a few times and be carried off the field by my loyal teammates and a doting doctor that falls in love with me.

When dreams of playing professional football feels a little out of reach I imagine that I am the team laundress for the Miami Dolphins and I get to wash Dan Marino's underwear and socks. He'll be obsessed with me and watch me from a distance. I'll be so beautiful he can't take his eyes off me. He'll fall in love with me and we'll play football on the weekends. It all works out in the end.

The end. There's no agent, no doting doctor, and no Dan Marino, only a basement full of clothes that I wash over and over and over. Besides the four invisible walls that seem to be closing in on me there's only the dangling bare bulb over my head observing me.

XXXII

Tom cornered me in Mother Helen's bedroom. I knew something was up immediately. I tried to pretend I didn't know.

"Hey. You sure got big fast."

"What do a mean?" I knew exactly what he meant.

"Ya know, tits."

"Tom, that's gross."

"Yeah, I know. I'm sorry. I shouldn't talk like that." He shut the door tight.

"Would ya show 'em to me?"

"Tom!"

"Okay … I'm sorry. I'm not tryin' to be gross. I just really want to see what they look like."

"Tom, you know exactly what they look like. You have magazines full of 'em."

He smiled mischievously. "Yeah, I know." He kept smiling at the thought of it.

"I've gotta go clean the bathroom." I tried to leave the room. He stepped in front of the door.

"I'll clean it for ya if you'll show me everything ya have."

"I can't, Tom."

"Why not?"

"Because of last time."

"I didn't hurt ya."

"Yeah, ya did. When ya used that stupid yardstick."

"Did that hurt ya?" He seemed genuinely surprised.

"Yes, Tom."

"Okay, I promise to be careful this time."

"I can't, Tom. Someone will come."

"I promise I'll make sure they don't." He was more desperate than I thought. I started to feel scared.

"Please, Tom, I would, but I can't." I tried to push him out of the way.

"C'mon, please? It'll be quick."

"No, Tom, I don't want to."

He was begging. I didn't like this Tom at all, but I had always protected him. We had always been on the same side.

When Father caught him smoking cigarettes in the bathroom I didn't tell anyone that I knew he was hiding them in his clothes drawer. Father made all of the kids take a drag on one of the confiscated cigarettes so we would know what we were missing. He brought out the wine at the same time. The one he used for the Sacrament. He said we needed to get the desire out of our systems. It was weird seeing Father with a smoke in one hand and drink in the other. It reminded me of something I saw in a black-and-white movie, like Humphrey Bogart in *Casablanca*. Only Father didn't look anything like Humphrey Bogart.

Tom's been in trouble with Father for a while now. It really started when he lied about his age and got a job at a local car wash. Shortly thereafter he found a girlfriend. Her name was Destiny. She lived a few houses down from Mrs. Larsen and I guess they met while he was walking Toby. He told Father about her and wanted to go on a date with her. Of course Father said no and then embarrassed Tom in front of the family by telling everyone he had a girlfriend using a mocking tone. I could tell Tom was upset but he pretended he didn't care. Later Father told Mother Kay to go through Tom's stuff. When he left to go to the garden the next day, Mother and Mother Kay snuck down to his room and rummaged through his things. I was so angry I couldn't see straight. I was going to have to re-hide all *my* stuff in a safer location.

Tom was persistent. I didn't give in and I think I made him angry. He walked out of Mother Helen's bedroom and slammed the door. I felt relief and guilt all at the same time. Pictures of that night locked in the schoolroom when I let him see me and touch me vividly returned in my head. I lost a piece of myself to him that I knew I could never have back. I have to save what is left. Tom made so many empty promises during our years together; his promise to *just look* meant nothing to me. I had a deep feeling that I would lose much more than my self-respect and dignity if I let him do it again.

I think I understand Emily's secret about what happened to her. I see the hollow place in her eyes where the shadow of her true self is hiding. I don't dare to ask her what else has happened to her. I don't want to know.

Now Tom is gone.

He ran away from home to who knows where. He didn't take much of his stuff but left things as if he would be right back. He left his bed unmade, the sheets still a tangle from his last night at home.

He's not coming back.

It's hard not to think about him the way he used to be: floppy brown hair in the wind as we skated around and around in the backyard on our twin skates; making jokes about Mother Kay's nose during long hauls in the schoolroom. He drove me crazy and I miss him so much I can't breathe sometimes. No one says much about him except that if he comes around we aren't to talk to him. He's an evil spirit just like Mother Kay had said. The devil got him and made him bad.

I hope he has somewhere to sleep.

XXXIII

A construction crew has been working on rerouting the creek behind the eight-foot fence in our backyard. I like to watch the men, with their lithe bodies and deeply tanned skin, through the holes in the fence. Most of them work with their shirts off, in holey jeans. We know all their names, me and the other girls, from listening carefully to their banter whenever we are outside filling up pitchers of water for dinner at the well on the north side.

Jim is the one we watch the most. The others have long straggly hair or some other unavoidable flaw, but Jim is perfect. His sandy-colored hair has just enough wave in it to stay put in the wind. He keeps it cut short but not as short as the Big Boys have to keep theirs. It curls up under his ears and hugs the back of his neck. He has blue eyes that sharply contrast his tanned face. His arms are all muscle and he holds his body in the most irresistible and masculine poses. Lately he's been noticing Ruby and Emily's odd zeal for keeping the upstairs windows clean and he whistles at them. Ruby has even emboldened herself enough to talk to him from across the yard. He told Ruby he likes it when she wears her blue-checkered dress. I think she's madly in love with him and Emily isn't too far behind her. I like watching him, but that's as far as it goes.

Sometimes I wonder if something is wrong with me because I don't daydream about being kissed by a guy. I don't think it would be that good. Once I saw Ruby and Emily kissing the beams holding up the roof of the sandbox. They confided in me that the beams were really the two motorcycle cops on the TV show *C.H.I.P.S.* I thought they were both pretty stupid.

That's not to say I don't daydream, I just don't get into the details of kissing and all that stuff. While Ruby and Emily are dreaming of romance on deserted islands, I dream of Jim finding my battered body floating in the creek one morning and saying "jeesus!" when he sees me. I imagine what it would feel like to have his arms holding my legs and back as he carries my near-lifeless body to the bank. Forget mouth-to-mouth resuscitation, I just want his hand to check for a pulse. I don't tell the other girls that I get more thrills about imagining a siren-filled ride to the hospital with at least two overly concerned paramedics than of all the passionate lovemaking I am not allowed to watch on TV.

I thought about jumping into the creek to stage such an event but worried that I would just drown and no one would find me. Mother Kay would tell everyone I deserved to die. I wouldn't be able to tell them otherwise. They might believe her.

"Guess why Jim likes the blue dress?" Emily's face was full of unusual mischief.

"Why?" I was sincerely interested.

"He told Ruby he can see through it." There was a mix of graveness and utter delight in her voice.

"No way!"

"Yes way! And I'm gonna ask Ruby if I can wear it tomorrow."

"Emily! Ya want him to see yer bra?!"

"Well, he can't exactly *see* it. That's the whole idea with sheer clothes. It gets the imagination going."

"You wanna get his imagination going?"

"So what?" Emily defended. "I'm bigger on top than Ruby anyway and I'm a true brunette."

"Okay, what does that have to do with anything?"

"Guys like brunettes and they like girls with big …" she pointed to her chest. "Ya know."

"Yeah, believe me, I know."

I have recently been faced with C-cup bras and bouncing when I run up the stairs and it has come as something of a shock to me, the men who suddenly became interested in shaking my hand at Meeting, where former eye contact has been exchanged for the shift—up, down, up, down. It wouldn't be so bad if it was just the guys my own age but it's men I've been calling "Uncle" out of respect or men I've just plain respected, up until their true colors seeped through their phony facades. It makes me want to slap their silly faces and strap my trusty belt back on. I don't want to be seen as property and can't imagine why it seems Emily does. If I want anything from guys it's their acceptance and camaraderie, not their adoration or their lust.

Sometimes I hate men. Mother says it runs in my blood to hate men. She says all of Father's sisters are men haters and I need to watch myself very closely so I don't turn into one myself. I'm not really a man hater; I just hate men who think women are inferior or stupid, which is a lot more men than I realized. In truth, it's women I hate, at least the ones who think they are inferior to men. I hate them even more than the men who treat them like appliances.

I try not to talk this way when Mother is around because it gets her terribly upset. She thinks because men hold the priesthood that they have some superior wisdom and know things that women don't. I told her I didn't believe in that crap and she got really mad at me for saying the word "crap." Then she told me I needed to counsel with Father. She said he could explain the whole "women should submit themselves to men" thing much better than she could.

I don't want it explained to me and if I hear the word "submit" one more time I think I'll throw up.

XXXIV

Ruby says she knows who she's supposed to marry. She says it's Glenn's friend Rich. Glenn and Rich work at the egg factory together. Rich is Uncle William's son, another of the unrelated uncles. Rich and his family don't go to Meeting. Mother says they're independents. She says they believe some of the things we do but they don't attend any church and have remained independent of a leader. They have no authority to baptize their children or give their sons the priesthood because all the men have lost their priesthood. But I don't know if Mother is right.

Ruby says she's been praying and the Lord has told her that she is supposed to marry Rich. I couldn't be happier for Ruby because Rich is one of those super nice guys who seem to care about everyone, including his best friend's sister. He's even been nice to me. She told me from the day she laid eyes on him she felt he was the one. Of course they haven't really talked to each other. Ruby told me she asked God for a sign. If she was supposed to marry Rich then it would rain the next day. Well it rained and Ruby is 100 percent positive that this is her course of action.

I am glad she got an answer because she almost ran away with Jim.

It all started the week before the construction crew had finished the job. They dug too close to our fence and it collapsed into the creek and they spent an extra month making repairs and rebuilding the fence. Meanwhile, with no fence, access and visibility was dramatically heightened. Ruby would sneak outside in her blue dress and talk to Jim when Mother Kay was at the doctor. Then Ruby got the idea to make Jim an apple pie, as if talking to him wasn't risky enough. She promised him she would bring it the next day. When she told me about it she asked me if I would help her. We had to steal all the ingredients, including the apples, and figure out a way to cook the darn thing. We got up early the next morning and Ruby had already stolen the needed ingredients and had them hidden in the basement sink. I helped her by peeling the apples and we baked it in the basement oven. Ruby was on cooking and had to make the pie in between making breakfast. We almost got caught while it was cooking—the smell of apples and cinnamon wafting suspiciously up the basement stairs. But Ruby had an amazing talent for changing the subject and then raced downstairs to tell me to open the basement window. I stood next to the stove, pushing the smell out the window with my hands while Jeanette frantically cleaned up the apple peelings. After it was cooled we had to hide it until she could give it to Jim.

Jim was becoming increasingly interested in Ruby to the point of worrying me. She told me everything he said to her. She told him about her life and how miserable she was. She wanted to leave. I'm still not sure how the conversation went but she came in late one night and told me that she was leaving with Jim in the middle of the night. She said he was going to leave his wife and take her with him. *That must have been one heck of a good pie*, I thought. She told me a tearful good-bye and I wondered why I didn't try and talk her out of it. Jim told her they were finished with the repairs and would be leaving the job for good. Ruby was desperate as she packed a bag with her most essential belongings. I went to sleep that night expecting to never see her again. When morning came Ruby was cooking breakfast as usual, except she was crying. When no one was looking I asked her, "What's the matter? What happened?"

"He never showed up!" She turned her head and kept stirring the oatmeal. "Do ya think he's okay? Maybe he got in an accident and couldn't make it. Maybe he saw Father or Mother Kay and didn't want to get caught. Susanna … why didn't he come?"

"I don't know. I guess he changed his mind. Maybe his wife talked him out of it."

"He didn't tell his wife, silly." Ruby chuckled through her tears. "I guess I shouldn't have gotten my hopes up."

"Well, if it makes you feel any better, I'm glad yer still here." I couldn't hardly say the next words but I wanted her to know. "I would have really missed you."

"Thanks," she said. "At least one person cares about me."

I do care about Ruby and I know she cares about me. When Glenn, Tom, and Danny were teasing me in the kitchen, calling me a pig and making oink-oink sounds in my face, I could tell Ruby didn't like it. Glenn asked me if I had a face or if my neck just vomited. I laughed with them at first, each joke crueler as it went. I laughed and finally I couldn't laugh anymore and instead of a chuckle that I was trying to emit, a sob broke loose from inside of me. I was so ashamed and embarrassed I ran upstairs, pent-up tears running to my chin, and hid in the closet. Ruby found me and sat in the closet beside me and told me all the mean things the boys had said weren't true. She told me not to feel bad for crying and she gave me a hug.

I was relieved that Jim was gone and would never come back. If she can only talk Father into letting her marry Rich. But I have a bad feeling that he won't like it.

XXXV

One of our regular bread customers gave me a Bruce Springsteen cassette. I told him I was a huge fan even though I had never really heard Bruce Springsteen sing. I had seen pictures of him in the newspaper and I thought he was cute and I liked the title of one of his tapes, "Born In The USA." So the man who buys two packages of brownies every week gave me a copy of his tape. I was glad he'd parked his car in front of the trees or Mother Kay would have made me give her the tape. I stuffed the tape in the waistband of my underpants and asked Mother Kay if I could use the bathroom. I've been hiding it under my mattress with my football scrapbook and my day planner. Actually, it's not really a day planner. It's one of those little calendar pocket books where I pretend that my life is interesting enough to record. It's mine nonetheless and I like thinking others have no right to see it.

It's probably no surprise that Mother Kay caught me listening to Bruce Springsteen on her handheld cassette player while I was cleaning the house. I didn't hear her coming or anything. The next thing I know, she's got me by the hair and is shaking me. I admit I had to pry into her dresser drawer to find the tape player. I thought it would be easier to hide if I had a small portable one rather than the big one with the cord. I was going to put it back after I listened to all the songs but … well. She started shoving cayenne in my mouth for being a smart aleck. She was really mad. I wonder how she would feel if she knew about all the other bad things I do, like stealing whole packages of brownies and cookies that I'm supposed to sell. I hide them up my shirt and manage to get to a bathroom where I dump the whole thing in the sink, fill it with water, get everything soggy, and gobble the entire thing up in a matter of minutes. I feel like a pig and I like it. Of course there's the matter of money. Mother Kay counts everything before we sell so she knows how much money she'll have at the end of the day. I use some of my allowance to pay for it. And I get to eat sugar and chocolate, which is illegal.

Mother Kay is a health nut—emphasis on the "nut" part. She goes crazy sometimes trying to make us eat spinach quiche for dinner or whole-wheat bran and soy flour, sugar-free muffins with our honey-sweetened oatmeal for breakfast. Mother Kay doesn't believe in sugar. She doesn't believe in chocolate or white flour either. She tries to make everything into something healthful. Even the word "healthful" sits heavy in my stomach like whole-wheat bread. Of course we could never sell whole-wheat carob brownies made with honey to anybody no matter how charismatic and persistent we might be as saleskids.

When the opportunity presents itself to have refined flour, sugar, and chocolate on a regular basis it is reason enough for me to steal a little every Friday.

After shoving a few tablespoons of cayenne into my mouth she made me sit on the kitchen floor while she humiliated me, telling Mother and whoever else might happen by what a little baby I was, and how I had to sit and fold my arms right in the kitchen where Mother Kay could watch me because I was too little to be trusted. She made me sit in the high chair and wear a bib. She made me take a bath and go to bed at six thirty. This has happened before and not just to me either. We call it "getting tending" or "being a baby" and it is said right in the same breath as "getting a whipping" or "sitting on a chair." It's just another way to punish. Mother Kay told Father everything she wanted him to know. I went Father's bedroom so he could talk to me. I pretty much just went into auto pilot, said what was expected and swallowed the rest. I'm really going to have to be more careful in the future.

Things have been going downhill fast for Ruby. Emily had a conscience blowout during one of Mother Kay's "let's be friends" talks. She divulged every secret Ruby ever told her including a letter Rich had written to Ruby. Mother Kay confiscated the letter and Ruby's other personal things and read the letter to Father on Sunday. He told the mothers to go through all of her stuff while Ruby sat outside in the lean-to. At first I was in the house but I could hear them hunched over her drawer, talking about Ruby, touching her things, deciding what was good and what wasn't. I went out to the lean-to and I stayed out there with Ruby and we talked while the three mothers violated the only privacy any of us have. I felt the intrusion inside of my own body, like pieces of shrapnel.

XXXVI

Ruby left, ran away.

Everyone is shocked. I am the only one who knew anything. Last night I walked in on Ruby in the bathroom, in her lavender robe, combing her hair. It was 8:30 PM.

"Why are you combing your hair right before bedtime?"

It was Saturday night and the swamp cooler had just been turned on for the season, emitting a musty reminder of last summer.

"I like to look nice before I go to bed."

Her answer didn't fool me for a second. "No, really, tell me why you're combing your hair." I looked down at her feet. "And why are you going to bed in pantyhose?"

"Okay, okay. I'll tell ya if a promise not to tell anyone. I mean ANYONE."

"All right, I get it. I won't tell anyone even if I am Chinese tortured."

"I'm goin' on a date with Rich."

"Nuh uh!"

"Yes, he's coming to pick me up at midnight." She hadn't looked that proud of herself in a long time.

"When are ya coming back?"

"Probably about two or three. I'll go to bed in my clothes and I'll sneak out when I see his truck parked in front of the telephone pole. When the date is over I'll come back through the window and no one will ever know I've been gone."

It sounded foolproof. I couldn't wait until morning to find out how the secret date went, but Sunday morning Ruby was nowhere to be found. I had a hunch she seized the day and did what any of us in the same situation would have done.

She had been in constant trouble with not only Mother Kay but Father since the letter incident. Father had her up in his room for hours, talking to her. She came downstairs crying and upset. I could only assume he was trying to convince her to find a better mate. Ruby had her testimony and her sign from God and if Father didn't know how stubborn Ruby could be … well, that speaks for itself.

If that wasn't enough, a few weeks ago Ruby went into the bathroom and cut her hair. Not an ambiguous trim off the back. She cut the front of her hair in thick bangs. I was stunned. No one had ever cut their hair like that before. It turned into a huge drama, with Mother Kay hollering at Ruby and Mother looking extraordinarily anxious. I realized Ruby didn't care and she hollered right back. The rest of us were too immobilized by Ruby's outburst to think. The only good thing about this situation, now that Ruby has left, is that Mother Kay eased up on the rest of us. When Ruby was doing all of her crazy stuff it made Mother Kay suspicious of all of us. Like we might all cut our hair and holler at the mothers.

The next day, Mother Kay assembled all of us in Father's bedroom and asked each of us, point blank, if we knew anything about Ruby's disappearance. I lied through my teeth and was proud to do it. She told us if Ruby made any attempts to contact us, we were to inform one of the parents immediately. And if she should make an appearance at the house, all the babies might be infected by her malefic evil. We were expressly forbidden to let her see or hold the babies. Of course, Mother Kay knows that Ruby is very fond of babies.

A week later she did appear in a wedding dress, seeking Father's approval. She didn't get it and was married in a courthouse by a justice of the peace. Later, I think one of the brethren gave her a proper marriage sealing.

When we had a moment she told me how it happened. Rich dropped her off at three thirty in the morning but when she reached the window she discovered the hall light was on and Lillian was gone from her bed. She assumed the worst and ran back down the street and hailed Rich, who returned and got her. In reality Lillian had merely gotten up to use the bathroom. Mother Kay made a huge deal about how Ruby had the disrespect and gall to leave on Mother's Day. That was the card that shot the deck. We had never made the slightest attempt to celebrate Mother's Day. In fact, we were told it was a monogamous holiday and full of pagan tradition.

I decided I won't ever run away. It brands you for life. I will have to find a different way to cope with things. I won't give Mother Kay the leverage to wedge herself between me and my brothers and sisters. I won't provide her with evidence of her accusations about me. I will stay so close she'll have a hard time lying to Father without me breathing over her shoulder, ready and armed to defend myself.

XXXVII

Cooking.

I never thought I would hate it as much as I hate doing the wash, but I do. In some ways it's worse. You can't hear Mother Kay coming around the corner and she has to walk through the kitchen several times a day. In other words, we run into each other more often than is good for either of us. She told me I'm getting to be too big to hit with the stick because last week when she gave me a whipping for leaving the milk out, I didn't make a sound, and when she was done all I said was, "Are ya finished?" It made her mad and she slapped my face eight times for saying it. I think she prefers slapping my face to hitting my back and legs; now because she can view her handiwork for several hours after while the redness and swelling goes down. It's embarrassing to me too. I might as well be wearing prisoner stripes, ankle chains, and a shaved head. Everyone coming up the playroom stairs to eat dinner can see her hand print on both sides of my face like the mark of the beast or leprosy. They turn their faces and pretend they can't see it. No one looks me in the eye like I'm some kind of Medusa. My face is red and blotchy all the time. Lillian let me feel her face and it's creamy and smooth as satin.

"I'm sure glad Mother Kay doesn't slap my face. I wouldn't want it to be all red and bumpy like yours." Lillian was touching her own cheeks when she said it.

"Maybe it won't be that way if she stops hitting me. Maybe when I get married the redness and bumps will go away."

"Maybe. Why does she slap yer face all the time, anyway?"

"Cause she's stupid and I make her mad." I felt the pressure in my throat rising like mercury in a thermometer. "Because nobody stops her."

"You shouldn't criticize her like that," Lillian said, looking toward the kitchen stairs.

"I'm not criticizin'. I'm tellin' the truth. I hate her guts and I wish she would die."

Lillian turned gray. Her voice dropped just above a whisper. "You shouldn't talk like that. What if it comes true?"

"I hope it does."

Lillian shook her head at me. "I gotta go. I don't want to get caught talkin' to ya."

I can't decide if I hate myself for not being good like Lillian or if I hate Lillian for being so good. It seems everything comes easy to her. When Mother wakes us up in the morning at six o'clock, Lillian always gets right up. Meanwhile, me and Claire remain semi-unconscious until the third and final call from Mother, punctuated by a glass of water in our faces. Even then, I turn my pillow over and sleep for five more minutes. I feel exceptionally guilty to find Lillian fully engaged in her morning work by the time I saunter to the kitchen to start breakfast. I always end up cutting corners so that I'm not late. We have to eat at seven thirty. Sometimes I don't even make it to the kitchen until seven o'clock. I can usually pull it off because Mother Kay is nowhere in sight. It's the one thing that makes mornings more bearable. Mother Kay sleeps in until prayer. She comes downstairs in her nightgown and robe, the entire family watching her in silence as we wait on our knees. Every morning feels like the coronation of Queen Elizabeth, only without the choir. Last week we waited a full five minutes, listening to the rustling upstairs while our legs fell asleep. When she finally appeared, floating down the stairs in her blue robe, Jacob, who could only say this because he's Mother Kay's kid, sang out in his big dramatic voice, "Here comes the bride, all fat and wide." It split the silence and everyone erupted in laughter. Mother Kay was not pleased being humiliated. Father asked her to say the prayer and she was extra long-winded and boring.

Sometimes I hide when it's time for prayer. I don't know why, but I just don't like going to prayer. I don't like saying my own prayers at night either. Lillian says them perfectly. She never misses a day. Morning and night, like the sun rising and setting, I can count on seeing Lillian leaning into the side of her bed, her hands to her face, deep in prayer. Sometimes I pretend to be praying, so I don't feel guilty or so Lillian will think I'm a good person too. Or I will tell Lillian I said my prayers in the bathroom. I feel bad, like God is looking down on me and shaking his head in disgust. I just wish it felt like I was really talking to him. Mother says if it doesn't feel like your prayers are getting past the ceiling you aren't praying with enough faith. I've never had my prayers get past the top bunk. Maybe I will find a way to get my prayers to ascend properly, to bust through the steel walls of the kingdom of God and make a seriously good impression on the Lord. Maybe when I get older. I have asked for forgiveness a few times when I knew I was really doing something wrong, but I'm still not sure that the Lord has forgiven me. I'm hoping.

XXXVIII

It's five minutes past twelve. I'm late. Lunch is supposed to be ready at noon sharp. Five minutes might as well be twenty-five. The split pea soup is boiling on the stove and I rush from setting the tables to prevent it from burning. That would be a fate worse than what I can afford right now. It's a big pot, twenty quarts if anyone is counting. The cornbread has ten more minutes before it comes out of the oven but that can be manipulated into the timing of the meal.

The tables are finished, the highchairs pulled up, and the bibs arranged on the trays. Napkins? Check. Water? Check. Everyone has a chair? Check. I pour the soup into two large serving bowls and place them in the middle of each table and send Nathan to give the five-minute warning. "Time to eat!" he yells all throughout the house. "Time for lunch!" Every bathroom door is beaten on, every corner of the house checked as the five minutes tick, tick away. Whoever doesn't make the five-minute warning will find themselves going without.

I cinch the ties of my apron and brace myself for the crowds, the kids clamoring to reach a favorite place, and all the things I know I have forgotten but can't remember for the life of me will be demanded. Mother Kay and the school kids appear and the pressure is on. I dish up Mother Kay's plate of food. Beef stir-fry over steamed rice and two slices of hard Wasa bread. Split pea soup gives her a stomachache. Cornbread gives her a stomachache. Everything, it seems, gives her a stomachache, everything that the rest of the family is eating. She gets special food for her special needs. It has an upside though; it makes her more amiable, sitting at the head of the lunch table with something infinitely more delectable than the rest of us are eating, looking down the long dining room at her subjects. Keeping the queen happy keeps all of us happy.

I slice the hot cornbread and arrange it onto two plates.

"Susanna, where's my tea?" Mother Kay has her chin up and her head cocked as if she can see my flaws as easily as a fly resting on the wall. Tea! I run to the fridge and pour her a mug full of previously steeped raspberry leaf tea and heat it up in the microwave. While it's heating up I rush the steaming cornbread to the table and then back to fetch her tea. Mother Kay is staring at me when I reach her place with the tea burning my palms.

"Butter?" she says like I might not grasp a complete sentence.

"You need butter?" I ask, not able to imagine what for.

"Oh, grow up and don't be such an idiot! How are these kids supposed to eat cornbread without butter?"

I knew I was forgetting something.

"Get a move on; we don't have all day. You know lunch was twenty minutes late today. I think you know what that means." I look at the clock. It's twenty two minutes past twelve. Whatever.

The butter is in the basement fridge. The basement. I run down the steps, skipping half of them on my way. I grab a pound of cold butter and slam the fridge shut. I stand there, legs stopped, trying to let some of the anger escape out the top of my head. I am too angry to cry, too mad to care, and too frustrated to realize I'm not breathing again. I take a long slow breath and let it out carefully, slowly blowing a controlled wind. She's yelling my name again. I forgot something else to be sure. I march back up the stairs, back up to the eating masses. They will leave soon enough, I tell myself. She will leave too. Upstairs for a nap, back to the schoolroom perhaps, or maybe, just maybe, she will walk down to Father's shop and be gone from the house until dinner. For now, I will just smile and endure, preparing dinner in my mind so that it is served at five thirty and not a minute later.

XXXIX

I saw Tom today. He looked terrible. He was wearing greasy mechanics overalls and his face was dirty. He looked really hungry too. I heard someone tapping on the basement window and at first I didn't recognize him, but there was something in his eyes, a kind of hollow desire that forced me to look twice. It was Tom. His eyes seemed even bluer than usual against the dark circles under them.

I opened the window. I hadn't seen him in months.

"Tom, what are you doing here?"

"Shhh …" Tom looked over his shoulder. "Do you have any food?"

"Sure, wait here and I will get it for you." I ran upstairs. I cooked today so it was easy to fill him a container full of potato chowder and a baggie of bread sticks without raising suspicions. For a moment I let myself imagine that Tom was the leader of an underground resistance group of a Communist government and was wanted in all fifty states. He had come to me for help. I went back to the basement door where Tom was huddled. I handed him the food for which he looked enormously grateful.

"Did you cook this yourself?" Tom said between mouthfuls.

"Yeah."

"Wow, I'm impressed. It's really good."

"You're just hungry," I protested, but his compliment was as warm inside of me as the soup that steamed in spirals off his spoon. I watched him eat until he was licking the lid of the container.

"Do you want a refill to take home?"

Tom looked at me for a moment when I said the word *home* and for the first time I wondered if he was living on the street. "You have somewhere to live, right?"

"Sure, of course I do. I just don't have enough money for food. I would love to take some home with me."

I refilled the container and the bag of bread sticks and returned to him.

"Thanks, Sus." He was very sincere.

"Sure, no problem."

"I have one more question: What happened to all my stuff?"

Tom had taken nothing when he left home. His favorite leather jacket with the eagle embroidered on the back was left hanging in his closet along with the horse trophies Grandpa had given him. He had left his clothes, his music, and his tape recorder. Everything.

"Mother Kay sold everything at a garage sale."

Tom didn't look too surprised. "When?"

"Probably a week or so after you left." Tom shook his head.

"They never wanted me back." He paused for a long second. "She sold my jacket?" There was a hint of real hurt in his voice.

"I'm sorry, Tom. I would have saved it for you if I could have."

"I know. It's okay. Thanks again for the soup." Tom looked so small, crouched low against the house and creeping toward the gate.

"Wait …" I called back to him. "Come back whenever you need anything. I will be here for you."

"Thanks, I will." He disappeared and I felt a deep sadness for him, stranded out in the big scary world. He was no longer the brave resistance fighter out to save his country and I reminded myself that Tom was my own age, fourteen. A hungry and lost little boy.

XL

I'm stuck on kitchen. Mother Kay says I have to do it until I can do it right. Doing it right is impossible by Mother Kay's standards. I have to clean something big once a week in addition to cooking, and if I serve dinner even five minutes late she makes me do the dishes by myself, which is almost every night. I already do the breakfast and lunch dishes alone because all the younger kids are in school now. It feels like all I do is dishes.

On Mondays I have to clean the fridges and freezers, on Tuesday I have to clean out all the cupboards. Wednesday is scrub the stove and two ovens day. Thursday is the floor, stripping off last week's wax and dirt with ammonia and reapplying another coat when the job is done. Friday is countertops and appliances and little things like that. I know I will never be good at kitchen.

Mother Kay tries to make cooking almost as awful as eating. Monday is leftovers, food nobody wanted the first time around because it was so weird, like zucchini and spinach casserole or salmon pizza. They're recipes she finds in her health magazines that I am absolutely positive no person has ever tried. Tuesday is canned salmon day: salmon casserole, salmon loaf, salmon patties, salmon gravy, even salmon pizza. We all hate salmon. Wednesday is chicken, Thursday is ground beef, and Friday is Tuesday again. Mother Kay seems to like seeing me wince as she hands me the menus for the week. I admit I don't put forth every effort to make the food very edible. She'll tell Father in the morning, before he leaves for work, that we will be eating some exotic dish that she has adjusted to satisfy her health conscience by removing all the fat, salt, sugar, and refined white flour—and essentially the flavor. Then she hands over the altered recipe and says to me, "This better turn out delicious. I don't see why it won't unless you do something stupid." I don't try to do something wrong or stupid, I just manage to do something wrong or stupid. She thinks I can read her mind and she forgets things and there's no telling her she's wrong. It wouldn't be so bad if she would just decide whether she's going to be mean all the time or nice. In the morning she'll be sullen and dangerous, and by afternoon she'll be sarcastic and even playful. She is unpredictable in her behavior and will turn on you at any second. Sometimes I wake up in the middle of the night to her jerking me out of bed by my hair and dragging me down the stairs to mop the floor again, which she was examining during one of her insomnia-induced AM inspections. Other times, when she is feeling nice, she'll sit on the kitchen stool under the phone while I do the lunch dishes and talk to me about her life when she was a kid.

She hasn't been in a good mood for a while. Yesterday, after breakfast, when she was out of earshot, I turned to Emily and said, "Who peed in her Cheerios?" Emily laughed out loud and then promptly went and told Father.

He didn't get mad; he just tried to hide a smile and then asked me why I would say such a thing. I told him sometimes Mother Kay can be a real bear. He said "Oh yeah? Like how?" I told him she makes a big deal out of everything and then I couldn't think of anything else. Well, I could think of a few things, I just didn't know how to say them. Sometimes I wish there was a hidden camera in the kitchen. Then at night I could show it to Father and he would see for himself. He would see how unfair she is and how she lies. Father doesn't think Mother Kay lies. Whenever she says she didn't do something that she did, Father looks right at me and says, "Who do you want me to believe? A mother or a kid?" That pretty much tells me he thinks all of us kids are liars just like Mother Kay tells him.

He almost found out that Mother Kay lies, one day when she slugged Emily in the arm when she forgot to put a bib on one of the babies. Mother Helen saw it with her own eyes and told Father. Mother Kay denied the whole thing. I never saw Father look as confused and frustrated as he did that day. Mother Helen was standing there with her hands on her hips looking flushed and Mother Kay was as uncomfortable as I ever saw her. Emily was stuck in the middle of it all, trying to be honest without getting herself in double trouble with Mother Kay the next day. After all, both Father and Mother Helen go to work. Father dismissed the case without a resolution. I don't know if Emily was as surprised as I was that everyone was making such a big deal out of something so minor. It made me realize how much Father doesn't know. Someday I am going to tell him about all the things she really does.

Someday.

XLI

"Homemade bread! Get yer homemade bread here!" I yell at the cars that speed past me. Lillian and Claire are sitting on the edge of the flowerbed, looking embarrassed to be related to me.

"Come and sit down, Sus," Claire says in her authoritative way. "No one's gonna wanna buy bread from a lunatic."

"Wanna bet?"

"No."

"Okay, you just watch. In the next hour I will get three cars to stop and buy something."

"No one's gonna stop. It's raining. People don't stop when it's raining." Claire had a way of bringing a dark reality to everything.

"Just you watch," I say. I grab two loaves of bread and walk right into the middle of the wet road and wait for the next car to get near enough to see me. I put the bread up to my nose and sniff it dramatically like I am being paid to do a commercial for Wonder Bread.

"Come and get the best tastin' bread you've ever eaten!" I holler at the green Ford Taurus before moving out of its path. The driver honks at me and races by. Claire drops her face in her hands.

"Hey, he honked. That's a good sign. He noticed me."

"That's a bad sign, Susanna. He didn't stop." Claire looks at the table full of bread and cookies that are hiding under a tarp. Her hair is wet like dark strings on her face. Lillian is sitting next to her, shivering.

"Why don't you guys get off your butts and warm up over here selling bread?"

"Ya mean, why don't we get off our butts and go make fools of ourselves," Claire says without flinching at the use of the word butt.

"You guys better be quiet before Mother Kay hears ya talkin' like that." Lillian is looking at the window where Mother Kay's back is turned to us, a sign of desperately slow business. I can see a line of cars coming in our direction and I get ready for the next show. With a butter knife in both hands I imagine each car is a huge airliner waiting for me to bring them in.

"Come on in!" I wave the butter knives back and forth. "Come on in and get yer bread!" The first few cars drive by and I notice some of the drivers are smiling. The fifth car slows down and pulls up to the curb and rolls down the window.

"Hey, what ya sellin' there?" says a middle-aged businesswoman.

"Let's see, I have white or whole wheat bread, made fresh today. I have the best brownies you've ever tried. I have chocolate chip cookies, oatmeal raisin, and orange-frosted cookies. What can I get for you, ma'am?"

"How about a loaf of your wheat bread and a package of cookies for my kids." I run to the table and got the best-looking loaf on the table and a dozen cookies.

"That's two dollars," I say holding out my hand. The lady hands me two crisp bills from her purse, and I set the baked goods on her immaculately clean passenger seat.

"Do you sell bread all the time?" she asks.

"Every Friday. You can be a regular customer if you want to. Just give us your phone number and we'll call you Thursday to see what you want to order."

"No thanks, but I might come back next Friday." She drives away and blends back into the traffic, heading south on our street.

No one else will stop. It's been two more hours of sitting in the rain. I don't know what else to try. It is seven o'clock and getting dark. We've only made fifty dollars and have a lot of brownies, cookies, and bread that will have to be frozen and sold half price next week. That is not good—the fifty dollars part.

I'm about to put the sign away when Bryan drives up to the curb. Bryan left home five or six years ago. The family isn't too keen on him showing up for any reason. He's one of the bad ones.

"You guys done sellin' bread?" he asks me, leaning toward the window of his car.

"Yeah, we had a slow day." Bryan reaches into his pocket and takes out four dollar bills.

"Here ya go," he says, his eyes twinkling.

"What would ya like?"

"Nothing. You keep it. Don't show Kay, either." He says Kay, not Mother Kay. I like the rebelliousness of it.

"Don't worry."

"Oh, by the way, there's a song in the hymnbook that you should read. It's on page ninety." It seems odd that Bryan would give me money and then recommend a religious song out of the hymnbook.

As soon as Bryan pulls away and drives off into the darkness, I hear Mother Kay calling me from the window.

"Who was that?" she asks craning her head.

"It was nobody."

"Don't tell me it was nobody! I saw a car parked by the curb. Now who was it and what did they want?!" The lull in business always makes her cranky; she treats us like it's our fault when things don't sell. "You better tell me right now young lady or yer gonna be in big trouble!"

"It was Bryan."

"What did he want?"

"Nothin'."

"Don't give me that! What did he want?!" I have no idea what she wants to hear from me and I feel pinned by my desire for the four dollars and getting Mother Kay off my back.

"He gave me some money."

"Why didn't ya tell me that in the first place? Now give it to me. He shouldn't be givin' you girls money without Father knowin' about it." I hand her one dollar bill. "Is that all he gave ya?"

"Yeah, he just handed me a dollar and said, 'I don't want to buy anything, you keep it.'"

"Next time he tries to give you money, you tell him you're not supposed to have it and if he's gonna stop he better be stoppin' to buy something. Ya hear me?"

"Okay, I will." I sound convincing even to myself. I finish cleaning up out front and put the big bake sale sign away behind the front shed and go in the house. I read the words to the song. Though I have sung it many times, I have never thought about the words.

Know this, that every soul is free
To choose his life and what he'll be
For this eternal truth is given
God will force no man to heaven.

XLII

I run down the street as fast as I can go. My dress flaps at my knees and I try not to think how ridiculous I must look to all the cars passing me by. Ever since I started selling bread I realize how odd I am. I've always felt weird but not in a bad way, just different from the other kids in the family. I didn't realize until now that not only am I different, I am weird to the neighbors across the street who stare incessantly, and to the clerks at Osco Drug, where I buy shampoo and nylons with my two dollars a week, who avoid eye contact with me. I am definitely weird to the kids who spit on my dress as they ride by on their bikes.

It is dark and I take comfort in that. I run until I my legs wobble underneath me. I sit down on the curb and rest a few minutes, breathing in my surroundings. Apartments to my right and a residential street on my left. I'm close enough to the intersection to see the traffic light changing colors. I think about running all the way to the 7–11 on the corner, but by looking back at the direction of the house I am reminded that my chains don't go that far.

I don't move, though I feel rested. I want to hold space between me and the house the way someone would wear sunglasses to prevent the sun from burning their eyes. After five or so minutes I stand up, take a deep breath, and run back home to Fifth East as fast as I can, refusing my legs any kind of reprieve. When I get near the house next door I slow to a walk, breathing hard and keeping close to the trees. I don't want to be seen returning from somewhere. Mother Kay already had her thumb pressing on my blood flow like a tourniquet. When I run across the sidewalk and into the front yard a red jacked-up pickup truck rumbles past me loudly, honking its horn. Mother Kay's head appears immediately through the curtains, the same moment mine disappears into the lean-to.

She saw me.

I go in the house through the basement but I know that I'm caught.

"What were you doing out front?!" Mother Kay's eyes are like steel screws.

"Nothin'." For once it is true.

"Don't you give me that. Who was honkin' at you?" She wears her suspicion like comfortable slippers.

"I don't know, just somebody." It wasn't unusual to be honked at by passing teenagers or whistled at by drunks that hung out on the street corners. She grabs me by the braid and shoves me upstairs toward Father's bedroom.

"I caught her out front getting out of someone's truck," she says out of breath.

Father looks at me carefully without saying a word. I stand there by the dresser planning my strategy.

"Is that true?" he says calmly.

"No."

"Are you telling me that Mother Kay just made the whole thing up?"

"Yes."

He looks surprised.

"Why would she tell an outright lie?" I shrug my shoulders. "Mother?" he looks at Mother Kay.

"I heard a honk out front, so when I looked out the window I saw Susanna get out of a red truck and run in the house. I'm almost positive it was Gerald. I caught her sneakin' through the basement."

"*That* is not true," I blurt, encouraged by Father mediating.

"Why would Gerald be honking at Susanna?" he says, looking at Mother Kay.

"I don't know. That's a good question. Susanna? What were you doing with Gerald?"

Gerald had gotten married and moved out of the house months ago. He had somehow slipped from honorable Big Boy status to disdained brother and bad influence. He was given a wife and Mother Kay doesn't like her. It didn't take long before Gerald wasn't on the good list anymore.

"How did Gerald get in the picture?" I feel things slipping out of control. My voice is defensive. "I haven't seen Gerald in months! Why would Gerald be picking me up? And why would he be dumb enough to honk at me when he dropped me off after we did our supposed secret thing that Mother Kay thinks we did?!" My face was red and my knuckles cold. "That is so stupid! I can't believe you would think that!"

"Hold on!" Father says. "Just hold on now. If you weren't with Gerald what were you doing out front?" I don't respond for several seconds. I don't know how to tell Father what I was doing. I don't have any words to say it. I feel trapped like he is holding my head under water.

"Running." I finally say it.

"Where were you running to?"

"Nowhere. Just running."

"Nobody just runs. Where were you going?" he says, still patient.

"I'm telling you, I was just running. I ran down the street and then I ran back. That's it. Believe it or not."

"I don't believe it for a second. Now you better tell me what's going on here." Father's voice is louder.

"Okay, I saw something shiny while I was putting the bake sale sign away and I ran down the street to look at it."

I lie. It's the best I can do on such short notice.

"What was it?" Father asks me. "What were you running down the street to look at?"

I am not prepared for the question and I struggle for a second to come up with something. "A hubcap."

"A hubcap?" Father raises both eyebrows.

"Uh-huh."

"You ran down the street to look at a hubcap?" Father is looking less amused and more irate.

"Yes." I am firm about it. "I looked at it and came back." I keep my back against the bedroom wall and fidget furiously with a thick string of hair that keeps falling over my eyes. Father is silent for several minutes and Mother Kay makes herself comfortable on the bed like she is settling in for a good TV show and a warm cup of milk.

"I'm sorry, Susanna, but I just don't believe you." Father looks serious and I can tell he is trying to pressure me into saying something. I am happy to tell him whatever he wants but I don't know what he thinks I did. I don't know how to lie my way out of it.

I can't tell him that running away is like coming up for air. It is the only thing keeping me alive. I can't tell him that running away is like filling up with the fuel I need to take more steps. I don't say a thing but drop my eyes. I can hear him telling Mother Kay what to do with me but the volume in my ears is turned down.

"Well … what do you have to say for yourself?" he says softly.

"I'm sorry you don't believe me."

"So am I."

XLIII

It's so early in the morning. Mother Helen shakes me again. "Get up. The bread isn't going to make itself." Bread. And what is it all for? Mother Kay. She is a money hoarder. If the day goes well and we exceed three hundred dollars then we can expect an uneventful evening, but if it rains or the road in front of the house is under reconstruction and we can't convince the crew to buy our bread, it will be miserable. I really don't mind selling bread, even in the winter when we have to alternate sellers because our feet get to where we can't feel them anymore. I have to go into the bathroom and run them under warm water to get things going again. I try to sneak a package of chocolate chip cookies with me. I have only a few minutes in the bathroom before Mother Kay becomes suspicious. It takes longer than that to consume a dozen cookies *and* get one's feet warm. I fill up the sink with hot water, dump all the cookies in the water, and take off my shoes and socks. I sit on the counter warming my feet and eating soaked, easily swallowed cookies at the same time. I can be back out to the freezing cold in no time at all with warm feet and a full stomach with no one the wiser.

I don't mind any of that too much, but this stumbling out of bed at 3:00 AM, sleepiness threatening to pound and throb in my head, and grating sand relentless in my eyeballs—this I mind. For this I hate bread, Fridays, and everything else associated with it. I can hardly make it down the stairs, my legs like gelatin stilts and my stomach churning in retaliation. Emily is beside me, sullen and resigned. Lillian tries to be cheerful, which only makes me madder. You can't be cheerful at three o'clock in the morning, I don't care who you are. I ignore her with great and specific intent. I will not enjoy this. I will make the bread because I have no choice but to do it, but I will not like it. Mother Helen turns on the kitchen light but I can't bear it.

"Please, can we make the bread by the stove light?"

Mother Helen seems unimpressed at my lack of enthusiasm but acquiesces in spite of her obvious disapproval. Once my eyes adjust I notice a small piece of paper on the counter. I recognize the handwriting as none other than Mother Kay's. It says:

Dear girls,

I know how hard it is to get up early and I know that you know how important it is that you contribute on Fridays to the work. Everyone has his or her job to make it happen.

I know it all seems difficult to bear right now but someday, years down the road, when you are all grown and gone, you will look on this time you spent together with great fondness. It is a wonderful opportunity you have, and mark my words, someday these will be priceless memories.

*Love,
Mother Kay*

Priceless? I would give it up for a buck. I can hardly believe what I am reading. Sure, it's easy to say when you are snuggled in your warm bed upstairs while someone else does the special work we will all feel so fond about in some distant, indiscernible future. Whatever. I hand the note to Emily; she reads it and shrugs her shoulders. If I was Mother Kay and all I had to do on Fridays—besides sleep in and have someone cook my breakfast, make my bed, run my morning bath, and massage my feet—was sit at the window and collect cash all day, sure I can imagine feeling fond of that. I finish my batch and cover it with plastic wrap. My batch alone will make at least twenty loaves. Mother Helen made two batches, and Lillian and Emily both made one. We made the other half on Thursday for Mother Helen to take to work to sell to the other employees there. She brings the money home to Mother Kay. I guess I wouldn't be so upset about all this if Mother Kay had any ethics, but she is more than willing to encourage us to lie about the freshness of our "fresh homemade bread." It's all about money for her. She'll do anything for money.

She tries to sell us pictures of her kids so she can have our measly allowance. I don't know why she thinks we want pictures of the kids. She will buy shampoo and then tell us we owe her ten dollars when we didn't ask her to buy us shampoo. Shampoo doesn't cost ten bucks. I can tell by the brand that it's the cheapest thing she can find. She marks it up hoping to make a profit. Sometimes I feel so angry at her sneaky and conniving ways. I feel like Samson, blind and broken, head shorn. I want to push all the pillars from underneath her world. I want her to die in the steaming rubble. I don't think I would feel badly about that. That scares me.

XLIV

Okay, I admit I did it. I stole a magazine from Osco Drug. It was called *Teen Bop*. I didn't have any money and I wanted it so bad; I stuffed it up my shirt and ran all the way home. Nobody suspected a thing until Mother found it in Emily's clothes drawer. I wanted it because it had a close up of picture C.B. Barnes in it. Emily insisted she keep it in her drawer, folded open to a picture of Rob Lowe so she could run upstairs and peek at him during every free moment she had during the day. She didn't hide it under her clothes like any normal person who was used to getting in trouble would. It was right on top of everything. I knew I should have made her keep it in my drawer. Mother took it to Father and we were called up to his bedroom—me, Emily, Claire and Lillian. Father had the book laid open on his bed when we arrived. Mother might as well have been standing there with a Polaroid camera waiting to capture the look on our faces. Father seemed pleased to have the upper hand as well. I gave them the best poker face I had. Father was upset. It was the fifth time this month I came before him.

The last time it was the radio. Mother Kay caught me with my ear pressed to Mother Helen's clock radio, listening to Alabama's "When We Make Love." Not a song I would want anyone to know I was listening to. She made me sit on the bed with her while she turned up the radio and listened to the rest of it, as well as several other songs. It was as if I was being personally blamed for the lyrics to each song as it waved and echoed through the room like a foreign language, and she shook her head in disgust. Reba McEntire, The Judds, Vince Gill, and George Strait. I was trying to hide the pleasure of listening to my favorite country artists at regular volume. I tried to look ashamed. When Father found out, I stood before him and confessed that I did indeed listen to the radio at every opportunity and I committed these acts on the clock radios in each of the parents' bedrooms. He was appalled and kept asking me why I wanted to listen to that garbage. I told him I didn't know why, but I liked it. He was thoroughly repelled by my actions. I promised him I would stop listening to the radio. I really tried to stop, too. For a while.

Sometimes when no one is looking I will switch the cassette on the tape recorder that turns ordinary hymns like "Do What is Right" and "Count Your Many Blessings" into Ronnie Millsap singing "Why Don't You Spend the

Night." I think having a magazine with boys in it is worse than listening to the radio.

Mother was right behind us as me and the other girls filed into Father's bedroom, Father looked at me and said, "Where did you guys get this magazine?" Lucky for me, I was able to say I bought and paid for it with my own money because two days after I stole it I couldn't stand the guilt and I returned it to the magazine rack and then five minutes later I bought it as if it was the first time I had seen it. I knew both Lillian and Emily would be able to say in all truthfulness that I had bought it. I tried to do all the talking and take all the responsibility for having the magazine so as to keep the other girls quiet. After all, I had reimbursed the store for my crime. Father doesn't know I stole it. He's more concerned that we are looking at pictures of teenage boys in provocative poses. He told us that he understands it's natural for girls to like boys, to have feelings for boys. But those feeling were not to be indulged, no matter how natural they may be. He told Mother to burn the magazine, but not before embarrassing us by reading the movie stars' names and asking us what it was that we found appealing about half-naked men.

We followed Mother to the playroom where she ripped pages out of the magazine and threw them into the fireplace. I begged her to let me keep just the one headshot of C.B. Barnes while she was lighting the match but she wouldn't let me and I watched his face go up in smoke and disappear into curling ash.

The parents think they've solved a problem. But I can always look at the magazines at the store. There will always be an abundance of movie stars for me to create fantasies about. I can watch TV, at least the programs that the Father watches at night after he comes home from work. I can read books that Mother Kay bought for school book reports like *King of the Wind* or *The Singing Tree*, though I can't let Mother Kay catch me reading any of them or I will get in trouble for taking the books out of the schoolroom without asking.

There's the newspaper too. I read it from front to back, from the classifieds to the comics. I just like to escape, even if only to someone else's dilemma of selling a swamp cooler in fair condition for two hundred dollars. I save the comics for last because it's my favorite part of the newspaper. I love to hear myself laugh. Great big spontaneous laughs that contradict everything I'm feeling inside. I read them in front of people so they can hear me laugh too. It feels like I am trying to convince them that I am happy. Maybe I'm trying to convince me.

I also like the sports section where I can cut out pictures of football players and tape them into my scrapbook. There are articles full of statistics from games the weekend before that need memorizing. I fold them up and put them in my apron pocket while I'm scrubbing the kitchen floor so I can have the reports on the latest College Bowl games at hand while I pretend to be the game announcer.

I have stacks and stacks of newspapers I keep in the closet under my dresses. I keep everything that I want to remember for reasons I can't understand right now, like the coverage of the 1984 Summer Olympics in Los Angeles or the rescue of Baby Jessica McLure from an abandoned well. I have commentary on the Reagan attempted assassination and pictures of the Challenger shuttle exploding in midair. I have coverage on Oliver North and the Iran Contra hearings and the trouble brewing in the Persian Gulf. Mother does not approve of me reading so much. She insisted that I throw away my newspapers when she saw the giant stack in the closet. I don't know what's so bad about them. It seems like everything that I like or have an interest in is wrong. She says if I'm going to read I should be reading the scriptures, but the scriptures are boring.

Now I have to hide to read the newspaper. I usually go into the bathroom. I take it in a section at a time so it won't be noticed. Sometimes if I take too long Mother comes banging on the door and demanding that I open it and show her whatever it is I am reading. I just tell her I don't have anything with me. She checks the bathroom high and low to find the missing section of the paper but I hide it really well. Sometimes if I have finished reading the whole thing I will fold it up and put it in the toilet tank. Or I will roll it up and slide it inside the shower curtain rod or inside the cover of the bathroom ceiling fan. It drives Mother crazy because she can hear the newspaper rustling while I am adjusting its size. She knows I have it but can't prove it. I don't know why she doesn't want me to read—that's probably partly why I like it so much. That's not the only reason, though. It makes me feel connected to something; it makes me a part of a world I know nothing about. That's why I took the magazine in the first place.

I figure I'm supposed to do bad things like listen to the radio and steal from drugstores. After all, I'm fourteen.

XLV

His name is Joseph Walker.

Mother would kill me if she found out I've been calling him on the telephone. I haven't told anyone but Emily, who promised on her life and the lives of all good men that she wouldn't tell. I know I shouldn't trust Emily but she loves to hear about all the bad things I do. She even encourages me to do it. She asks me at least once a day, "Did ya call Joe?" I call him constantly. Sometimes two or three times a week. Now that school has started I have a lot more opportunities. Mother Kay is in the schoolroom all day and Mother is in the playroom tending the babies and it's just Emily and me. We take turns cooking and housecleaning. Mother keeps the laundry going until Lillian and Claire get out of school and they fold it in the evenings.

Joe is different from anyone I have ever met. I haven't met that many people but I am convinced there aren't many out there like him. Father talks about how dangerous the world is, full of kidnappers and murderers and thieves and policemen who would leap at the chance to throw Father in jail. I don't think the world is full of dangers and ugliness. I don't believe Father. I think he's trying to scare me away from the world, scare me into being good. I know it's wrong of me to be talking on the phone with someone out in the world but I don't care. It's worth it.

I first read Joe's column when I saw that the former TV editor had been replaced by this young, handsome, dark-haired man with a lovable name like Joe. When I read his words it was as if I could hear his voice. There was a powerful feeling between the lines. I sat with the newspaper in my lap for a full five minutes, looking into this man's eyes. It was there. I have no words for it. It was something so tangible that it hooked me to him; it emblazoned his face into my mind and I wondered if I was telepathic or something. I knew in that instant I was going to send him a letter and tell him, somehow, the impact his picture and his words had on me. I went straight to my room and drafted a letter using a television show as a way to introduce myself. I told him that my mom thought I was nutty and strange and didn't even come close to understanding me. I told him his smile was so powerful it could turn lemons into lemonade. I felt welcome and useful and appreciated all from gazing at his face. I poured on the flattery and my awkward charm without restraint. I wanted him to remember me if nothing else.

I kept the letter in my drawer for a few months while I accumulated enough nerve to send it. When I mailed it I taped a quarter to the right hand corner of the envelope and left a note to the mail carrier to please attach a stamp. I watched from my bedroom window as the mailman placed a stamp on the envelope I had stolen out of Father's desk and put the letter safely in his bag.

Joseph Walker noticed me and three weeks later he printed my letter in the mailbag section of his column. He added a thoughtful postscript that read, "By the way, Susanna, I don't care what your mom says, I don't think you're nutty … for a fourteen-year-old."

He spoke to me; he wrote my name. I touched the print as if it were his very own handwriting. I stared at those words and read them over and over and over. I laughed and cried and promised I would never throw that paper away. I felt as if my name had been inscribed on the pages of history, on the tablets of time. I had been documented. I was *real*.

He's the first friend I have ever had. I've long since quit asking useless questions about television shows I only read about in his column. I tell him about my life, my worries, and my fears. I don't tell him about the religion or home school or anything that will take him out of my life. The best part is he just listens. He tells me he understands my frustrations and he asks me all kinds of questions about me, like he cares. The first thing he says when I say hello to him is "Hi, Susanna! It's good to hear your voice!" It takes all the words out of my mouth and sometimes I cry when he says it and I have to get my bearings straight in a hurry. I don't want him to know it means so much to me. I want to be normal so I just say, "I'm great, how're you?" After one of our talks I have more energy. I clean faster. I whistle while I work. Mother thinks I'm starting to grow up and be responsible. I'm glad she thinks that. She thinks that all Mother Kay's lectures and reprimands are finally having the desired effect. Heh heh.

XLVI

Glenn showed me how to make someone pass out. A friend he worked with at the egg factory showed him this place on your neck, pressure points, that will make you faint. I begged Glenn to show me how it was done. He finally consented and I woke up with Glenn peering into my face asking me if I was all right. It was wonderful! I slipped out of consciousness to a silent dark world that felt similar to curling up on couch next to a warm fire. Glenn felt bad for showing me and told me to never try it on anyone. I said I only wanted to see what it felt like. I would never do it to someone else. I didn't tell Glenn I planned to try it on myself.

I usually do it after lunch when Mother Kay goes back to the schoolroom. It only takes five minutes. I'm not exactly sure where the pressure points are, so I wrap a dishtowel around my neck and after hyperventilating with my head between my legs I stand up fast and straight, letting the blood flow backward while I squeeze the towel as tight as I can. I can hear the static and see the blurring as I slip away to dark small place. It's like the genie being sucked back into the lamp. When I wake up I am on the floor, sometimes I have a bruise on my head from hitting the dresser or the bedpost on my way down. I try to place myself near something soft so I don't make too much sound when I fall. I only wish the time I was gone was longer. It is the only time I get to be alone and I am truly free of Mother Kay's grasp. Mother Kay says it is bad to want to be alone. I don't know why she thinks that. Maybe she just wants to know what I am doing every second of the day.

So she told me I'm not allowed to be alone. Well, I guess that isn't it exactly, I can be alone if Mother Kay tells me to, I just can't do anything of my own free will. I have to report to Mother Kay so she knows where I am all the time. I have to get permission from her to leave my work for any reason. Sometimes she'll come knocking on the bathroom door and demand to know what I'm doing in there. She's looking over my shoulder one way or another. If I'm on kitchen duty she says I have to receive her instructions about how to make even the simplest of projects that I already know how to do. She even made me ask her how I was supposed to set the tables. She says she's trying to teach me responsibility. She says it's part of my job to remember all the foods she's allergic to and make her special meals, to remember to take her a glass of warm lemon water in the morning while she's asleep and her raspberry leaf tea two times a day to keep her feminine organs in shape, whatever that means.

I just pretend I am in a play and I have the lead role as Cinderella and Mother Kay is the wicked stepmother. It's nice to believe that the cameras are rolling and I am convincing as the ragged child of the cinders. I have to do what she says and be loving and sweet about it because that's the role I am in.

Sometimes, though, it's not enough to pretend and I thieve a little time for myself out on the hood of Glenn's car in the front yard after dark and stare at the lamppost, but it's not long before someone appears at the front gate with the dreaded words on their lips: "Mother Kay wants you."

I stand in front of her at the dining room table, folding my hands in front of me. I wait and watch her draw house plans for an illusory home we'll have some day on five acres of property that doesn't exist. She's lost in a world full of half-baths and master bedrooms. I can feel I am an itch on her nose. She shifts her face from "lost in thought" to "wicked stepmother."

"What are you doing?" she doesn't look at me but keeps drawing and measuring.

"I was just outside."

This time she looks up. "You don't belong outside. Why are you isolating yourself again? You know what I have told you about that."

"I just like to think."

"You mean you're daydreaming. Say it like it is. You're not so innocent. You know better than to isolate yourself." She looks back down at the graph paper. "Isolating yourself is the first sign. Next thing you know you will be just like Ruby, lost and miserable and married to the wrong man. Is that what you want?"

"No." There's nothing else to say but the anger inside is clenching my teeth and making the room spin.

"I'm not a robot." The words come shooting out of my mouth unbidden. "You can't make me do what you want with your little remote control."

Mother Kay flies up from her seat and starts slapping me in the face. "Don't you start that with me. I'm not going to have you going around mouthing off to me. Do you hear me, young lady?" I nod. She grabs me by the hair. "Not a robut, huh?" ROBUT. I can't believe she calls it a robut. It's the stupidest thing I've ever heard.

It's the end of the day and I don't know where to go. There is no place that affords me any quiet, any relief, except for here, the wonderful empty darkness. Eventually I wake up, lying on my back on the bedroom floor. I don't know how long I was out but I hope it was a long time. I have a secret place where I hide and I can't be found, not even by myself. I can get lost in a forest of blackouts where I feel no fear and have no memory. I can go where nothing is retained and everything is lost the minute it all rematerializes in front of me.

XLVII

There are three phones in the house: one in the kitchen, another in the playroom, and one in Father's bedroom. Father's room is the only logical place to call Joe. I can usually hear if anyone is coming up the stairs and I can pretend to be cleaning. I always take a rag and some furniture polish just in case.

Mother suspects that I'm up to some kind of mischief because the other day she came in right as I was hanging up the phone.

"What were you doing?" she asked.

"Uh, just washing the phone … It gets really dirty on the earpiece." I knew my face was red and obvious but I couldn't tell her the truth. Mother just stared at me, words wanting to come out of her mouth, but she said nothing. I held my rag firmly in my hands and washed the telephone, trying not to glance up at her face. When she finally spoke her words were chosen and calculated.

"I hope you're not lying to me."

I didn't look at her. "I'm not."

She looked straight through me and I shifted uneasily on my feet.

"Okay," she said and walked downstairs. That night when Father came home I was called up to his room but she couldn't pinpoint exactly what wrong thing I had done, so Father turned to Mother and said, "She's a Big Girl now, Mother. She knows what she is supposed to do." He was looking right at me when he said it.

In a way, he was right. I do know what I'm supposed to do. I'm supposed to make sure no one finds out about Joe.

I called Joe again today.

He asked me a lot of questions about my family. He asked where I went to school, what grade I was in, etc. He wanted to know all about my life, about my mother and father and family. I told him I was in a private school that I had twelve brothers and sisters, and I had a bunch of friends. This is kinda true, because the other kids that aren't Mother's own are my friends.

I thought I did pretty good, making up such untruths on short notice. The whole time I talk to him, I imagine myself in a pair of jeans and a short-sleeved sweater, my hair scooped up in a ponytail while I twist the phone cord around my finger. I am sitting on the floor of some imaginary kitchen, talking to my best friend on the phone in front of my mom (not Mother), who is cooking dinner on the stove. My boyfriend lives two blocks down the street and my dad calls me "Princess." I am living the American dream or at least some drunken version of it where I ride comfortably on clouds of normalcy.

I've thought all day and I wonder why I lied to Joe. My *friend* Joe. If anyone deserves to know the truth it's him. I feel guilty rotten about it. He believes me. He believes my made up family, the private school, all of it. Normal seemed like the right thing to portray at the time, but what do I know about normal? It lives on suburban streets with a dog in the yard. It has kids in tank tops and shorts running through the sprinkler and mothers carrying pitchers of Kool-Aid in frosted cups. It's the next-door neighbors, it's television, it's a foreign country. Do I have a right to steal it, to pretend it's who I am? I've done worse things, I suppose.

I can't tell Joe who I am. If he knew he would hate me. He wouldn't want to talk to me again. He's the enemy, only he doesn't know it. I am not supposed to like the enemy and I am definitely not supposed to talk to the enemy. I am supposed to hate him because he is out in the world. What if he learns about me? What if I slip up and tell him that my father is married to three women? That I really have forty brothers and sisters? If he saw how I look he wouldn't like me anymore. That is why I have to let him believe what I have told him. I will lie to him when I have to; I will lie to him in spite of how it feels inside of me, because that's all I have—lies.

XLVIII

It's four thirty in the morning. I wrap my bathrobe around me and tie it at the waist, closing the back door inaudibly behind me. The warm pavement is sensuous to my bare feet. My hair, usually pulled back into a braid, hangs freely about my shoulders. I have to squeeze between the station wagon and the suburban to get to the street, which is abandoned and empty. The dim orange light of street lamps casts rectangular shadows on the houses that line both sides of the street. All the neighbors are asleep and I am deliciously alone.

I don't know why I do it, why I feel compelled to come outside in the wee hours of the morning. Friday morning. Bread day. It's the only morning that I am awakened at three o'clock in the morning the still of sleep interrupted. Claire, Lillian, and Emily stumble out of their beds alongside me. Mother Helen's persistent nudge is the only thing keeping us from falling asleep on the stairs. We're ghosts, shadows of the daytime versions of ourselves. After mixing bread and covering the greased dough in plastic wrap, each of us washes our hands, wipes everything down, and goes back to bed. Big stainless steel bowls line the counters like sentinels of the night. We try to finish the job as quickly as possible and then quietly slip back into bed for the last forty-five minutes before morning. Like the little elves in the story of the shoemaker who awakens to find his shoes cut out and sewn while he slept, we use up secret hours making hundreds of loaves of bread in the small nightlight above the stove, in a dead silence that only the truth of night can evoke. Only it's no surprise to anyone to find the kitchen overflowing with bowls of soft dough spilling over onto the counters on Friday mornings. There is bread dough everywhere.

I pretend to go back to sleep and as soon as I hear the other girls beginning to snore I sneak out of the house.

It starts at the edge of the curb, a small drop off, a mini cliff. It's me and the warm black asphalt. It's my body hugging the convex surface of the road. I lay down, calmly, quietly. It is my space for now, this main artery that in a few hours will be humming with corporate businessmen racing to tall buildings, balancing cups of hot coffee in their hands. But for now it is mine. High school adolescents will cross at the stoplight on their way to morning classes, worlds unto themselves, but for now it is quiet. Joggers will sweat in the sunrise and curtains will open and blinds will be drawn and I will be sucked back inside with the dawn. But for now, it is mine.

I am here, holding the space between giant meteors about to collide. Lying on the road, facing the fading stars, I clasp my hands as they might appear in a coffin, resting them gently over the knot in my robe tie. I spread my hair in a fan around my head and point my feet toward the east, and I lay myself on the altar of rebirth, on the edge of fear and resolve.

I saw a picture once in the *Guinness Book of World Records* of a man walking a tightrope over a raging Niagara Falls. That is how I feel right now, lying in the middle of the road. I like feeling that I am daring, taking a great risk leaving the inside world at an attempt to steal a bit of my freedom. No one knows that I am here, that I am wondering what it might be like to die. But if I am not careful I might fall. I might get caught and drown in the crushing water.

I can hear the truck roaring, muffler-less, in the distance. I can feel the deadly weight of its wheels crushing my internal organs, the shattered bones and the broken ribs piercing my heart. I want to be able to do it. I imagine myself leaving so clearly, an exit through a tiny mouse hole in the top of my head, and I leave my body behind me. I leave all of it behind me.

But a thread tugs at me; it holds me in my body, like an uncut umbilical cord. The truck is very near and fear clutches me.

I leap up from the street, a fleeing pink robe dashing through the night. The honking horn is a blast back to where I belong, standing on the curb, the house behind me, waiting for me.

XLIX

"Guess what?" Emily's face is all animated at the prospects of my interest.

"What?"

"There's a new dentist working at Dr. Jonsson's office." Emily had just returned from having a cavity filled.

"So, what did he look like?" I knew Emily wouldn't wait very long for me to ask.

"Ahhh, he was sooo cute, way cuter than Dr. Jonsson. His name is Barry. I call him Dr. Barry. But that's not the best part. While he was filling my cavity he laid his arm across my forehead like this," and she showed me with her own arm how close he was to her face. Emily sighs. "The nurse was out of the room and everything."

"But, Emily, he was looking in your mouth. How romantic is that?"

"He wasn't really paying attention to my teeth. Besides, I have nice teeth. He was talking to me the whole time. I can't wait to get another cavity."

"Was he as cute as Dr. Vorhees?"

"Course not! No one will ever be like Dr. Vorhees." She disappeared for a moment in thought. "I'll probably never see him again."

"Maybe you'll get another tumor," I said, half-serious.

"I wish, but I doubt it."

Emily had found the tumor four years ago, when she was fourteen. She had me feel it when she was lying on her back, a hard round ball in her abdomen. It took her a long time to get up the nerve to show Mother Helen, but when she realized the tumor was growing she felt she had to do something. She told me later that Mother Helen had taken her to Father who actually had the gall to ask her if she was pregnant. Emily couldn't believe the thought had even crossed his mind; it seemed insanely ridiculous. But after that we had many shared fantasies about some imaginary man who was the father of the calcified cyst.

Father told Emily to wait and see if it didn't go away. But it didn't go away. It just grew and grew. Finally she was taken to a doctor, Dr. Vorhees, a curly-haired physician with muscular arms and soft eyes—at least that was Emily's version of it—who stole Emily's heart if for no other reason than that of being a doctor, healer of wounds. I would sit on her bed in the weeks following the removal of a grapefruit-sized cyst from her ovaries that turned out to be benign, and listen with awe and envy to the stories she told of her stay at the hospital and of the dashing Dr. Vorhees, who seemed to become more handsome with every retelling. I loved to hear the story over and over and Emily loved telling me. I knew she was embellishing but there was something about the long scar on her belly that made even the most outlandish flourishes seem absolutely true.

I wanted nothing more than to have my very own tumor, to have a loving Dr. Vorhees check in on me and rub the top of my foot over the hospital sheet, a gesture of real, genuine concern. I dreamed of the day when I would find myself awaking from a coma, looking around the room and saying, Hollywood style, "Where am I?" But that's where the dream would end, because there would be no reply. Of course I could imagine a kind-faced social worker like the ones I had seen on TV, telling me that my family had all been killed in a terrible explosion and I was the only remaining survivor. There would be a handsome police officer waiting to interview me. He and the social worker would get into an argument about my state of mind. Meanwhile I would lie in the hospital bed, tubes going in and out of me, smiling.

I don't tell Emily about my own fantasies but I listen to hers with an appreciation that is unequaled. I understand Emily, her intense needs and hungers. I can see the vacuum, the wormhole, the sucking sensation when she looks at me. I know she will never have enough of what it is she wants. She wants acceptance but has no container for it, she wants validation but has no end of her need for it. This scares me because I have my own vacuum, my own bottomless pit that can never be filled.

L

It's a typical Friday: work, work work. Mother Kay took me off of selling bread. I do kitchen every Friday now. I wish I could say this morning has been worse than most Friday mornings but it's about the usual. Breakfast was a disaster. I burned the eggs and the muffins were dense and flat. Everyone complained. I'm still doing breakfast dishes. The bread has to be made into loaves and I still haven't started lunch. It's eight fory five. I'm still sleepy. I'm wearing my ugly clothes too.

"Where is my lemon water?" Mother Kay appears on the bottom stair, her robe trailing behind her and her wide bare feet are poking out, unashamed, beneath her flannel nightgown.

"Umm, I guess I forgot it." I head to the fridge to get a lemon. Better late than never.

"Forgot? What kind of an excuse is that?" Mother Kay stands in my way.

"Not a good one."

"How many mornings do I have to come down here and ask for my lemon water? You know very well that I am supposed to drink it first thing in the morning before I get up. What's the matter with you?" I shrug. She steps down from the stairs and into the kitchen.

"What is this milk still doing out? Is this clear from breakfast?" Her tone is rapidly gaining volume.

"No, I got it out a little while ago, and I forgot to put it back." I can feel my face getting warm. The milk had been out for several hours. She walks over to the five-gallon bucket of milk sitting on the end of the counter. She places one of her white, smooth hands against its side, breaking the beads of condensation.

"It's warm! You lied to me, didn't you?!"

I can't back down now. "No, I got it out about a half hour ago."

"Don't you lie to me!"

She slaps my face several times like I knew she would. I knew it when her face appeared at the bottom of the stairs. The tone of her voice, the tilt of her chin—it was over before it started. She slaps me into a corner until my head is up against a wall. She keeps me there until she has had enough. She turns on her heels and glides back up the stairs. I turn back to my dishes, touching my face several times with cool water, grateful that this time I was alone. No witnesses to either feel sorry for me or give a "that's what you get" look. A few minutes pass before I hear her whistle for me at the bottom of the stairs.

"Yes?" I smile up at her.

"Would you please bring me up a glass of milk and the olive oil?"

"Sure thing!" It's difficult to make the words come out, to be a part of the cover, the game of pretend. I carry a full glass of creamy milk in one hand and the bottle of oil in the other and stand in the bathroom while she pours both liquids into her bath water. She hands everything back to me and says, "Go tell your mother I want her." I seethe at her words.

Mother Kay wants to see *my mother*, as if she is a prisoner and Mother Kay is a Supreme Court judge calling Mother into the courtroom to give her a ruling. I can hear them from my post at the sink, Mother Kay with aggravation in her voice and my mother apologizing. She's sorry that she didn't change Mother Kay's bed sheets like she said she would yesterday. She knows. She'll remember to do it next time; in fact, she'll go change the sheets right now. I can hear the bathroom door close and I know Mother Kay will be soaking in her own concoctions for at least an hour. Emily will massage her feet and legs for the next hour in the playroom. At least it keeps Mother Kay stationary.

Mother works in the kitchen beside me. She makes all the cookies and brownies to sell. I understand why she isn't pleasant with me today. I am part of the reason her and Mother Kay have troubles. I am my mother's child; she is partly to blame for my behavior. She yells at me when she finds out I didn't put the bread bowls to soak in the sink. She shakes her head in disgust when she sees me slicing bread for sandwiches. "Do ya have to be so sloppy? Look, you are getting crumbs everywhere."

Mother works so hard all the time. Her face is red like a pressure cooker about to blow a lid. She's always looked that way. When I was little, I told her she looked like an Indian without the feathers. She laughed but I could tell it hurt her feelings a little. I've felt bad for saying that.

Mother is up before dawn cracks, scrubbing the tile in the playroom bathroom. The vacuum is going before 6:00 AM, Mother in her perpetual white apron vigorously pushing the vacuum back and forth, somewhat oblivious to anything but the floor needing a good cleaning. By the time I finish making breakfast Mother has half the house cleaned. Fridays are worse. I have no idea what time she starts the laundry and the cleaning but it's earlier than usual because of the extra cooking she has to do. It makes her irritable on days like today. She rushes around the house trying to hold the world together. I just survive. I don't feel I should contribute any more than I do. Every Friday Mother and I end up angry. I want her to stop working so hard so I can stop working so hard.

It's Friday night. Bread is sold, dinner is ready, and Father is about to come home. The kitchen looks okay considering what it's been through. I've been in the bathroom several times today to hold my breath, to force as much blood to my face as possible. After a minute a blood vessel breaks somewhere on my face and neck. I check in the mirror to find it. The first one's on my neck and looks mysteriously hickey-like. The next one is on my forehead, right in the middle, a big reddish-purple stain in plain view, with several others randomly appearing throughout the day. Father asks me when he sees me what happened and I gladly reply, "I dunno," and finish clearing the tables. I can hear Mother Helen offering her diagnosis: an allergy. Mother thinks it's an infection and Mother Kay says I'm low on minerals. Only I know it's self-inflicted and it thrills me to be the one holding the secret, the one looking off stage at the bewildered faces and laughing.

LI

Her voice booms through the house. "*Susaaaaanna!*" I'm in trouble for sure. I fold up my newspaper, stuff it quickly behind the toilet, and hurry out to the kitchen.

"What is this?" Mother Kay points to the pot boiling responsibly on the stove.

"It's the beans you told me to cook." I'm thinking hard and fast as to what could be wrong.

"Why aren't they cooked? I told you I wanted them done for dinner!"

"They will be!" I defend myself. "Dinner is six hours away."

Mother Kay slings her open hand across my face. "Dinner is at noon. It's a quarter to twelve and I told Father to be here for dinner because we were having chili. Damn you girl!" She's wound up. She never swears, only when she is seriously mad. She slaps me twelve more times until I am backed into a corner. She's towering over me, rage in her green eyes. The kitchen is buzzing with activity.

"Father's going to be here any minute!" She slaps me three more times. "You rotten little snot. You think you can do whatever you please." She slaps me again. My face burns from both pain and humiliation. Everyone around is frozen, unable to turn away. When she is finished with me I slip under her arm and take my station at the stove, stirring the troublesome beans. She grabs me by the arm and flings me away from the stove.

"Get out of here," she growls. I can't move. I stand there looking at her, unsure if I should really leave.

"Get out of here," she repeats. "I can't stand you. I can't stand the ground you walk on or the air you breathe!" Her face is twisted so tight, her mouth open, explosive, her teeth bared. Her words are new, true. It's the first time I have heard her speak the truth about me. I back up slowly toward the stairs.

"Get away from me. I can't stand you!" she is screaming now, her own demons loosed and crazy and dancing in her eyes. I turn and run up the stairs. But I am afraid to be upstairs and I am afraid to be downstairs.

It's quiet down below. I stand at the top of the stairs listening.

"Don't just stand there," she says to Emily, her voice slightly calmer. "Get some dinner on the table before Father gets here."

Emily will have to finish the sandwiches I had started, and after a while I hear Father drive up. Mother Kay's out in the lean-to, no doubt, before he can get out of the car. I hear them come in the house and Mother Kay's voice describing the events in her usual manner. Father doesn't say much. Everyone eats and to my great relief I hear her ask Mother to drive her to the store. Mother Kay can't drive.

When everyone leaves I call Joe.

"Hi, Joe, it's me." My voice is shaking. I hold my hand out in front of me and notice the trembling.

"Hello, Susanna, how are you?"

"Oh, not too good." I can't think of how to tell him what happened today. I want to say my stepmother was horrible to me today but I can't because he would wonder if my mother was dead. I can't tell him about all the mothers. He'll never want to speak to me again. He will know that I'm a freak.

"My mother yelled at me." I can hardly swallow the lie. "She told me she couldn't stand the ground I walked on or the air I breathed!"

Joe sighs. "I know it hurts when your mother says things to you like that. But you have to understand something. Sometimes parents say things that they don't mean. Even I say things to my son that I don't really mean."

"I know."

"You have to remember that grown-ups make mistakes too."

"But sometimes it's not a mistake; sometimes they try to hurt you. Like when she …"

Joe interrupts my ranting. "Did someone hurt you, Susanna?"

I want to tell him everything. I am so desperate. But I can't. I am afraid he will hate me. It is for myself that I refuse to tell him the truth.

"No, not really." The lie burns my tongue and leaves a deeply bitter taste in my mouth. "I know what you are saying; she was probably having a bad day."

"Susanna," he says, his voice grave, "are you telling me everything?"

"Oh yes, it was nothing." There is a terrible silence on the other end. "Really, Joe, I should just be more understanding."

"If you need anything you call me, okay?" His voice is full of kindness.

"Okay, thanks, Joe. I gotta go." I hang up the phone. I am still shaking a little. What if I could make it go away? What if I could make Mother Kay go away?

I open Father's desk and find the phone book. It takes some time but I find the number I am looking for. It's a child abuse hotline. I don't know if it's a place where I can talk to someone about what is happening or if it's connected to the police department and they dispatch a herd of officers to come and arrest Father.

I run my finger thoughtfully across the number. Someone could know today. They would take Mother Kay to jail. We, the kids, would all be taken in by foster parents. Split up. What if they took me away from Claire and Lillian? What if Glenn and Danny were mad at me? What if everyone in the Work hated me for sending Father to jail?

I slam the book shut. I will live with things the way they are. Being split up would be worse than what I have to deal with now. I couldn't live with myself knowing I could cause my family to be destroyed. The thought of Mother Kay going away forever is tempting but it would be at too great a cost.

Knowing I could do it, that feels good enough.

LII

"I got your letter," says Joe, a few notches lower than his usual chipper voice.

"Oh, good." There is a tense silence that I have never felt between us before. "What?"

"What do you mean 'what'? You know very well what." He is starting to sound like Mother.

"I do? Did I say something that offended you?" I am beyond baffled.

"It was what you said in your letter," his voice still parental.

I can't remember. I have written Joe several letters and all of them are a bit off the wall but I must have said something in this last one that jarred him. He doesn't seem to want to tell me what it is.

"I don't know what I could've said that would have offended you. What did I say in my letter? I really don't remember." I'm worried. Maybe he has figured out that I have been lying to him.

"Oh, I think you remember."

"Really, I don't. Please tell me. I can't stand to think I've upset you in any way." Tears stream down my face. I am about to deal with my worst fear. He is going to get rid of me. Joe hesitates like he is at a loss for words.

"You said you think about committing suicide all the time." His voice is grave and has a concern that seems unnecessary.

"Oh, that ... um," I stumble over the words. "Yeah that's nothing." Whew. What a relief. At least he doesn't hate me.

I completely forgot that I wrote about committing suicide. Doesn't everyone want to kill themselves? I guess that isn't normal to Joe. I figure it's normal. I would never have written it if I thought it would make him angry.

"Is it true?" he asks.

"Well, yes, it is true."

He sighs and I can almost see him shaking his head, struggling for the right words. It feels good to have him believe me, to have him anxious about me.

And it is true. I get to tell him something that is true. I haven't had the nerve to actually attempt it but I think of ways to die. It feels warm inside me when I think of it.

"I don't ever want you to say that word again! Do you understand me?!" Joe sounds different, like someone angrily worried and not just angry.

"Okay," I say, feeling meek.

"I don't ever want you to think about it again," he says a little softer this time.

A panic rushes through me. If I can't think about killing myself, what will I think about?

"I … well, I …"

"Promise me, Susanna. Promise me you will never say those words again. Promise me you'll never think about killing yourself again!"

"Okay, I promise." I feel a deep river open up inside me and a great rushing is released, like furious rapids down a steep crevasse.

Joe is worth this promise. This is the only promise I have ever made where making a promise seems solemn and breaking it would be like breaking a part of myself. I am quiet and still, just breathing, trying to take in all that I feel. Joe interrupts.

"Can we still be friends?" he says. I can tell he's worried that he upset me or hurt my feelings. His voice is warm and soothing and I wish he would get mad a hundred times so I could have him say to me a hundred times, "Can we still be friends?"

"Of course. I'm sorry I said that word. I just didn't realize what I was saying. I didn't mean to upset you. Really I didn't."

"It's all right. Are you sure you're okay now?"

"Yeah. I'm good."

"Are you sure? I only said what I did because I care about you. You know that, don't you?"

"I know."

"So you are okay, right?" he says in a tender voice. "You call me if you ever need me, okay?"

"Okay."

The words barely escape before the tears and the lump in my throat choke me. His words feel like a velvet hand caressing me in a pile of thorns. I hang the phone gently on the cradle. I sit down on the floor near the dresser and sob the sweetest tears I have ever tasted.

LIII

Joseph Walker is my life. He is my breath and my beating heart. I know I shouldn't feel this way, this dependant on someone, but there is nothing else. Without him there is nothing. I dream about him at night and think about him every waking hour. I've asked myself if maybe I am in love with him but I don't think I am. It's more like I want a father out of him than anything else. I want him to protect me and take care of me. But he has his own kids, a fact I am all too eager to ignore. Sometimes I do stupid things. I call him and disguise my voice and pretend to be someone else. Sometimes I call three times a day. I hate myself for doing it. I hate the deception. I hate the secrets that are so familiar and pressing. Joe doesn't pretend with me. He has been honest. I once pretended to be my own friend just so I could hear Joe tell someone else what he thought about me.

When I talk to Joe as myself, I like the person that I am, the person I feel I am capable of being. That person would be a stranger to Mother and the family but it is the truest version of myself I could ever imagine. I hate to think about it but Joe is not going to be in my life forever. The very thought of it makes me want to close my eyes and not see anymore. I only have this time, this bit of life with him now. I want to hold onto whatever gifts he is trying to give me, to let those gifts guide my feet to where lasting happiness is. I don't know why he is willing to spend time with me, to talk to me about my life and the challenges that I face. I only wish he knew it all. I only wish I could tell him everything.

It's hard to explain how I feel about Joe. All of this isn't really about him, the person. It's as if Joe is something inside of me that I am hanging onto with the last ounce of strength that I have. I've never seen him in person; I don't know what sort of man he is outside our phone calls. But he touches something in me that has never been touched. It is raw and pleasant all at once, it is both pain and joy. He makes me like myself in spite of everything and that, to me, is miraculous.

When I talked to Joe today he asked me what my prospects for life were. I wasn't sure what the word *prospects* meant, but I probed him a little. He asked me what I was going to do with my life. I hardly knew how to answer. I had never been asked that before, and as I stood there leaning against Father's dresser hoping no one would catch me on the phone with him, I felt my future crystallize in my mind.

"I'm going to be a mother," I told him. "I'm going to love my kids and help them feel all the happiness that I want. I'm going to get married to someone that loves me and I am going to adore him. I don't know many things that I am really good at doing yet, but my life here on earth is going to count for something, that much I can promise you. My life will count for something." I was startled by the conviction and I think Joe was too. Those words, those promises to myself, were like pure red blood coursing through my veins for the first time. Now I can feel those promises slipping carelessly through my fingers.

Today has been a horrible day. I want to give up. I am too tired to be angry; I'm too sad to cry. I am numb and it actually feels good not to care.

It's dark outside, very dark. Everyone has gone to bed and I am still up, mopping the kitchen floor. It is quiet except for the sloshing of the rag on the linoleum floor. The blankness swirls about me. When the floor is clean and dry, I walk outside to get the rugs from the railing by the front door. The wind catches my hair and the stillness outside fastens me to the moment. "I don't care. Do you hear me? I don't care!" A soft summer wind brushes my face. I can feel it like a father's hand that cradles his daughter's chin. I won't be comforted, but I can feel the edge of hope like the fringe of a warm blanket. I walk in the house holding the rugs over my arm. It's cool inside and all the lights are dimmed. It is at this moment that I see myself. There is a mirror mounted above the mantle in the living room. My hair is hanging out of its braid and looks droopy; my skin is pale except for the faint lines of irritation from my face being slapped. From the outside I look exactly like I looked this morning when I combed back my hair. I drop the rugs on the floor and walk up to the mirror until I can see nothing but my own face.

On the inside there is something new. I look into my eyes and I see it there as plain as it can be. I see a light, a burning ember of light. It smiles at me somehow and I smile back. I can see someone beautiful for just one moment. I can see goodness, no, greatness inside the depths of those eyes. I can see the soul, my soul, and it is glorious and brilliant. It is as white as the whitest white and as pure as a new day. I hold myself to the spot, gazing, admiring, and knowing that I am good, that I am this light that shines from beneath the blemished skin, the bedraggled hair, the broken body, the despicable person that I believed I was not five moments before. I am this. It is who I am; it is who I always was. It is a gift that not even Mother Kay can mock and destroy. I bask for a moment in this new knowledge before it fades, and like a jolt I am looking at my body again, this chamber of preparation. I am being prepared to be who I was born to be, and I will activate it like a switchboard when the time has come. It is not today.

But today I saw God. He was smiling at me, through me, for me. I saw the piece of me that is God, that was crafted in his image, like a great bone from his body. I remember ... I remember that I have always been this close to infinity; I have always been touched by the divine love. I am hidden from it, but today I remember it.

I want to see who I will be when this person is released from this timely prison. I want to know what I am capable of being, who I am without the shackles of self-hatred. I will live, I will go on, and I will see again, someday, who I am.

LIV

Emily comes out of the bathroom, her long black hair twisted up into a tight bun at the back of her head. She is wearing a pleated skirt and a look on her face I'm not too anxious to see.

"What's with the new hairstyle?"

"Nuthin'. I just think it's time for me to start wearing my hair like a mother." She sits down on the bed and begins tying her shoes.

"Why do you want to look like a mother?" I ask her, dumbfounded. A smile crept up on Emily's face, a smile that tells me she knows something.

"What? What is it?" Emily purses her lips together, but the smile won't go away. "Emily, tell me. C'mon! You know you want to." Her face reveals that she does indeed want to tell me. But she enjoys my begging.

"Okay, I'll tell you … if you can guess." She's going to make me work for it. It's not every day that Emily knows something that I don't.

"Yer getting married."

"Close. I know *who* I'm gonna marry."

"Nuh uh! Who is it?" I blurt out.

"I'm not gonna tell ya; it's a secret."

"Have you talked to Father about it?"

"Yes."

"Well?" I don't like being played with. If Emily knows who she is going to marry it won't be long before she will be gone.

"Sorry, I can't tell you." She seems pleased with herself.

"Well, whatever. I guess if you can't tell me, *you can't tell me.*" I chuckle to myself knowing that Emily can't resist. Besides, I don't want her to know how badly I want to know.

"All right, I'll say yes or no and you ask me questions about him. If you guess who it is, I'll tell you if you're right.

"He's older."

"Yes."

"He's already married."

"Yes."

Several older men pop into my head, and I begin to systematically eliminate them with specific questions. After I exhaust the list of everyone I know, it hits me. She is going to marry someone from Down South.

"Does he live Down South?" I ask, cringing.

"Yes." My heart sinks all the way down. This means I won't see Emily, and she will change and turn into a mother! Yuck! I don't want to know anything else but Emily says, "Do ya know who it is now?"

"I think so."

"Who? Tell me and I'll tell you if you're right."

"Is it Russell?"

Emily smiles so big she doesn't need to say yes; it is written in plain language on her face.

I know who Russell is. He comes up from Down South from time to time. He's nice enough, but he definitely has the older look down. He's around forty, has big hound dog eyes, and a slightly receding hairline. He's pretty well built except for a small pot just above his belt. He isn't typical of the older men. Russell's the silent type, easy to respect because much of him remains obscure. I heard he was in Vietnam and that he doesn't talk to anyone about it which makes him all the more mysterious. He has two other wives and at least three sons, with one just about Emily's age.

"There's more. He's coming over tonight!" Emily says.

"What for?"

"Well, Father said when he told Russell about me, Russell said, 'Now which one is Emily?'"

"He doesn't even know *which one* you are and he's marrying you?!" I can't believe my ears.

"I don't care about that. I know he's the man I belong to."

Russell arrives at seven in patched up work pants and a red plaid shirt. Father opens the door and invites Russell into the playroom. Emily stands at the top of the stairs. I can't help but think she is presenting herself as if she were wares on a cart about to be sold. He looks nervous, keeping his hat held tight in his hands in front of him. Emily has removed her apron and combed back her hair. I feel sorry for her. If this is marriage, I don't want it. The way it looks to me, Russell is coming over to view his purchase, like Emily is a milk cow being swapped for a basket of eggs.

LV

Everything is finalized. Emily's getting married next Tuesday. She comes into the bedroom in tears.

"What the matter?" I ask, expecting it to be about Russell.

"Father wants you."

"What for? Do ya know?"

"I had to tell him. I'm sorry, Sus, but I had to tell him." She is genuinely upset.

"Tell him what?"

She looks at me and I know. "You didn't!"

"Ya better hurry. Father's waitin' for ya."

"Are the mothers with him?"

She nods and walks away. Emily can't keep anything a secret. She has to be a good policeman and clear her own stupid conscience. I guess it's easy for her—she's leaving.

"Did you want me, Father?" I ask, poking my head around the doorjamb to his bedroom.

"Come in and shut the door." Father looks at me while I chew on the corner of my mouth. Mother is sitting on the bed, looking soberly at her feet. After a minute I raise my eyebrows at him, as if to say, "Well?"

"I've been hearing some things about you. Do you know what they might be?"

"I don't have a clue." I have learned not to trust even Father.

"Are you sure?"

I nod.

"Why would I be hearing things if they weren't true?"

"I don't know."

"Well, what do you think it might be?"

"I don't have any idea."

Father doesn't want me to know how much he knows. I can see that I am aggravating him. Mother jumps in.

"Susanna, *we know*, so you might as well tell us what's going on."

"You'll have to tell me about it," I respond calmly.

Father's face flushes and he looks like he might leap from his chair and punch me in the face. Instead he carries restraint in his every gesture.

"Emily's been telling us some pretty unbelievable things and we want to know if they're true."

"What has she been saying?"

"You've been talking to some man from the newspaper on the phone." I can hear his teeth gritting in his mouth when he says it.

"That's right. I have."

"I want to know why you would do a thing like that?" he asks.

I shrug. "I guess I wanted someone to talk to."

"You have your parents to talk to. I don't want you talking to some Gentile who doesn't know anything about us. How did you meet him?"

"I read his column in the newspaper and I wrote him a letter, and then I started calling him on the telephone."

"How long have you been talking to him?"

"About a year and a half."

Father closes his eyes and shakes his head in disbelief. "Why on earth would you do something like that? Do you realize how dangerous it is?"

"He's not dangerous; he's nice."

"Do you realize I could go to jail if the law found out about us?"

I nod.

"Why would you do such a thing?" he asks again, sincerely baffled.

"I told you, he's my friend. You don't understand. He's a good person. Besides, I haven't told him anything." I feel a tear tugging at the corner of my eye. I pinch the inside of my arm to make it go away.

"How old are you?"

"Fifteen."

"Do you think a fifteen-year-old knows as much about the world as dear ol' dad?"

"No."

"Don't you think I know a thing or two?"

"Yeah."

He sits up straight in his chair. "I don't want you to ever talk to this person again. I mean it. It's over. I want you to promise me you will never talk to him again."

"Okay."

"Is that a promise?" he asks.

"It's a promise."

It's a promise I'm not going to keep.

Emily apologizes when I come to bed. She says she wanted a clear conscience when she left home. Well, she should have it now.

LVI

Emily is leaving. It's a dull November day, with enough gray saturated in every molecule of the sky that the memory of sunshine seems impossible. The leaves that ricocheted reflections off the living room window through the summer days have fallen from their hosts in heaps and have amassed themselves in the gutters. A few strays, wet and clingy, stain the sidewalk. Their color is gone and all that remains is an unflinching reminder of death. Not the sort of death that brings relief, but merely a shift from one form of existence to another. The way summer has died, and must buried in the cold and unforgiving snow.

It's almost dark. Father has started the car, where he sits in his dark blue suit and tie, occupied by thoughts that reveal themselves in the fine lines of his forehead. His hair remnants are wet and combed back, and his face is smooth, smelling of after shave. Emily wears a familiar white dress and looks as nervous as a hummingbird. She skits across the kitchen, her white shoes in her hands. Her black hair is combed in rolls at the back of her head that are mounted on one another, producing a headdress. Each of the mothers, in their own white clothes, hasten down the stairs to the car with Emily following them, flushed and tugging at the cummerbund around her waist.

I watched Mother Kay in the days before the wedding, the way she pretended she liked Emily, embroidering flowers and green vines on the yoke of her wedding dress. With everything in reverse, Emily sat on the living room chair while Mother Kay combed her hair just hours before her departure. Did Emily forget everything she'd been through? It must be easier to simply know you are leaving it all behind, forever. Emily's been distracted all week, no doubt thinking of being kissed for real, by a real man with real lips, forgetting that the rest of us are being left behind. Does anything matter now? She's getting married. It is the final polish, the last nail in a long and tedious project.

The tail end of Emily disappears when she pulls the length of her white dress into the car and shuts the door. The car pulls out of the lean-to and into the street where it disappears in a cloud of its own exhaust. Emily is on her way to wherever it is that girls go to get married. I didn't even hug her good-bye.

I've thought all day about my turn, my day in the white dress. But it's like a blank page in my mind; it waits for me, revealing nothing. I have seen them all get married, the sisters ahead of me. There was nothing confusing about it. It was a simple word, married … gone. Simple, like a children's rhyme—diddle-dee dum, diddle-dee-dee—all words and no meaning. Simple like death, mysterious as the earth's interior. Emily will die, our time together forgotten like a dream.

I turn my attention to the task at hand. I am in charge. It's distracting business, changing diapers and rocking little ones to sleep. I forget that tomorrow will bring a long and boring session of rearrangement of chores. Mother Kay will point her finger in my direction and say, "You, young lady, had better get your act together. No more goofing around. It's time to grow up and start taking responsibility. There's no one to do it for you now." She'll be glaring at me with those green eyes and I will look at my fingernails while she says it. If she says anything that might bring tears to my eyes I will fold my arms and firmly pinch the insides of them, the crook where they bend and where it's most tender. She will tell Claire and Lillian they're finished with school and they will be placed on the roster. When it's all over, she'll dust her hands, stand up, and say, "Now all of you, get to work!" At which point she'll head upstairs for a nap and the entire room will exhale simultaneously.

It's late. The parents ought to be home soon. I chase kids to their beds and tidy up the playroom. I intentionally bark orders to my subordinates, providing them with the security and the belief that someone is in charge.

I am the Big Girl now.

LVII

I've never seen Mother Kay jealous. She looked like she was being turned inside out when Father married Daisy and Laverna Johnson. Of course, she tried to hide it, which only made it more obvious. Daisy and Laverna were widowed when their husband died five months ago. I don't know why Father married them except that Laverna wanted to have children. The two of them refused to separate. So, like Mother says, two birds with one stone.

Mother appears unflappable but she wears the tension on her face and in the clench of her jaw. When I ask her about it she says the ceremony was very simple and that life goes on. Then she fastens her apron around her waist and leaves the room.

Daisy confides in me, while I help her with her suitcases up to the room she will stay in, that she does not intend to live as one of Father's wives. She considers Father to be more like a brother and a priesthood influence that she feels she desperately needs for her own survival. It was a logical choice. It seems odd to me, being married to someone you consider a brother, but she wants to stay with Laverna at all costs.

She pulls out an eight-by-ten picture of her deceased husband and sets it gently on the dresser. It was Milton who had converted her from her strong Catholic ties to the truth, to the real gospel. Milton has her heart. She shows me pictures of them together. It was like something on TV, with his arms around her waist while she is cooking over a camp stove out in the wilderness, his jet-black hair wet in the style of the day. Another one shows the two of them grinning broadly, sitting on a checkered picnic blanket, basket and all, eating lunch together, Daisy's curly red hair aloft in the breeze. I can see that they loved each other in a way I didn't think existed. I can't stop looking at the pictures. It's like breathing clean air for the very first time.

"Was that before you came into the Work?" I ask, looking at this younger version of Daisy, her legs bare.

"Oh heavens, yes! Look at that makeup on my face!" She smiles at herself and then at me. "Ya know, I didn't know any better. I was such a vain woman, so fashionable. Here, look at this one." She hands me a snapshot of her and her girlfriend, hand in hand, dressed to the hilt in 1950s attire. It looks like she stepped right out of an episode of *I Love Lucy*. On the back it reads *Daisy and Gretchen, age fifteen*. I wouldn't have guessed she had ever looked that way by looking at her now in her polyester blouse and plain brown skirt. I feel sad for the laughing girl in the picture, unaware that someday she'd find herself in our family. I want to warn her, to prepare her, but I better not.

"My whole life changed when I met Milton," she says. "He was perfect."

I have a hard time believing anyone is really perfect, but it's obvious that he loved her. *He* loved her. That's what looks so different to me. Man loving woman and not exclusively the other way around. I've seen adoration and wistful glances in all the mothers' faces before. I've seen Mother reach over and take Father's hand in her own while she sat at his feet. He didn't look down at her or take notice of her eyes looking up at his for mutual love. He simply continued to watch television from his big rocking chair, neither warm nor cold.

I have seen this in other women at Meeting. I have watched them gaze at their husbands. The women look so demure with their hands folded neatly in their laps and they wear a hunger on their faces that they aren't aware of, like small dogs waiting to be fed. I want to stay away from them, like I might be swept up in a secret substance that keeps the women hungry. I don't like men; I don't trust them with their chins up and their shiny black shoes and stiff suits. The power to take the terrible hunger away is hidden inside their jacket pockets, where it is doled out according to the will of the man. I think the men love their wives, just not in the same way. The men do not respect their wives or so it appears to me; but they love them like one loves a pet expecting obedience.

I help Daisy arrange the bedroom to her liking, and before I leave she catches me by the arm and gives me a hug.

"I like you," she says earnestly. "You remind me of myself at your age." I assume she is giving me a compliment so I say thank you.

Laverna is going to be Father's wife and is the opposite of Daisy in every way. She is shy to the point of total introversion and still painfully awkward at twenty-seven. She seems hyper-aware of herself, her clothes, her hair, her glasses that she keeps pushed close to her face. She's petite with small eyes, small ears, small feet. Laverna is as stiff as a two-by-four. She sits on the edge of her seat, literally, with her back straight and her hands folded in her lap like she's posing for Leonardo da Vinci to paint her portrait. Her face, unlike the easy glance of the Mona Lisa, is cemented, unyielding of the folded lines of her forehead and the creases of her brows. She looks as though she might just erupt in tears at any second, but she never does. When I look at her I feel compelled to take a huge deep breath and exhale long and slow.

I heard Mother Kay talking to Mother once before Milton died and she said something like Milton was "done, ya know, *done*" and that's why Laverna couldn't have any children.

That's why she's marrying Father I suppose, to have babies. She doesn't look like she could be a mother though. She already has one child that she and Milton adopted from a couple with mental disabilities. I heard his real parents nearly shook him to death. I guess he's our new brother. His name is Adam.

Laverna arrives with her green suitcase packed with her clothes and Adam by her side. Adam sits on the toy horse in the playroom and rocks back and forth, with the whole family looking at him. He is content in his own world.

He looks like he comes from another country with his curly hair and brown eyes, a distinct contrast to all the straight-haired, blue-eyed faces I am familiar with. I feel sorry for him. I can see his future like it is written in stone, disadvantaged beyond belief. I look away from his unsuspecting brown eyes, full of hope about to be drained and a spirit on the precipice of being broken.

"It's a good thing you got him away from his parents," Mother Kay says, looking at Laverna. "He would have been ruined being raised by retards."

Maybe he would have been better off being shaken to death.

Part III

Beginnings

LVIII

I knew we were moving Down South but I didn't know that I was being left behind at Fifth East. I told Joe I was moving to another state. I can't believe that I did that; now I can't call him. I miss him in the most dreadful way. I still read his column faithfully. I memorize every one of them. I memorize every word he writes. My heart aches that I can't tell him what he has done for me.

Last fall, I went Down South during the construction of the new house. I swept up sheetrock dust and gathered nails from the plywood floors. Mother and I cooked on an old-fashioned wood stove in the basement of the house during construction. The erratic heat of a wood stove made cooking more difficult. We did the dishes out of big bowls and threw out the water into the red dirt. Mother said she remembered the days when that was how dishes were done all the time. She said they used to hang the washbowl right outside the kitchen door. I don't mind doing dishes like that—Mother and I, with most of the family still back home in the city. I felt I was contributing in some way. I felt it ensured me a place down here. I guess I was wrong.

I found out I was staying at Fifth East the night before everyone left. I looked over at Mother but she only said, "You won't be all alone. Mother Daisy will be here too." I know this is a punishment. Mother said it wasn't but I don't believe her.

I know why I am being punished. Mother says beatings don't work very well, although it doesn't stop Mother from turning her head when Mother Kay reaches for the stick on top of the fridge or makes me follow her upstairs to Father's bedroom where his Sunday belt hangs in his closet right alongside his ties.

It's a cold January morning. The semi-truck is loaded with furniture and everyone's beds and clothes. They took a bunch of the dishes and kitchen utensils. I wanted so much to go with everyone. It feels like my heart is being torn from its cavity. Lillian and Claire are crying and trying very hard not to show it. I watch them leave; everyone and everything I have ever known is leaving me. I hold my suitcase, feeling angry and foolish. Mother Daisy and I stand in the lean-to and watch the cars and semi-truck pull out onto the street, one by one, until it is quiet. I want to cry in this moment; it feels enormously appropriate but Mother Daisy starts chattering pleasantly about her friend Elizabeth who is coming over for tea the next day. People don't come over for tea. That doesn't happen in any reality that I know of. It especially doesn't happen when the world is falling apart.

Mother Daisy seems distracted as she fusses with the knob on the kitchen stove. She makes lunch for the two of us and we eat it in silence. The empty places at the table stare back at me. I bite the inside of my lip to make the tears go away but they push relentlessly at the cracks. But after a while, the urge descends back to the place where all my tears are stored. I unpack my suitcase into a box.

The house has a new terror. The emptiness is suffocating. Some days I run through the house screaming at the top of my lungs until I collapse on the floor of my barren room and let the tears have their way with me. It surprises me that I find this change to be so difficult. I have waited for a change all my life. Now that it's upon me, I find the uncertainty almost too much to bear. It is more than this external and obvious change; there is a restructuring of the landscape inside of me. I imagine how Noah must have felt coming out of the ark and seeing the earth a wasteland after the flood, everything gone. The only humans left.

It's been two weeks since everyone left and I haven't done anything today. I roller-skated in circles in the backyard until I grew bored of it. The lights are off in the house and there is a muteness that hurts my ears. I made me a cheese sandwich for lunch and watched TV. I'm still not supposed to do that, but there's no one to catch me watching it. Mother Daisy stays locked up in the sewing room, filling orders and making nurse's scrubs. She's in charge of me during the day until Mother Helen comes home at night.

Mother Helen acts like I'm not supposed to be here at all. She doesn't talk to me when she comes home, but instead asks Mother Daisy if I was good. Mother Daisy always says yes and Mother Helen looks suspiciously at me as if that is highly unlikely and Mother Daisy is ridiculously naive. I'm not sure what I have done to make Mother Helen upset with me so I stay out of her way as much as possible. I heard her talking to Mother Daisy last night after she thought I went to bed. She said some mean things about me. I don't want to remember them right now. I have to hug her in the morning like I never overheard her talking about me.

I keep breathing and my heart keeps pumping blood but I don't know why. My mind keeps busy, calculating, measuring, and deciding, while I remain in the background somewhere, a tiny buzz in my ear. It's as though all the functions of my body have been turned off to preserve whatever energy is left for moving my legs and remembering how to make scalloped potatoes. Perhaps now that the urgency that has focused my life is gone I don't want to look at what is there, what is left. I am trying to earn the right to be in this family. I just want to belong. I would take a thousand beatings, I would endure the most horrendous workload, I would smile through the ugliest rebukes and the most abusive insults to at least belong, to at least be with the other kids. I always thought I would be happy if I could leave and run away but now I don't know. I just want to be with Lillian and Claire. It feels like a cruel game of musical chairs. The music stops and all the seats are taken and I am left standing. Maybe there was never a chair for me to begin with. I have always felt like one of the many and there was a sense of safety knowing I was in a crowd. But now, I feel vulnerable and singled out. I just want to blend back in, to become part of the landscape.

There's a huge Chinese elm tree that hangs over the fence. It drops little seeds all over the place during the summer and fall. Mother used to say, "They ought to cut that tree down," when she was sweeping the driveway and the little seeds just kept coming. In the winter it bears loads of snow on its extended branches, protecting the car that's parked beneath it. In the summer it shelters whatever is beneath it from the heat of the sun. It doesn't matter whether it's useful or hated, the old tree simply exists. I should be a tree.

LIX

Russell came over today. He didn't have Emily with him but he had one of his older sons. He is working on a job across the street and wondered if he could lock his tools in our lean-to at night. Mother Helen invited them both to eat dinner with us—corned beef hash and vegetables. Mother Helen and Mother Daisy were overly attentive to Russell and his son, giving Russell the head of the table and generally acting like they were hosting the king of some country. Mother Daisy says it feels so good to have a priesthood holder in the house again. Russell acts like all the attention makes him a little uncomfortable, but no one else seems to notice. He always says hi to me when he comes over. I ask him if he is treating my sister properly, to which he smiles and says absolutely.

He brought letters from Claire and Lillian today.

It's weird reading letters from your own sisters. I've never been separated from them before and I leave the dinner table to read the letters in private. My room is empty. The impressions in the carpet from the beds that are now gone remind me further of the absence of my two best friends. I curl up in the corner of the room on my sleeping bag and open Claire's letter first.

Dear Susanna,
I sure wish you could come down here. I'm really missing you. It's awful lonely without you. Don't get me wrong, me and Lillian are getting along great but it takes all three of us to make me really happy.

Right now Father and Mother Kay are gone to St. George. It is very boring down here. It is terrible, just like I thought it would be. The only good thing that has happened is Mother Kay took us to the store Saturday and there was free ice cream. Lillian gave me a cute stuffed animal. She said it was for my birthday but she couldn't wait until then. It was a yellow dog. I named him Jake.

Most of the clothes that Mother Laverna gave us, fit, so that's pretty good. So, how're things up there? Having fun? I hope so. Well, I don't have anything more to say except I am missing you a lot. All right, go sew your shirt buttons back on. Ha ha!

Well, I'm supposed to be tending the kids, so bye!

Love,
Your friend and sister,
Claire

Dear Susanna,
I can't wait for the time when we are reunited. Hopefully it's soon. I realize more and more what it's going to be like when we're all separated and on our own. It will be hard at first but we'll get used to it. (Maybe, if we try hard.)

Well, you would say it's a beautiful day outside. I wish you were here to share it with me.

Boy, I really miss you guys. Especially Mother. Please tell her hi. I don't see Emily much, only when I go to Meeting. It's been horrible down here. I'm getting a lot of unwanted practice on cooking. I'm surviving I guess

I'm sorry this letter is so short, but understand it's eleven o'clock at night and I'm on breakfast in the morning. Wish me luck. Please write back, okay?

Love, your sis,
Lillian

I wait a long time before I open my door. Russell is gone and Mother Helen and Mother Daisy are downstairs watching TV. I go back to my bedroom and listen to the cold wind whistle through the cracks of the window. I know I'm feeling sorry for myself. I write two five-page letters to Claire and Lillian, making light of my situation and imaging I can see them laughing at my words, but I am not laughing. I am making do.

"You are strong." I can hear Mother's voice in my head. "You don't need the same things as the other girls. I have always known that about you."

"I am strong," I repeat out loud, before folding the letters and placing them safely under my pillow.

LX

I am waiting for Russell to come.

I made a huge pan of soup and ten loaves of bread to send Down South to Claire and Lillian. Hopefully it will make life easier for them and maybe I won't be forgotten. Russell is going down for the weekend and he told me he would take it with him.

I found out where Russell works. It's right across from the park in a big building. At nights I like to go see Russell, when Mother Helen and Mother Daisy think I am at the park.

He does sheet rock and works long hours after the other construction workers go home. It's cold and dark outside but he has a small heater and big flood lamps to work by. He walks on metal stilts and mounts the big slabs with grabber screws or he smears white paste on the ceilings and walls. I like to hand him screws or move the lamps around to better his workspace, but mostly I enjoy talking to him. He doesn't act like I am stupid. He doesn't talk down to me like everyone else does.

I know exactly when he will be here. Six forty five. I have already decided what I am going to be doing when he arrives, and I set up the chopping block and arrange several logs around me. Since I am the only one at home, I have been chopping the firewood for the stove in the playroom. It's our main source of heat in the winter and everyone depends on me to do it. I find unusual pleasure in swinging a mighty weapon around and chopping big things into small pieces. I cut the logs into four pieces and I have taught myself to swing the ax like a man.

I arrange an impressively large log on my block and am careful to hide the giant crack that will make splitting it in a single stroke possible. Then I wait. Russell is right on time and I raise the ax over my head and bring it down hard the moment his headlights shine on me. The log creaks and falls into two pieces. I pretend I hardly notice him and set up another log, and with the ax above my head I throw my weight into the second log. I have never split two in a row but the universe is on my side and in one blow it splits into two. Russell shuts the truck door and walks toward me as I raise my ax again.

"Whoa, whoa, whoa!" he says, a smile evident on his face. "Slow it down there, missy." I set the ax down on its head and lean my left hand into the end of it, just the way I had seen the man on PBS do it. The only thing missing was a red plaid shirt and greasy overalls. Instead I am wearing a dark brown skirt and a man's shirt, which I convinced Mother was a woman's. I wear it untucked over my skirt with the sleeves rolled up, revealing my muscled forearms. I'm proud of my physical strength and I work hard to maintain it.

I reach out my hand and shake Russell's with more than a little ebullience.

"Hello, Russell, how are you doing today?"

He grins. "I am just fine, and how are you?"

"Good. I take it you're ready to be on your way?"

"That's right." Russell shakes his head and I notice a weariness in his eyes.

"Let me go get the bread and soup." The feeling of control is so intoxicating; it feels like its taking me for a bouncy ride. When I return Russell is making room in the back of his pickup for the bread and soup. I leap up over the side of his truck. Russell steps back, a look of surprise on his face.

"Hand me that stuff and I'll load it for you." I say to him. He slowly hands me the food and I arrange the soup and bread neatly and cover it with a dusty gray blanket.

"There ya go!" I say, dusting my hands more than is really necessary. But Russell doesn't speak. He just looks at me with his hands on his belt.

"What? What did I do?" I leap off the truck and swoop up my ax again, ready to show off my skills.

"Come over here," he says.

I set my ax down, for the first time feeling a little vulnerable, and walk over to where he stands near his pickup. He puts both hands on my shoulders and looks into my face.

"How old are you?" he asks me.

"Sixteen."

"That's what I thought," he says, still firmly gripping my shoulders, which are feeling smaller every second. He doesn't speak but keeps looking into my eyes like he is trying to find the right words for something that doesn't have words.

"You don't have to be invincible, you know," he says finally.

"What do ya mean?" I know exactly what he means.

"It's okay to just be who you are. I have a sixteen-year-old too, who believes he's indestructible." He laughs at the thought of his son. "He lives on the edge, trying to prove his worth to the world. The funny thing is, he has nothing to prove. I already love him the way he is."

I know Russell is telling me something important but all I can feel is the weight of his arms on my shoulders, and the way his tone is breaking up the glacier inside of me. He lets me go and climbs into the cab of his truck and begins to pull out of the lean-to.

"Wait …" he says, holding an envelope out to me. "I forgot to give you this letter from Emily."

"Thanks." I fold the letter and stuff it into my skirt pocket. Russell looks at me for a long second.

"Being strong isn't everything, you know."

"I know."

It isn't the thing I wanted to say.

I wanted to tell him that I'm not allowed to be anything else but strong. If I let go of it, even for a second, I will break apart like the logs at my feet.

I stand with my feet apart and both hands planted firmly on my hips as he pulls out of the driveway.

LXI

Dear Susanna,

How are you doing? I hope you're doing just grand. I'm not. I miss you so bad. I miss the little things you used to do. If you can believe it, I miss your laugh. I'm writing to you because I know how it is to get a letter when you're not expecting it.

I miss you coming to me with your problems. There's one bit of advice I'd like to give you: Don't be too anxious to get married like I was. It comes all too soon. I'm not saying I'm having second thoughts about getting married, because I'm not. Just enjoy what you have.

I want you to know I miss the talks we used to have. I want so badly to give you advice and help you. It makes me feel good when you say how much you miss me.

Please be honest with me about something. Mother Kay said you won't be coming Down South because you were telling Claire and Lillian that they didn't have to do what they were told and you were acting just like Ruby used to. By what your letters have said I just can't quite believe it.

Now that I've been the big sister, how about you being one for me? Marriage is hard. I need to open up my feelings to Russell but I don't quite dare and I don't know how. Around him I feel so dumb and I can't find the right words to say. Everyone has been so sweet to me. Russell is always telling me I look lovely and if I fix dinner I get told by everyone how delicious it is. Does that sound like home? NO! Then other times it's so difficult and I feel like screaming! I wouldn't want to be un-married though. There are a lot of good things about marriage but a lot of heartache and hurt too. You never know how much jealousy is in you until you live in a house with two other women married to your husband. I know I have a good husband but there are times I feel like kicking the _____ out of him. I guess that's my emotions getting the best of me. Well, enough of me telling you my problems. I would like to know what severe trials you have gone through.

I want to tell you I understand how lonesome you are. Remember that time everyone went to Thompson's and I had to stay home. I was lonely. Remember when I almost had to stay home from Brother Patterson's funeral? I would have been terribly lonely. <u>I understand.</u>

I want you to hang in there and please, for your sake, don't be in too much of a rush to get married until you are sure you can live without ever seeing your mother again.

Well, I wish I could talk to you more often but I told Russell I better not write to you anymore. You shouldn't ask for my advice either because I'm married now and not a part of your family anymore. Let's keep the letters few and far between, okay?

I better say good-bye for now. With much love,

Emily

P.S. You can still write me back to this letter real quick and please don't show this letter to anyone.
Thanx.

I know Emily will write to me in spite of what she says. She might take a little break but I am confident I will get another letter. I put her letter in a box in the closet with the others.

There's a picture of Emily, Claire, Lillian, and me that I have placed on the windowsill. It was taken last year. Mother was offered a free eight-by-ten from Royal Studios and she gave it to us. We went on a Saturday and took half the day off to get ready. Mother was with us and she bought us sandwiches on the way home. The picture is still in the flimsy metal frame I bought at the thrift store for ten cents. I slip the picture inside my sleeping bag and turn off the light. There is a full moon outside and I know it will not get truly dark tonight. I can see the faces in the picture in the moonlight and though I don't really want to, I find myself crying. Tears find their way out of my body and I cry because I can. It feels peaceful to do this, to honor the sorrow like this until the door swings open and the light flips on.

"Where's the shampoo?" Mother Helen's voice is matter-of-fact. I try to hide my face.

"I didn't use it. I don't know where it is." My voice gives me away and Mother Helen comes closer.

"What are you crying about?" she asks, like I have no right to cry. I can't speak; no words will come out of my dry mouth. She sees the picture, the edge of it poking out of my sleeping bag. I hope she will let me be but there is something in her face that I have never seen before. The lines soften and her eyes get thoughtful. She turns off the light and for a moment I think perhaps she is gone until I feel her kneel down by my sleeping bag.

"You really miss the girls, don't you?"

I nod and she brushes the hair from my face. I have never been touched by anyone this way. No one has ever touched my face this way before. There are many more tears that come, whose meaning has nothing to do with missing the girls, tears that come because they are beckoned. They are the tears from a thousand nights when I held them back, when I refused to feel. I lay there and let her soothe me and she tells me it's going to be okay because I don't know what else to do. I feel myself resist her kindness and gentleness and I want her to leave me alone. I hug her before she leaves me because I want her to know that I care and because I think that is what she wants me to do. It is hard to hug her and let her love me. This is a Mother Helen I have never seen and will probably not see again. I am relieved when she leaves and closes the door behind her. I am also sad that her love made me feel uncomfortable. But it did touch me somewhere deep down inside. It changes something inside of me; it softens this something that had nearly hardened into a permanent form.

LXII

We've been driving for four hours. I was happy to leave Fifth East behind me. The only pull I felt was that Joseph Walker was still back home. But I can't call him anyway so I might as well be Down South with Lillian and Claire.

I was packed in the car with extra pillows and boxes of things that were forgotten from the first move. I looked behind me as we were driving away and I made a face at the house—so there. I don't mind being here in the back of the car while civilization disappears as fast as the fields and orchards are replaced by shimmery desert road. As far as I can see there is nothing but sagebrush and squat juniper trees growing out of the red-orange sand. The long, flat space is broken up by huge boulders that look like they've been pushed up from beneath the sand by giant hands. Their irregular shapes loom over the valley and cast monstrous shadows across the lone yellow-striped road that is taking me further and further into the quiet desert. The grazing cows and tail-swishing horses from the hour before are gone. There are no houses, no fences, and not even a lone trailer to stand itself against the relentless wind. After five hours and a long bumpy ride on a dirt road a few homes appear in the distance. There is one yellow and gray house that is straight and tall, a full three stories high. Father chuckles as we pull up to the house and park.

"They call it the cracker box. It does sort look like a cracker box, doesn't it?" I step out of the car and suck in a breath of clean, dry air. Father disappears up the deck stairs.

"Bring something with you," he calls down to me. I look around me and wonder how long I will be here. There is hardly a hill in sight and the smoky green sagebrush seems to stretch out across the land in every direction. I carry my clothes up the deck stairs and stand against the railing in the afternoon light. The sun is mere spot in the vast robin's egg sky.

There is something very familiar about the new house. It carries the same energy as the old house except it is new; it is a new space that is holding some old secret. I can feel the weight of the unspoken in the new house. This house doesn't have its hold on me yet. We are like two acquaintances who don't yet know if they will become enemies or friends.

I am glad Mother Kay disappeared into the back bedroom with Father. I help right away, doing dishes and preparing dinner. I am one of the many again, and I can interchange with Claire or Lillian as one of the Big Girls—except I am on probation. Probation. That just means there is no room for error. But I am going to be so helpful that they will want to keep me.

Nights down here are unbelievable. The sky is so big I can actually see its dome-shaped ceiling, covered with stars. I can feel the immensity of it and the smallness of myself looking up at it. I have always liked nighttime. For some reason the darkness doesn't scare me like I think it ought to. It's true, sometimes at night when I go out to the woodshed it feels like someone is there, hiding in the shadows. I run back to the house with my beating heart in my throat. It's a thrilling idea to be chased, always outrunning the demon by a few steps. But there is a darkness that I can't run from, inside of me. It is a place that surpasses rage, beyond suffering and confusion. It hides an ominous depravity. It is deep, like the belly of the earth; it is a free fall into my own corruption, my own hateful heart, hatred so lucid and so rank in its own putrid that hell is but a single empty thought away. My very own thriving hell.

I walk in the dark tonight, and I want to feel that this is my new home. I miss Joe Walker. I am startled when I hear his voice in my head. "Do you know what a special person you are?" he says. I let the words settle down around my shoulders, wanting to believe them. A rabbit scuttles across the dirt road and a deep and sacred silence rests over the place like a giant fleece. I look at the house from a distance, its colors muted and its interior revealed only through big rectangular eyes. *It is not my home.* A new panic rushes through my veins. *I have no home. I have never had a home.* The adrenalin surges and before I can stop myself I am running. Running away from the darkness inside, knowing full well it is futile.

LXIII

Jennifer knocks at the kitchen door.

"Can you go for a walk?" Jennifer wears her dark hair in a French braid and I am envious of her narrow waist and her clean pink skirt. Her white blouse hangs delicately off her small shoulders. I am larger than Jennifer in every way although I can see that most everyone is larger than Jennifer. Her frame is tiny and her hands are half the width of mine.

I step outside onto the deck and close the door behind me, hiding my dry, cracked hands between a greasy apron and black skirt that has a safety pin where the button used to be.

"I'll meet you at the corner of the road in ten minutes."

"Why? What do you have to do?" Jennifer still doesn't understand my situation as she props herself on the railing.

"Just wait for me. I'll explain it when I get there. I have to finish the dishes and wait for the bread to get out of the oven. I won't be long."

Jennifer doesn't even try to hurry down the deck stairs. I don't tell her that I have to get permission from Mother Kay and my work has to be checked before I leave the house.

Jennifer lives on the lot next to ours. I met her the first time I came Down South to help with the construction. I didn't wait to unpack my clothes or take a tour of the beginnings of our house. I saw a dark-haired girl watering pansies in her front yard and I knew I was going to make a new friend.

"Hi, my name is Susanna," I said, dropping into the red dirt in front of her. Jennifer looked up from the flowers, a watering can tilted in her hand. She didn't answer me but her face was saying "So?" I was undaunted.

"What's your name?"

"Jennifer." She immediately went back to the task at hand as if I had walked away.

"So tell me about yourself," I asked.

"There's not much to tell."

"Sure there is. Why are you watering these flowers? Is it your job?"

"No, I am watering them because they're dry."

"Well, what is your job?"

Jennifer tried to look annoyed. "I don't have a job," she said sardonically. "I go to school."

"Really? You mean with a real teacher and classmates?"

She looked up from the dirt, trying to determine if I was making fun of her. "Yes, I have a real teacher and classmates." She raised both eyebrows and smiled ever so slightly.

"Tell me *everything*. That must be so fun! I wish I could go to your school."

"You could if you wanted to. I mean, now that you're living here." Jennifer stood up and brushed the dirt from her skirt.

"Right. That would never happen."

Jennifer was curious. "Why not?"

"I have to work. Besides, my parents don't want me going to school."

"Where do you work?"

I was startled by the question. "At home … where else?"

"Oh, you mean you have to stay home and work?" Jennifer scrunched her face.

"Yeah, don't you?"

"Course not. Mother does all the work. I only milk the goats in the mornings and clean my room. Hey, would you like to see the goats?"

"Sure. Is milking a goat hard?"

"Not once you figure out how to do it. I've heard it's easier than milking cows. See, you put the goat up here on this table and put this pail underneath her." Jennifer secured one of the goats on a makeshift platform with a chain connected to a small collar around the goat's neck. She showed me how she milks the goat and how long it takes her to do it.

"What do you do?" she asked me.

"Everything." I sounded bitter, even to myself.

"C'mon, it can't be that bad."

"Oh believe me, its bad. I have to get up at six every morning and cook breakfast for the whole ungrateful family. I have to make bread every single day because the oven isn't big enough to hold more than four loaves at time. I have to tend kids or do the wash. I have to scrub the kitchen floor with ammonia every day because the red sand gets everywhere. I don't get done with my work until seven o'clock and that's if I'm lucky enough to get help with dinner dishes. Should I go on?" I was out of breath. Jennifer didn't say anything and I wondered if perhaps I shouldn't have said anything. I could hear how pathetic I sounded to my own ears. "Sorry, I shouldn't be telling you all this."

"No, it's fine, I just didn't know or … well, it's fine. Do you want to go for a walk?"

The first thing I told her, my new friend on our first walk together, was about my other friend, Joe Walker. My first friend. Jennifer and I have been friends ever since that day.

Jennifer is propped on a large rock in a perfectly ladylike pose when I meet her at the corner of our lots. She rests her chin on her fist and pretends to be annoyed. "It's about time. I was almost ready to go back in the house and do something else."

I smile. She would have waited a lot longer. Together we saunter up the dusty road.

"Where are we going?" Jennifer asks.

"I need to say hi to Valentine." I tear up a handful of alfalfa growing in someone's field next door. Valentine is a horse that lives in the field across from our lot. He's a sorry-looking creature, his head pulled to the ground by some invisible force. His not quite black coat is dull and dry. His hooves are cracked and misshapen and every rib in his body can be seen when he plods toward the fence to say hello to me.

"Hello, Valentine." I try to get him to pick up his head by bringing my hand in the air but he'll only raise it to take the fresh alfalfa. I wonder who he belongs to because I have never seen anyone feed or brush him or lunge him on a long line. He appears to be orphaned except for the fence that keeps him captive.

I scratch his head between his ears while he eats the alfalfa I have brought him. I try to brush off some of the dirt that has hardened on his coat with my fingers and he sidles up to the fence for more.

"I don't know why you like this horse." Jennifer keeps her distance from the fence. "He's so dirty and ugly."

"He's sad. He doesn't have anyone to love him and he is definitely not getting enough to eat." I pick another handful of alfalfa and walk it back to his pasture. Jennifer follows me but the look on her face shows that she doesn't understand.

"He's like the losing team in a football game, the team that hasn't won a single game all year. Do you see his eyes? He's lost hope." I almost choke on the last words.

"Since when do you know everything?"

"I just know some things."

Jennifer tolerates the interruption in our walk. I put my hand beneath his nose and he blows warm horse breath on me and I instinctively sniff the air to catch his smell.

"Don't you just love the way horses smell?" I lean in close to Valentine for a deeper whiff. "They smell like new leather, like … like a good-looking guy wearing leather."

"Oh please," Jennifer rolls her eyes. "Personally, I don't care much for horses."

"This isn't just any horse, can't you see that? Look at that face, so forlorn and lonely. I'm probably the only person in the world that cares about him."

Valentine picks up his heavy head at my words and stretches his thin neck across the barbed wire and nuzzles my shirtsleeve.

"He likes me. He knows I care about him."

Jennifer laughs. "He doesn't know. He's only doing that to see if you have more alfalfa in your hand."

"Maybe, maybe not. But I think he knows. Would you think I was dumb if I said I can talk to him?"

Jennifer looks at me for a second. "Probably."

We both laugh.

"Definitely."

Jennifer and I walk to the end of his pasture and turn up the road toward the school. Valentine follows us from a slight distance and whinnies when we turn into the school grounds, barred from following us further by the fence.

I wake up in the morning to a desert sunrise. I sleep on the third floor, on the top bunk directly across from the window facing the eastern horizon. The light pours in my room and I find waking up more pleasant than I ever have before. I like to sit here at this window and think. There isn't much time in the mornings but I take a moment or two before putting on my apron and starting my day to open the window and let the wind that never stops blow into my face. This morning is no different than past mornings except for the small dark lump in the field across from my window. I wouldn't have noticed anything at lower elevations but from my vantage point it is a stain on the red dusty pasture. I cannot investigate what it might be until tonight when my work is finished. But inside I already know and I push it out of my mind; I push it somewhere safe and let the warm penetration of hope drive me on.

Valentine doesn't appear at the fence all day. I don't see him sniffing the ground for an overlooked blade of grass when I take the garbage out to the trash cans. I keep telling myself that he is at the other end of the pasture; he has survived like he has all the days before today. I don't want to believe that things come to an end, that some things are not redeemed. When evening falls I ignore the sight of turkey vultures overhead and the faint smell of dead flesh that permeates the gusting wind.

LXIV

Mother Kay is stretched out on the couch. Her shoes have been kicked off and lie in a disorderly fashion near her feet. She keeps one hand resting lightly over her eyes. I have seen her like this before and I wonder if she is pregnant.

"Susanna?" she calls, a touch of anxiety in her voice.

"Yes?" I wipe my hands on the towel on my way to the living room.

"What are you fixing for lunch?" She keeps her eyes closed and little beads of sweat dot her nose.

"Um, sandwiches?"

"What kind?"

"Tuna fish."

"Oooooh," she moans as though I had stuck her with a fork. "Don't even say that word. What else?"

"Vegetable sticks."

"What else can you get me?" she whispers.

"I have some tomato soup from yesterday."

"I'll try that. Bring it in a mug. And make sure it's hot this time."

I warm up the soup on the stove. I thin it down with a little hot water, add a touch of salt, and it should be good enough. I ladle a couple of cups into a blue plastic mug and set the mug on a saucer, adorned by three crackers. I hope this is the last thing Mother Kay eats for a while.

"Here you go."

Mother Kay doesn't move. "Mother Kay?"

She very slowly pulls herself upright and grasps the cup with both hands. "Oh, that smells good."

I'm relieved and I almost make it out of the room when Mother Kay shrieks.

"What's wrong?"

"Take it away," her voice is shaky and she holds the soup out to me with one hand and covers her mouth with the other.

"What's the matter with it?"

"Hair," she manages to get out.

"Where?"

"Look … in the mug." She barely gets the words out or her mouth before she starts gagging. With one hand pressed tightly against her mouth she disappears into the bathroom leaving me standing in the living room holding her untouched soup, a long dark hair coiled on the surface. There is nothing left to do but leave it on the table and finish making the sandwiches.

When Mother Kay appears, her face is white and she comes straight toward me, having discovered some hidden energy.

"Open up these windows! What's the matter with you? And get rid of that soup! I'm never going to be able to eat tomato soup again. Get one of the boys to empty this garbage and get rid of this tuna fish smell!" She makes her way back to the couch and all is silent once more.

"Susanna?" she calls again after a full ten minutes. "What are you going to feed me?"

LXV

Things have changed a lot since Father was ordained the bishop. I'm not sure what his job is or what is expected of him, or me for that matter. People treat me differently since Father was ordained. Men are coming over all the time now to see Father. Each one of them, both young and old, has to walk right past me through the kitchen to get to Father's office. I make sure I am nearby or that I brush up against their arm just a little on their way in.

This morning James Wiles came by. He looked at me like I was a brand new Ferrari and I let him look. I have an importance I have never known before. I know it's because I am of marriageable age now. James Wiles doesn't know I'm not marrying him and taking care of his seven kids whose mother left them for whatever reason. Even Claire and Lillian are getting new attention. Max Malone came to see Father last week and on his way out of the house he heard Claire tell me her back was aching. Without a seconds notice Max stepped up behind Claire, wrapped both arms above her waist and gave her an impromptu adjustment. Claire reacted by giving him the elbow and he released her and smiled as if he expected her to protest. When he left I thought Claire was going to blow a gasket, she was so mad. We both decided to hate Max Malone along with a few others who have taken their interests one step too far. Lillian avoids too much attention by disappearing if she hears one of the many knocks at the kitchen door.

At Meeting several men say hello to me and shake my hand. I am not the prettiest girl or the thinnest but obviously I have something they want; I can only guess at what it is. I pretend I don't notice their eyes following me down the aisle and I ignore their glances throughout the service. I wonder what causes their wives to sit there next to them with a long row of slick-haired children and take painful care to look the other way. I wonder how it feels to know your husband is always looking. None of them know that I am not even considering them as a prospective husband. I like the attention though and I like being the one holding the secret cards.

Mother Kay doesn't want me to be a woman, to be attractive to men. I overheard someone tell Mother Kay what a pretty girl I had turned into, when they believed I was out of earshot. Mother Kay said, "She's not, really." She went on to tell this person all kinds of nasty things about me. I couldn't ever really be pretty.

Mother Kay's been acting strange lately. Maybe because she just announced her pregnancy, which we all knew about. Or it could be that Father married another widow, Mother Beverly, leaving one less night a week for her to spend with him. Maybe because Father is gone all the time on church business, leaving her in charge of everyone. She seems tired and irritable all the time. I know she likes the power of Father's new position, I can tell by the way she talks on the telephone to her sisters, long distance. But I think she wasn't prepared for the burden of being one of the bishop's wives, not quite the glamour for her as it seems to be to Father. She appears to be scrambling for something that is out of her reach. I want to feel sorry for her. I think that would be the right way to feel, but I don't. My only concern is the way she takes out her frustrations on everyone at home, especially when Father is out of town.

Father asked me to take a job at Mother Beverly's sewing factory where Mother has started working. Of course I won't be seeing any money, I don't expect that, but it is kind of prestigious to get up in the morning and go to work. Just like Father. I walk the mile and a half to the factory and work in pleasant conditions until five or so in the evening, then I walk home.

The sewing factory is split into two parts. The Pattersons and Colemans run one-half and pay Mother Beverly rent, and Mother Beverly and our family work in the other half. The Pattersons and Colemans are the important people down here, the popular ones you might say. Their fathers have been ordained apostles and their families are so huge they take up half the meetinghouse. I really wish I was working in the Patterson and Coleman side of the sewing factory. I want to fit in somewhere. I want to belong.

LXVI

"Jacob? Is that furnace going?" Mother shouts from the deck stairs to Jacob, who is carrying an armload of wood. The ground is frozen and the wind blows an icy desert cold. There is a glazing of frost on the sagebrush.

"I'm workin' on it," Jacob says through chattering teeth. I close the upstairs window and turn the water on in the bathroom. Adam and Timmy stand in the hallway waiting to take a bath. Their wet diapers sag to their knees and they both work at getting their pajamas off while I gather towels from the closet. Once the tub is half-full, I don't waste any time dropping the naked two-year-olds in the water.

"Cold," Timmy says, standing up.

"Let me check," I put one hand in the water, and sure enough the water isn't even tepid. I take the boys out and wrap them in towels, then I run downstairs to boil some water. After returning with the kettle I pour warm water into the tub making it just warm enough for a bath.

"It's cold," Timmy complains again.

"I know, we'll hurry." I soap him down and am just ready to get him out when I hear someone at the door.

"What do you think you are doing?!" Mother Kay's eyes are ablaze. She puts her hand in the water. "This water is ice cold! Look at that poor soul; his lips are blue!"

"The water isn't very warm this morning, so I was hurrying to get the boys bathed."

Mother Kay bumps me out of the way, grabs a towel, and removes Timmy, shivering, from the bathtub.

"What's the matter with you? Don't you have a brain?!"

Mother turns the corner. "What's going on here, Kay?" she asks.

"Look what she did. She bathed this poor little soul in ice-cold water!"

"What did you do that for?" Mother asks.

"The water wasn't warm this morning. I boiled the kettle but it didn't warm up the water very much and Timmy was already in the tub before I realized the water was cold."

"That's true, Kay," Mother says in my defense. "Jacob was slow getting the furnace started."

"That's no excuse for her to bathe him in cold water. She's just lazy. Lazy and irresponsible. You are going back home, young lady." Mother Kay's green eyes, round with self-satisfaction, look straight at me before walking out with Timmy in her arms to dress him. Adam is still standing in the corner wrapped in his bath towel.

"Why didn't you check the water before you put Timmy into it?" Mother looks frustrated.

"I didn't do it on purpose, Mother."

"I know, but that's no excuse."

"But, Mother, I didn't realize ... I was trying to do the right thing."

"Well, you've got to think of these things ahead of time if you're going to stay out of trouble."

Father told me tonight that I have to go to Fifth East. I know I will come back, perhaps in two weeks. Mother Kay isn't going to rid herself of me that easily. I will find a way to get back. That much I know.

Mother Laverna will be leaving Down South and going to live at Fifth East permanently, Mother Laverna and her new baby Eliza. Mother Kay doesn't like Mother Laverna and puts her down every chance she gets. She doesn't like baby Eliza either.

Baby Eliza cries. She cries a lot. Mother Laverna stands at the bottom of the stairs wringing her hands while Mother Kay marches up to the crib, as if she's going to fix the baby once and for all. I can't stand to hear Mother Kay hit her. I try to eject the picture from my head: baby Eliza stripped of her diaper, draped over Mother Kay's arm while she smacks her tiny bottom until it is red. I can't make the picture disappear. But I can run to the cellar with the potatoes that are stored underground, away from the sounds, but the image follows me, as well as all the other images that I have tried to hide from: images of Jonathon getting a beating out in the lean-to; Carl in his yellow pajamas, crying; Annie getting dragged across the room by her hair; Danny's black, bruised legs and Tom waiting for a whipping and so many others. They all come out and collect themselves together for an appearance.

I take a deep breath and force myself back upstairs. I smile, even though the insides of my belly are trembling, and speak softly as if nothing is wrong, as though I have power to neutralize Mother Kay's actions with the sound of my voice.

It tears Mother Laverna up inside. Her eyes are red from crying and she is relieved when Mother Kay appears midway down the stairs.

"She's asleep now."

"How did you get her to stop crying?" says Mother Laverna in a faltered voice.

"You have to let her know who's boss, Laverna. That's all she needs," Mother Kay says impatiently while rubbing her right hand. "She has you wrapped right around her little finger. When I'm dealing with her she knows I mean business."

"You're right, Kay. I guess I need to be more firm." Mother Laverna's head is down and she bites the inside of her lip. There is a peculiar agitation on her wrenched face and a stiffness in every movement of her limbs as she walks away from the stairs, like a machine or a robot.

I wish I could talk to Joe right about now. I long to hear his pleasant voice, his kind wisdom. Of course I couldn't ask him what to do, or how to cope with the world I am in, but I could tell him how I feel, the emptiness, the bleak hopeless feelings. He would tell me that it was going to end someday, that teenage years are hard for everyone. He would tell me to hang in there because he was counting on me. He would remind me to smile because a smile can fill your heart up even when it's empty and dry.

There isn't much snow but it's cold outside. The wind presses into me; it swirls the cold sand around my feet and in my shoes. I just walk, walk, walk. There is finally peace inside my head. The wind whines and whistles in my ears and all the other sounds in my head are drowned in its mighty voice. It keeps blowing and blowing. Nothing stays the same in this wind. Even the dirt roads change shape as piles of sand are redeposited along the banks. It seeps inside the cracks of the trailers that are grouped together like a wagon train. It leaves a transparent film of sand on the tops of all the run-down vehicles in the yards.

"Hey!" I yell. The wind cuts my words into tiny pieces. "What's the matter with you?!" Again, the wind wipes the words from the air as if they had never been spoken. "You think you have me, don't you? You think you can control me by sending me away. You're wrong!" My words are nearly sucked up before I hear them. "I will never be like you. *I* will decide how I am going to feel. You can't make me feel anything I don't want to! DO YOU UNDERSTAND! YOU CAN'T STOP ME! AAAAAHHHHH!!"

Claire and Lillian would hush me if they were here. They would tell me to be quiet before someone heard. But the spoken word has a life all its own, escaping my body like a trapped moth that's been suffocating in a jar for a long time. I offer the words up to the wind and the wind whisks them away.

LXVII

I feel bad for Annie. Mother Kay has been so mean to her lately. She makes her go to bed at six thirty every night and she gets whippings almost every day. I don't know what to do for her because I know how she feels. I'm afraid to be seen talking to Annie or Annie will be stuck spending the rest of her childhood with that apprehensive look on her face. Last night I saw her sitting up on her bed, waiting for the sun to go down.

"Hey, how many weeks do you have left until your punishment is over?"

"Six," she said glumly.

"That's not too bad. It will go by fast."

"I haven't been good for even one week yet. I have to be to bed at six o'clock and stay in bed all night and be quiet." Annie said, tucking her nightgown around her knees. "I am not doing good."

"You mean, in Mother Kay's estimation."

"Isn't that what matters? I'm never going to get off this punishment. She will keep adding week after week until I'm married."

"You know, I read somewhere that if you get a lot of sleep in your preteen years you will grow up to be tall. I'm tall. Five feet six inches. That's an inch taller than Mother Kay." Annie's face wasn't encouraging and her cynicism at nine years old was a little upsetting for me to hear.

"At this rate, I will be as tall as Paul Bunyan before Mother Kay lets me off this stupid punishment."

"That would be good. Then you could squash her like bug." Annie laughed out loud. I sat down on the bottom bunk next to her.

"I know how you feel, Annie, like nobody cares. But I care, and if it makes any difference I don't think you deserve this punishment."

"You don't?" Annie was genuinely surprised.

"Nope. And you wanna know something? Someday you're going to be grown up. You will leave all this behind and Mother Kay will have to stay here for the rest of her life. We get to leave." Annie looked at me, not quite pleased with my speech.

"What about Mother? She has to stay here forever too. With Mother Kay."

"I have an idea. When we all get married, we will let Mother come and take turns living with us."

Annie laughed. "Mother would never do that."

"Well, for now, you just worry about getting off this punishment, okay? I'll help you as much as I can. I'll remind you and check up on you until you've made it, okay?" Annie nodded her head and I could tell she felt better.

"Good night," I said before I left the room. Annie had tears at the corners of her eyes.

"Thanks, Susanna," she said and I halted in my tracks, the sound in her voice, the hauntingly familiar sound of my own voice, echoing in the back of my mind.

"Any time, Annie, any time."

Mother tries to help Annie too and she sometimes comes up to Annie's bed and talks to her, telling her what she can do so she won't get punished by Mother Kay the next day. I asked Mother why she didn't try and help me when I was being punished. She said Annie isn't as strong as me.

Maybe Mother is right, because I am worried that Annie might just die in her sleep. I'm afraid that she will simply give up and her heart will stop pumping and her oxygen-starved brain will shut down. I am afraid I will go into her room one morning to wake her and she will be cold and hard and dead.

I wish I wasn't strong.

LXVIII

"Someone wants to marry you." Father doesn't smile or wink at me like he's joking.

"Really." I try to sound uninterested.

"That's right."

"Whoever it is, he's desperate."

Father laughs. "Sit down and shut the door." I sit in the only other chair in the room and tuck my skirt around my thighs self-consciously.

"Are you going to tell me who it is?"

Father looks at me for a moment, deciding whether or not to tell me. "It's Brother Potter."

I nod my head thoughtfully but my insides shrivel at the thought. Brother Potter is old. He has children older than me, married with children of their own. Besides, he's ugly and has wrinkles on his big boxy face. His eyes are hidden under bushy gray brows that turn up slightly, giving him an angry-looking face. He looks at least six feet five inches, and has hands … he has these gigantic hands that swallow up anything he takes in them. He isn't fat but he is big, linebacker huge.

His wife is no stranger to big either. She is a solid-looking woman with red-colored hair that rises up a full eight inches above her head. She has a generic smile on her face all the time. Not exactly the kind of woman I want to spend my life with.

I squirm uncomfortably in the chair; a picture of me standing next to Brother Potter with his first wife on the opposite side rotates in my mind. I would be the new wife. New in a bad way. Fresh and unbroken, but purchased.

"What did you tell him?" I lean forward in the chair.

"I told him you were still too young."

"Good," I say after a moments thought, "I am too young."

Father smiles. "What makes you say that?"

"I don't want to get married right now. I am not ready for that." I take a breath before finishing. "Especially not to him."

"What's the matter with Brother Potter?"

"I don't like him."

"What makes you think you will like your husband?"

I think about this for only a moment, assessing the realities of marrying a complete stranger. "If I don't like him, I ain't marryin' him."

Father laughs heartily. "How do you know Brother Potter isn't the man you made covenants with in the preexistence?" he asks, the smile slowly fading.

"Some things you just know, Father, and that's one of them." Father looks surprised by my certainty so I quickly change the subject. "What did he say when you told him I was too young?"

"He told me to let him know when you were old enough."

My mouth drops open. I must look awfully comical because Father is smiling. I can't believe what I am hearing. When words finally come out of my mouth they are cracked with anger. "What did you say to him?!"

Father shifted in his chair. "I said, 'Let's get her there first.'"

Let's get her there first. The words poked at a hardness inside of me.

"Well, you can call him right now and tell him I'm never going to be old enough to marry him! You tell him I'm not some stupid appliance in the factory that he can order over the phone!" I could feel my face getting hot. "You tell him … tell him … to go fly a kite!"

Father is amused.

"You feel strongly about this, don't you?" he says.

"Of course I do. I will not marry that man. I won't. I'll go to hell first." I am breathing hard and I can feel the sweat running down my tensed shoulders. Father raises his eyebrows when I say hell, but continues smiling and leaning casually on his elbow in his big office chair. "I'm serious, Father."

"I can see that. I guess I don't need to see if you want to pray about him?"

I shudder. "Definitely not. I don't want him to have the slightest hope."

"Okie dokie," he says cheerfully. I leave his office hot and mad and go straight to the basement to tell Claire and Lillian what happened.

"That's is so *sick*." Claire twists her face. "You *should* be mad. I would clog my nose every time he came around if I were you." Claire presses her fingers against her nose to demonstrate the effectiveness and clarity of the message it would send. I am grateful for the comic effect it has on me.

"Boy, I'm sure glad that didn't happen to me. I hope nobody icky asks for me, because then I would have to pray about them." Lillian looks positively worried.

"I am *not* going to pray about him, believe me!" The anger is massive inside me and I feel it all trying to surface like a huge lump in my throat. "He is such a pig, thinking he can have me when I'm ripe on the vine like I'm a stupid watermelon in Father's little garden. Sure, come on by when she's ready and you can have her. OOOOOOHHHHHH!" I stomp my feet and spit on the ground. "I'm so mad, I could scream."

"Here." Claire hands me a pillow. "Scream into this."

I should be flattered that someone finds me attractive but I'm not. I don't want an old man finding me attractive. It would be different if he was my own age. I hope he wishes he had never asked for me. No one will make me marry him. Not Father, or the brethren. Not even God.

But I am starting to feel guilty. I know that Father would never force me to marry Brother Potter and I have nothing to worry about. Some part of me knows that this anger doesn't have anything to do with Brother Potter. A little part of me feels ashamed that I am allowing myself to hate him. I didn't know I had this wild fire inside of me. I already know I am not going to marry Brother Potter; the real question is why am I still so angry?

LXIX

It's a one-and-a-half-mile walk to the sewing factory. I refuse to ride with Father when he drops Mother off there before his daily onslaught of appointments. Mother tries to talk me into at least wearing a coat before I leave the house but wearing a coat is a concession. It says Mother knows what's best for me. Mother doesn't know what's best for me. I'll skip breakfast too if Mother tells me I need to eat before I leave for work. It's a kind of safe defiance, a battle I can always win.

There is another reason I walk to work. I like people to pull over and ask me if I want a ride. I like to tell them no thanks and see the look on their faces, like I know something about walking in freezing temperatures with a dusting of snow on the top of my head, something that they don't know.

Women rarely stop; it's mostly men, and I would say at least half of them are being genuinely kind. Sometimes I really want to accept the invitation and be driven to work, but that would nullify the reasoning behind my insistence on walking in all kinds of terrible weather in the first place. So I hold my head high and walk with purpose while the car peals back onto the dirt road. I hope the driver is watching in his rearview mirror. I hope he wonders what it is that causes me to refuse his offer. I walk because the rest of the world remains huddled in warm cars and heated homes. I walk the path alone, the way Galileo stood against the tide of cemented beliefs, the way Dickinson sequestered herself, the isolation a gift to the world in the form of poetry. I am part hero, part martyr, part activist, changing the world, light years ahead of my time.

At least that is what I tell myself every morning during the thirty minutes it takes me to walk to work. It's how I confront the snubs of all the women's faces when I open the door to the sewing factory. I don't belong down here; I am a foreigner. I want to be accepted in their circles but they won't even say hi to me when I walk in the building. It is quite a sight. All these women sitting at a sea of sewing machines wearing headphones, a muffled Neil Diamond out of sync with the hum of the machines and the bang of the foot levers.

Every morning it's the same thing. I open the door and all the women look up from their machines and then look right back down. I said good morning once. It was met with silence, and then the drone of the machines. So now I make a quiet entrance and ease my way down the aisle, trying not to bump anyone's sewing desk and knock off a pile of fleece sleeves on my way to the back of the room. Once I am safe on my side of the factory, Mother Beverly looks up from her machine, a more advanced version than the other machines in the factory, and hands me a stack of stylish suit jackets for serging. I spend most days making covered buttons, serging inseams and hand-sewing hooks and eyes on ladies slacks. Mother stands at the cutting table all day with an electric blade, cutting out expensive cloth from patterns. Mother Beverly does the most important part, making the actual articles, getting each pleat just perfect. Each item is then hand ironed by Sally, a slightly heavyset woman with thick glasses and a somewhat eccentric personality. She tags and individually bags each item, making it ready for shipment.

The only time our little business ever received attention from the other half of the sewing factory was when we received a clothing order from Sundance Catalog. The women clambered about asking if Robert Redford himself called to make the order. The attention was short lived though and I continue to overhear snide remarks about my hair, Sally's glasses, or Mother Beverly's inflexible demand for the rent payment.

I always believed that women were the more compassionate of the sexes, with a few exceptions, but I have discovered that the opposite is truer. All the more reason to feel I have been unjustly burdened with a female body. I told Mother once I thought God had made a mistake, that I was a man forced into a woman's body. She actually got quite mad at me, and told me to stop talking so ridiculously. I didn't exactly mean what I said, because my recent induction into womanhood gives me a deep sense of wholeness. I wouldn't dream of telling this to anyone but I like being a woman in that sense. I have been trying to tell Mother that my spirit isn't meant for the kind of stifled existence expected of me. I am trying to warn her that I am not going to be like her other daughters. Mother doesn't hear that part.

LXX

I got fired from the sewing factory.

No one bothered to tell me why. It was hard not to feel angry when I found out that Mother Beverly hired someone to take my place even before I was fired. But the worst part is I found out from Mother. She just said one morning when I was getting ready to go to work, "You've been fired."

"So, I'm not going to work this morning?"

"You're finished. You'll be staying home and helping Claire and Lillian with the house and the cooking," she said, slipping her arm into her coat. "You know you haven't shown the dedication that Mother Beverly was looking for. You shouldn't be surprised."

I was completely surprised. Mother Beverly had been very nice to me and gave me no indication that I wasn't performing up to her standards. Mother grabbed her purse and headed out the kitchen door.

"I don't know when you're going to learn to take responsibility, but I hope it's soon."

I guess I didn't even deserve the dignity of being fired in person. And now there are all these unspoken words between Mother Beverly and me. I have to admit, though, I didn't have a strong affinity for professional sewing.

I have been put back on house duty. I really don't mind too much now that Mother Kay teaches fifth grade at the elementary school. She is gone from eight o'clock to three o'clock. That leaves the three of us, Lillian, Claire, and me, a lot of time without any parents at home. Of course, in the hours from three o'clock to nine o'clock Mother Kay makes up for the hours she missed during the day. The minute she walks in the door she is yelling at one of us for something. Yesterday she cleaned Lillian's clock when baby Isaiah fell down the stairs. Lillian of all people. Mother Kay gives her no room for error. Lillian is supposed to be perfect. Mother Kay would expect that from me. I would probably let babies fall down the stairs twice a day, I'm sure that is what Mother Kay thinks. That's why I'm not allowed to take care of the babies.

She doesn't like us girls going for walks at night so she makes us do everything before we can go for a walk. Sometimes she wins and it's too late. She is also trying to get our bedtimes changed. She wants us to go to bed at eight o'clock. Can you believe it? I am nearly seventeen and she wants me to go to bed at eight o'clock. It's stupid things like that, that make me want to get married just to leave this place.

I know Lillian is desperate to get married. I keep telling her she's too young at fourteen but she starts to cry when I say that. Maybe she can't live this way any longer. For one thing, she has to work on Mother Kay's feet every day. I've had to do it myself a few times when Lillian was sick and it was awful. The only way I got through it was imagining that I was a witch and Mother Kay's foot was voo-doo doll. There is the one advantage to doing it though; she treats me a little better when I work on her. Maybe that's why Lillian does it.

Father is having a new addition to the house built and Lillian told me she hopes she is married before the new addition is finished. She has her eye on one of the missionaries. The missionaries come over every day and work on it. Right now it's a jungle of two-by-fours. I'm not sure why the missionaries are building our house. I get the feeling that it causes some problems.

The missionary program is fairly new. At first I didn't know what was meant by *missionary*. I was thinking along the lines of Martin Luther and John Wesley. Then Father explained to me that the men who sign up are agreeing to go on a work mission. They can't be married because they pretty much work for free. Each missionary signs up for either one or two years and it seems to be some kind of status though I can tell all of the young men involved are sincere in the belief that their work and sacrifices are important to the building up of the kingdom of God. Father is in charge of each mission. Last summer they landscaped the school grounds with lush lawns and desert honey locust trees. Tithing pays for the enhancements. In fact, tithing pays for the meetinghouse and the school—the school I don't get to attend.

The only good thing that has happened to me of late is art class. Frank Williams teaches the class and Father said we could take his six week course at the school. Every Thursday Claire, Lillian, and I walk to the school. It only lasts an hour but I get to be with all the other high school kids taking the class. I wish so much that I could go to school. Frank has told me several times that I have a gift for art. My watercolors, he says, are exceptional. I think I deserve to go to school, not just art class. I suppose Father is worried about me flirting with the boys there, or maybe there is some other reason left undisclosed. Whatever it is, one thing is clear: No one seems concerned about our education. It's enough that we can read and write.

Mother tells me all the time, "You can't learn to be a good housewife at school." She says the most important things I will ever learn, I will learn at home—taking care of kids and cooking. It's true in one sense I suppose. I have learned a lot about dealing with people and I don't lack experience in the domestic, but what I really want is to explore the other half of my capacity. I want to find out where I really excel. I don't want to do what Mother has done with her talents. She has stacks of pencil sketches of her children and portraits that are so true to the likeness of the person it seems to be a soft gray photograph. She hasn't drawn anything in years and never took an art class in her life. It seems such a waste to have her gift lying undeveloped and unnurtured at the bottom of her soul. I am always telling Mother that she can be a Mother and an artist but she says they are incompatible. I wish I knew the part of Mother that is a woman, the part of her that is an artist. I imagine her sometimes, painting at an easel, others admiring her work and me admiring my mother.

LXXI

Mother Kay's come up with a new punishment. Actually, it's not that new, she just put a name on an old idea. She calls it "jail."

She announced this shortly after Father left last week to spend some with Mother Helen and Mother Laverna. I dread the times that Father leaves but this week has been the worst so far.

Malachi was the first to push the wrong button. I wondered if she would be a little softer on him because he's one of her own kids, but she wasn't. I'm not sure how Malachi got on her bad side, but Father wasn't gone four hours when Malachi was sentenced to jail. She was eerily calm about it too. "All right, you're going to jail," was all she said before grabbing Malachi by the arm dragging him to the chicken coop. It's a small space, holding only thirty chickens. She slammed the door and locked it on the outside. The day turned to night and I overheard Mother and Mother Kay arguing about the length of time to leave Malachi in the chicken coop. I didn't stick around to hear Mother concede but I could tell Malachi wasn't getting out any time soon. I went outside to check on him after dark. There was only a tiny screened window at the top of the coop. I couldn't see Malachi unless I was standing on something, but I could talk to him.

"Malachi?"

No answer.

"Malachi, it's me."

"What?" His voice was full of anger.

"Are you okay in there?"

"What do you think?" I was unprepared for him to take his hurt out on me.

"Hey, I'm here trying to help you. I'm not the one who is treating you like an animal, now am I?" There was a long silence and I could tell that he was thinking.

"Sorry."

"I heard the mothers talking about how long you are going to stay in here. It might be a while; I'm sure you're going to have to spend the night."

"What?!"

I felt terrible giving him bad news but I learned a long time ago that knowledge is power. I wanted to arm him with as much as possible.

"I'm sorry, Malachi, but I thought it was better that you knew instead of sitting in here waiting to be let out any minute. I wish I could give you something to sleep on but I can't."

"It's fine. I'll just lay down on the floor here with the chicken poop. It's soft and cozy."

I ached at his words. Ten years old and a developed sarcasm already.

"Good night." There was no answer and I understood completely. I also felt better having done something. Anything was better than remaining silent. It was the only alternative to wishing it wasn't happening.

The next morning came and went. I felt like I couldn't breathe properly until Mother Kay finally opened the door that afternoon. She tried to give Malachi a hug but he wouldn't have it. He was mad. I admire Malachi for his spunk and his honesty. He doesn't pretend for anybody. In a way, I wish I was more like Malachi.

Nathan was next. I wasn't prepared for the piercing of my heart, seeing his little face, all sorry and penitent while she pushed him in the coop. At seven years old he didn't know to be angry. He cried and cried, upsetting the hens. I didn't know what to say to him except to try not to worry; Mother Kay would let him out soon but I really wasn't sure. "Tell her I promise to be good," he said through the crack in the door.

"I can't, Nathan. She'll know I've been talking to you and then you'll have to stay in here longer. Do you understand?"

"No!" he wailed.

"I'm sorry, Nathan. You know I care about you, right?"

"Yeah."

"It's gonna be okay. I bet she'll let you out real soon."

I was so mad when I went back into the house I was ready to hit something.

Mother Kay eventually let him out at Mother's behest. I heard her arguing with Mother Kay, saying, "He's so young. You can't leave him in there all night." Mother Kay went out and let him out around eight o'clock. I was glad. I wasn't sure I could sleep knowing he was spending the night out there.

Mother Kay has been on rampage lately. Malachi calls her Old Dinosaur Eyes. She's that scary. She gave Annie a serious beating out under the deck. I had to run in the bathroom and turn the tap on so I couldn't hear her screams. I avoided Annie the rest of the day. I don't think I can handle this stuff anymore. She beat Jonathon too. I thought she would never quit. Then she came in the house, the anger like steam escaping from her every pore. She can't possibly be that angry at two nine-year-olds, no matter what they did. It's all spiraling out of control.

I used to think Mother Kay hated me, but now I can see I didn't even mean that much to her. I was merely the punching bag for her to take out her frustrations. I'm all grown now and she can't beat me anymore and she knows it. So she has turned on Annie especially. And Adam too. I have to be careful about what I say and do, or one of my little charges, someone that looks up to me as a protecting Big Girl, will be unjustly punished. I hate Mother Kay's ability to keep everyone under her control.

I don't know what I'm going to do. I guess I'm going to have to talk to the one person who can make a difference, the one person who would set things right if only he knew how bad it is. I guess it's time for the truth be heard by the one person who controls Mother Kay.

Father.

LXXII

"C'mon, guys, please go with me?"

"No way." Lillian wants nothing to do with my plan. "Do you know how mad Mother Kay will be when she finds out it was us who told Father?"

"She has point," Claire says. "What happens when Father leaves again? He won't be taking us with him."

"Listen to me, she's already railing on everybody, how much worse can it get? She yells at us the minute she gets home from school until we go to bed. She's beating Adam several times a day for wetting his pants. Annie gets humiliated in her class all morning and then she gets beat in the afternoons. The boys are getting out of hand and we are the ones who get yelled at for what they do and then Mother Kay throws them in the chicken coop. What do we have to lose by telling Father?" I sound convincing, even to myself, but inside I'm scared.

"I still can't believe they wanted Mother Kay to teach at the school." Claire tries to veer things the other way.

"Somebody needs to say *something*. The only reason she is teaching at the school is because she has pulled the wool over everybody's eyes, making people believe she's this nice person who loves children. She has to be stopped and Father is the only person who can stop her."

"You guys don't have to work on Mother Kay's feet like I do. I can't do this with you," Lillian says. It's true; Lillian is not in a position to be making Mother Kay angry. Every afternoon she spends an hour rubbing Mother Kay's feet and shoulders. Mother Kay buddies up to her, trying to wedge a wall between Lillian and me. But she's been doing that for a long time.

"Okay, I have an idea. I'll do all the talking and you guys just back me up. I'm afraid Father will think I just have a beef with Mother Kay and I'm trying to get her in trouble. If he sees you guys with me he'll take it seriously. I can't do this without you."

"I'll go with you, but I'm not saying a word," Claire says.

"Fine. I'll go too," Lillian concedes. "When are we going to do it?"

"Tonight."

"Wait, what about Mother Kay?" Claire knows that she doesn't leave Father for a second when he's home.

"Have no fear, I've got that covered. Mother Kay has that parent-teacher thing at the school tonight. It'll be our only chance."

"Father?" My voice is shaky and I clear my throat to get my bearings together. Father looks up from his newspaper. "We need to talk to you."

He sets the paper down on the table, and by the look on his face I can tell he knows something. "What is it?"

"It's Mother Kay."

"What about her?" he says, his eyes looking drained.

"She has been unbearable to live with lately. She yells at us for everything and she is giving spankings like they are going out of style. She locked Malachi and Nathan in the chicken coop. I can't deal with this; none of us can."

"Is this true, girls?" Father says, looking around me at Claire and Lillian. Claire and Lillian nod their heads.

"We're only here telling you this because it needs to be stopped. She is worse than ever. I don't know if it's because she is going to have a baby or if it's the stress at school but she is unbearable. You have to believe us, Father."

Father doesn't move but looks at the carpet under his feet. I bite the inside of my lip and I can hear Claire shuffle her feet behind me.

"What do you want me to do?" His voice is deep and serious.

"Just talk to her, make her stop hurting everyone. It's just been crazy around here, especially when you're gone."

"That's not what she tells me."

I look uneasily at Father. He can't really believe her, can he? "Well, it's the truth and Claire and Lillian stand behind me as well."

Father glanced at them for a minute and I see it in my mind how it looks to him. Claire and Lillian don't want to be here, anybody can see that. They are standing a full two feet behind me. I appear to have recruited them to get even against my old archenemy. I suppose I did recruit them. I can no longer feel the wind in my sails. Father looks long at me before he speaks, but when he does his words are firm and precise.

"I don't ever want to hear you talk that way about Mother Kay again. Do you understand me? Don't you think I have enough to take care of without you creating more problems for me? She is doing the best job that she can and you need to be supporting her."

I can't open my mouth. Father looks at all of us expectantly. All I can muster is a nod. My head is reeling. I won't believe that he's on her side.

LXXIII

Father calls me to his office. Mother Kay is there and she shuts the door behind me. The office feels really small with the three of us in here.

"What do you think you are here for?" Father opens with his famous hook.

"I have no clue." I keep my voice stoic and emotionless.

Mother Kay looks particularly pleased with herself.

"Kay, why don't you tell her?"

Mother Kay holds out a stack of pictures. I recognize the people in the pictures, all boys from the high school.

"We've found out about your little secret," she says wagging the stack in front of my face.

"What secret?"

"You've been taking pictures of boys at school."

"When would I do that?"

"During art class. I told you, Father, it would be a mistake letting her go to that class."

"Whatever."

Father looks at me sharply. "You have some explaining to do," he says frowning.

"I didn't take those pictures.

"But they're yours, aren't they?" Mother Kay says leaning in toward my face.

"No. I've never seen them before."

"You can't lie to us. We don't believe you. I have proof that these are yours." She seems pretty certain of herself.

"You don't have proof because I didn't do it. I don't even own a camera."

"Kenny Reid says you paid him to take these pictures." Everyone at the school knows that Kenny is the budding photographer.

"I paid Kenny with all my gobs of money. Right. I don't care what Kenny says, they aren't mine."

"We don't believe you."

"I've never even said 'boo' to him before, let alone paid him to take pictures of boys. C'mon, pictures of boys? I'm not *that* lame!" I surprised myself with my confidence against the two of them.

"Why would Kenny Reid tell Kay that you paid him to take these pictures?"

"Ask Kenny. Personally, this is the silliest thing I've heard all day."

"Silly or not, we have a serious problem on our hands, and you are the suspect." Mother Kay was groping on a slippery slope.

"You know what, you guys are free to think whatever you want, but I have no reason to pay Kenny to take pictures of silly little boys."

Father looks at Mother Kay. "You said you were sure?"

"I'm telling you, Father, Kenny told me personally." Mother Kay's voice sounds defensive now and so I stand up to leave.

"Can I go now?"

Father tries to hide the uncomfortable look on his face.

"Go on."

Mother Kay stays in Father's office for several hours. I took a huge risk defying her like that. It helps that I was being accused of a ludicrous lie but I am a little worried about what's going to happen because of it. Mother Kay has never let anything I have done to her go unpunished. I've been sent back home to Fifth East twice but I am needed too badly down here for her to keep sending me away. Work crews come over every day, building the new addition. Someone has to feed them lunch. Mother still works at the sewing factory and Mother Kay is gone to school. Claire and Lillian are only fourteen. I am the oldest so my place here is pretty much secure. But there's a storm brewing somewhere. I can feel it.

LXXIV

Work on the new addition has stopped and Mother Kay has designated a new jail. It didn't take her long to round up a few prisoners. Father will be gone for a week and I have a bad feeling about this. I think Mother Kay has gone too far. Way too far.

It started when Mother Kay got home from school on Monday afternoon. She had four kids in jail before dinnertime: Annie, Lucy, Benji, and Nathan. I heard a lot of hollering from my post at the kitchen stove, so when Mother Kay left to go to the grocery store in town I went up to the third floor of the new addition to see what I could do. The four kids were tied with ropes to the two-by-fours. Benji was determined to free his hands. Mother was on my heels when Benji freed himself and began climbing up the half-constructed wall toward the roof.

"Benji, what are you doing?!" Mother was clearly worried. "Benji, get down from there!"

"I'm running away and you can't stop me!" With that he disappeared onto the roof.

"Benji, you're gonna fall!" I screamed at him from the window.

He flashed me a grin from the roof of the three-story addition as he climbed from window to window on his way down the outside walls of the house and disappeared into the alfalfa fields.

Mother Kay came back and the first thing she did was go check on the kids in jail. They would be punished further for Benji's actions. I stayed in the bathroom but I heard her yelling at Mother and then for me. I corroborated Mother's story that Benji had escaped and that we tried to stop him. Mother was following Mother Kay, wringing her hands. She was definitely taking the blame for this one. Mother Kay kept pacing by the window. I don't blame Mother Kay for being worried; Benji is only eleven years old. After all, Benji was one of Mother Kay's kids—one of her favorite kids at that. Maybe that is why he felt emboldened enough to run away. Of course there wasn't anywhere to go so I assumed Benji would be back when he had cooled off. My main concern was the other three still up in the drafty addition.

When Mother Kay was frantically calling Father, I snuck up the stairs. The sight in front of me stopped me in my tracks. Annie was nearest the stairs and I could hear her muffled sobs. Her hands tied around the two-by-four behind her back were purple, the ropes chaffing at her skin. Her head was completely covered with clean cotton diapers and tied to the two-by-four, her facial features protruding through the fabric like the muted features of a ghost. Her mouth was opened in a wide O. Mother Kay had stuffed it with rags before covering her entire head with the diaper. She was crying and the tears left two wet circles in the concave space. It made a gruesome picture, like a skeleton, still protesting after death.

Annie didn't know I was standing in front of her. The other two kids looked exactly the same, their little bodies rigid up against the two-by-fours in complete submission. I loosened the ropes around her hands. She stopped crying.

"Shhh, it's me, Annie." I wanted to take all the ropes and rags off of her but I knew I couldn't. I loosened them just a little. Not so much that Mother Kay would notice but enough to relieve Annie a little. I loosened the ropes on Nathan and Lucy, their small faces unmoving beneath the white cloth. I burned at the sight of them and I was sickened by my own fears. I will never forget that sight.

Nathan and Lucy were let out after a few days, but Annie was left alone for the week. Mother Kay untied her and removed the rags from her face, but she left her in jail. I sneaked some dinner up to her but I couldn't talk to her. The guilt I felt for not doing something forced me away. I could hear Annie crying but what was I supposed to do?

Malachi told me that Benji has been sneaking into the basement at nights and then disappearing before anyone saw him. I found some food missing from the pantry in the basement too so I left Benji a can opener on the dryer in the basement for him to find. I envy Benji being able to leave. Hiding out somewhere in the desert like an action hero in a movie. I am here lying in my bed tonight knowing exactly how Annie feels. Day after day, night after night, isolated and locked up on the third floor of the addition. Father is coming home in a few days. He has to believe me now.

LXXV

If I have to live one more day in this house I will surely die. Annie is still in jail and it has been eight days. Alan Patterson's wife came over to talk to Mother Kay about something today and Mother Kay was upstairs beating the kids, one after the other. I told her that Caroline Patterson was waiting in the living room for her and she said, "Tell her I'll be down in a minute." I wondered if Mrs. Patterson could hear the crying upstairs but I pretended everything was okay. When Mother Kay finally made her appearance ten minutes later she was rubbing her shoulder and grinning. "Boy, it sure makes your arm sore when you spank that many kids." I shook my head at her stupidity. Couldn't she see the look on Caroline's face? She wasn't impressed. Anyway, it's been a typical day.

I'm glad I finished my work early so I can go to Ralph Denton's house to get his horse. He told me a week ago I could ride his horse, Chanta. He tried to talk me out of it several times because he said Chanta is a bit too spirited for an inexperienced rider. He has a lot of horses but I have eyes only for Chanta. She is a tall American Saddlebred, seventeen hands high. I used to go see her on my lunch break when I worked at the sewing factory. Her field was next door. There were ten other horses in the field but she stood out among the crowd. Her height as well as her feisty spirit attracted me. She snorted and stomped her foot while the other horses sidled up to the fence for petting. It was as though she was showing off her spunk to me. She galloped around the field, tossing her head and black mane in the wind. When I try to pet her she acts like I have no more right to touch her than I have a right to rub shoulders with royalty. I want nothing more than to ride such an elegant creature. Ralph helps me saddle her, with a warning. "Be careful. She has a mind of her own."

"I will.

I have Chanta at a controlled walk when I reach the driveway. I want to show off this amazing animal to the other girls.

"Get that horse out of here!" Mother yells from through the living room window.

"But, Mother, you said I could ride a horse." After all I went through to talk Ralph into saying yes, I wasn't about to turn around and put her back in the pasture.

"I never said any such thing. You turn right around and take that horse back to Ralph's and apologize to him for taking advantage of his kindness."

"But, Mother, I just barely got her."

Mother Kay appears at the window. "What are you doing?" she says, edging Mother out of the way.

"Mother told me …"

"It's almost eight o'clock. Isn't that your new bedtime? Get that horse put away and come in here and get to bed."

"My bedtime is not eight o'clock and Mother told me I could ride this horse." I was mad.

"You get that horse and put it away or you will never ride another horse again! Do you hear me?!"

Chanta nervously backs up. I'm not giving Mother Kay an answer. Chanta prances and tosses her head and I adjust my seat on her back but I do not say a word.

"I asked you a question, young lady, and I better get an answer!" Mother Kay pounds her fist on the windowsill. It is just enough.

Chanta bursts forward as if a starting gate had swung open and the gun sounded. Her sleek black body is like an immense machine pounding the earth beneath us both. Mother Kay gasps and a renewed sense of freedom overtakes me as the two of us bolt out of the yard and up the road. Chanta picks up speed just at the moment I thought it was impossible for her to go any faster. I can see the turn in the road up ahead. A sharp turn. "Whoa, Chanta." But her body is in a perfect momentum, rhythm like drums. "Turn, Chanta," I whisper as I give her a signal with the reins. She turns at the last second, skidding in the slippery sand. The two of us almost go down but she finds her footing and then we're off, the long stretch to home. I lean down low next to her neck, her black mane tousled in my face. "Go, Chanta," I whisper and two sleek ears turn back to catch my words. We two, like one, ride into the wind, into the darkening sky like a single unstoppable force. I know I should be scared. Chanta is doing exactly what she wants. A runaway. But I trust her like I have never trusted anyone or anything. I want to *be* Chanta, unstoppable. I can see her field just up ahead. Chanta isn't slowing down and I close my eyes. I know what she is going to do and I can't watch. I cling to her mane with one hand, my entire body gripping hers as we sail over the fence and land on the other side of the pasture. It was a smooth fly through the air and over the fence. The landing wasn't jolting as I imagined it might be. But Chanta hasn't slowed down and we speed through the pasture, stirring up the other horses. The entire field is soon a giant dust bowl. The other horses, inspired by Chanta's spirit, chase each other until finally Chanta stops, both of us breathing hard. The reins fall to the ground and without warning I start to laugh. I pat Chanta on the neck, throw my head to the sky, and bellow.

My legs quaver underneath me as I start to dismount. Chanta is as calm as I have ever seen her. Then, with my left foot still in the stirrup, she bolts forward, dragging me through the sagebrush. I hold my head just above the ground but she drags me through sagebrush and other prickly plants. I can feel my bare arms making contact as the sleeves of my shirt are torn. The other horses pick up the pace behind us and all I can hear is the thunder of the hooves on the ground. I suddenly decide my foot should stay where it is, lodged between Chanta's warm, heaving sides and a flapping stirrup. The last thing I want is to be stomped on by an excitable herd of horses following their matriarch. But Chanta stops at her feeding trough. I am hanging half off the ground looking up into the nostrils of nine horses. I manage to free myself and dust off my clothes. I pull a piece of sagebrush out of my hair. My face burns from the scratches. Chanta snorts at me and walks right up as if to say she's sorry. I remove her bridle and saddle and leave them near the gate.

It's a long, long walk home.

LXXVI

"Father's home! Father's home!" Malachi ran through the house calling out the good news. He's a day early. We weren't expecting him until tomorrow. Annie is still in jail and Mother Kay hurries up to top floor to tell her she can come out.

Benji is still gone. We know where he has been staying and we have been keeping him in a supply of food. Occasionally I've caught him sneaking out of the basement in the early morning, but as far as Mother Kay is concerned Benji is still missing. She is going to have to tell Father something and shoot herself in the foot. She will have to tell Father that Benji ran away because she was trying to tie him up and gag him with rags. Benji will come home when he sees Father's truck parked in the driveway. It's hard to explain how it feels to have Father walk in the kitchen door. I know Mother Kay's going to shift all her attention from angry rampaging on all of us to desperate needy affection for Father.

Father looks exceptionally tired tonight and Mother and Mother Kay follow him to his bedroom, unpacking his suitcase for him. Mother Kay hollers to the kitchen to tell me to bring a tray of dinner to Father. I can hear the TV in his bedroom click on and the sounds of the three voices float down the hallway to the kitchen where I stand at the stove. If only Father could have seen Annie's purple hands and Lucy's soaked up tears. If only he could have heard Nathan crying in the chicken coop. If only Father knew how it felt, what she has done to us. If only he could see her hitting one of us, I think he would change his mind. I prepare a bowl of steaming beef stew and buttered slices of soft white bread and place them neatly on the tray. If only Father could see the look on Adam's face when Mother Kay walks into a room, or feel the jolt of fear in any of us when she walks past, all of us holding our breath.

I walk slowly, carefully down the hall, focusing intently on not spilling the soup. With my fist about to knock on the bedroom door I notice the TV has been muted and Father is talking.

"You what?!" his voice, upset.

"I'm sorry, Father, I just didn't know what else to do. The kids were unbearable while you were gone. I tried everything I could and nothing seemed to help." Mother Kay is crying and I wonder if Mother has left the room because I can't hear her talking.

"You don't tie people up; that's just not right no matter how you look at it," Father says sternly. I lean forward, closer to the door, trying to make out each word.

"But Father, you told me to put them in jail when they wouldn't do what they were told," Mother Kay wails.

"I know what I told you. I didn't say to tie them up with ropes and gag them. It's just not right."

"Oh, Father," she's crying again. "I can't deal with these kids any longer. I've been throwing up and I'm sick all the time. I feel just horrible but I still get up in the morning and teach school and deal with all the bull-headed parents over there. I'm going to have a nervous breakdown if something doesn't change."

I think this is a good time to knock on the door. I open it at Father's bidding and graciously set the food on his end table near the head of his bed. Mother is sitting on a chair in the corner of the room. Father is sitting up on his bed, his shoes discarded near the door. Mother Kay is comfortably situated on the end of the bed between Father and Mother. There is a wonderful death-like silence in the room and I feel like the butler in an engrossing murder mystery. I leave the room, still playing the part, leaving the door ever so slightly open. Then, after walking back to the kitchen and carefully clanging dishes in the kitchen sink, I slip off my shoes and inch myself in perfect silence down the hall, my back hugging the wall until every voice in the bedroom is clear. Father is upset and I feel a growing surge of support. This is the end. Mother Kay has finally done enough damage and Father is going to stop her. Retribution will be paid. I can see it all playing out in my mind: Father taking each of his children to ask them what has happened to them, how Mother Kay had abused them. I can't wait for my turn and I see myself in Father's office, hour upon hour, the tale of my frightful past unfolding before his astonished face.

"This is terrible. Where's Benji now?" Father says.

"We don't know," Mother offers.

"We need to find him tonight," Father says, pausing for a long moment, "and …"

I hold my breath waiting to hear more good news when Father speaks in a near whisper. His words stop my heart. I want to rub my ears to make sure they are working properly. I tiptoe back to the kitchen without blinking. I hyperventilate at the sink until my face and extremities are tingling. I know now what I have always known but never wanted to believe and Father's words are scorched into my being. I will never forget his words as long as I live.

"… and let's keep this whole thing under a hat."

LXXVII

We named her Nutmeg.

Father was reluctant to let us keep her when Ralph Denton' son Craig showed up to our house on his horse with the tiny puppy nestled between his body and the saddle horn, but Father finally gave in with a warning: If she ever gets pregnant, she's gone. We promised to watch her and take care of her. She was six weeks old, a tiny bundle of black and brown. We named her Nutmeg because she looked exactly like the spice, and called her Meg for short. She was the first real pet any of us had ever had. Meg was the realization of a dream. I had been wishing for a dog since I was old enough to wish. Not even a dog so much as an animal. It didn't matter to me. Mother told me that when I was a baby I reached under the neighbor's fence and pulled a puppy that had wandered too close and was enamored with it. I was always trying to adopt the many city strays that found their way to me on cold winter nights. I would steal cans of tuna from the pantry to feed the thin creatures. I tried to make them my own pets but they were always gone by morning. There were even dogs who came into the lean-to looking for a little shelter but I was sure they had heard my mental yearnings and had responded. We found an orphaned duckling in the park once and tried to make it our pet. It died after a few weeks. Nathan found a turtle once but accidentally drowned it in the bathroom sink. One of the Big Boys gave us a hamster he no longer wanted and after a month we found him dead in his cage.

Meg was the first bona fide pet that the whole family embraced. The boys made her a little doghouse in the yard, and when she was small we let her sleep in a box in the basement. She learned to play tug of war with me when I shook the kitchen rugs every afternoon, tugging on the tassels. She was a presence that made existence seem meaningful.

One of her favorite things to do was follow us to Meeting on Sundays. We liked to go early and walk to the meetinghouse before Father and the mothers got there. We would always catch Meg slinking in the tumbleweeds, following us like a sneaky private detective.

"Go home, Meg," one of us would call out to her. She would stand erect at the sound of our voices and look directly at us, with her nose in the wind. "Go home." She always turned on her heels and retreated back to the house. A few times though we came out of Meeting to find her curled up next to the door, waiting. I secretly enjoyed this but worried she might seem a nuisance to Father and I desperately wanted to keep her.

I fed her dinner sometimes. She didn't get dog food, at least not much. I guess it was too expensive so we fed her table scraps. Oatmeal for breakfast like the rest of the family. For dinner, though, I would treat her. I stole packages of beef from the freezer and made her bowls of homemade dog food with thick gravy to go with. I was careful to keep it a secret so I sat out next to Meg at nights while she ate. I worried she wasn't getting enough meat because she only ate what we ate: split pea soup, biscuits, spaghetti, etc. It didn't seem like the right diet for her and I found her vomiting several times.

She loved to be petted and I loved to pet her. My favorite thing to do at night after our walk was to sit with her on top of the root cellar, a place where no window could find us, and watch the sun go down. Meg seemed to know the importance of this ritual because she always sat calmly next to me until it was dark and then, as if a switch inside her turned on, she would leap down and trot back to her doghouse. I told Meg an awful lot of things. I don't know what part of it she understood except the part about me needing a listening ear. Sometimes while I talked quietly she would lay her head in my lap and sigh. I could almost hear her voice. "Man, that's no good," she would say in my mind, "I wish there was more I could do." But Meg did what no human seemed capable of: She gave of herself. She was so eager to give love and so quick to forgive.

"Forgive me, Meg." The words sound like a stranger's coming out of my mouth. I realize just this minute how desperately I love her. She would have been two years old next month.

We didn't know if she was pregnant for sure but it was enough evidence for Father when we found her this morning chained to her house like we left her every night. Only this morning a big male Weimaraner was attached to her. She seemed perfectly content with the proceedings as Claire and I went out to scare the strange dog away. But it was too late. Father saw the dog glued to Meg from the kitchen window. After breakfast he opened the back of the pickup and called Meg. She loved to go for rides in the truck along the dusty roads. This morning was no different and she bounded up wagging her tail intently and sat down in the corner awaiting the adventure, her tongue lolling out of her mouth. The truck disappeared into the field and I assumed Father was dumping her off somewhere to fend for herself. I watched the truck until it was gone and I turned back to my dishes at the sink. I was already preparing rescue strategies when I heard it.

BOOM! A gunshot—though I tried to tell myself otherwise. The sound broke the silent dewy morning, startling the desert to life. He didn't do it. He was scaring her away. He wouldn't kill Meg. But Father came home without her. I couldn't ask him what he did with her but some of the little kids were wondering where he had taken Meg. She was shot in the head. Father had a police officer from town come and kill her, left to die in the field alone. I asked Father if he would bring her back so we could bury her but he said she was just a dog. Just a dog.

I still can't believe I will never see her again. I look out the upstairs window into the field where it happened, disbelief hanging inside of me. I want to go find her but I am afraid to see her as she might be: cold, eyes still open but empty and hollow. I am afraid of her body being hard and stiff and unnatural. I want to keep the vision of her the way she was, in my mind forever, curled up at the bottom of the deck stairs. When I open the kitchen door she will be there, her head up and ears alert when she sees me, her tail sweeping the red dirt off the step.

I stand here at the window today, memorializing her life in my heart. I want to make her death matter, I want it to be more than meaningless, but I don't know how to make it so.

LXXVIII

Jennifer and I walk along in an unusual silence.

"What's wrong?" Jennifer finally asks.

"You mean besides the fact that Father had Meg killed?"

Jennifer didn't answer.

"Trust me … you don't want to know." My voice is low and bitter.

"If I didn't want to know I wouldn't have asked you."

I remain silent. I have no idea what to say to her, where to begin or where to end, what to disclose and what to keep secret. I don't know what I have a right to say and what I don't.

"It's my life. It isn't the greatest."

"Like how?"

"It's Mother Kay mostly. She does things, has done things …" I shake my head, not wanting to talk about it and wanting to with the force of a hurricane all at once.

"Now, which one is Mother Kay?"

"Brown hair, medium build." It is beyond strange describing Mother Kay's appearance as if I am outside of my body. It makes her seem normal. "Mean." I finish somberly.

Jennifer looks amused. "Mean? C'mon. The Wicked Witch of the West is mean."

Her words burn. I walk quietly, disconnected from the conversation, kicking up small round balls of dirt in front of me. Jennifer is quiet too. I wonder what she must be thinking.

"I would trade any day." I am pleased to have found a good response to Jennifer's skepticism.

"Trade what?"

"I would trade Mother Kay for the Wicked Witch of the West any old day."

"If it's so bad why aren't you telling me about it?" Jennifer looks positively indignant.

"It's hard to talk about. It's hard to say things that have happened to you that you hardly believe yourself. It's hard to say things that others won't believe." Emotion starts nagging at my insides. There is a short silence. "Do you know what it feels like to be beaten?" Jennifer hides her surprise but I can still see it. She shakes her head and keeps walking just to my left and close enough that I can feel her sleeve brush my arm. "Then I am sure you don't know what it feels like to be starved and locked up. Do you really want to know some of the stuff she's done? She locks her own kids up in the chicken coop all night. She beats them till they bleed. I bet you didn't know that!" I can feel an anger inside of me that I have never felt. It swells and falls like the ocean tides, always threatening to burst through the dike I have built. Jennifer shrinks back a little, the skepticism mingled with shock. "Do you want to see my scars?" I secretly hope Jennifer doesn't want to see my scars because the physical ones are gone. I take a moment to hold the anger, to calm it once more. "She hurts babies." I know that Jennifer absolutely adores her baby sister Michelle and maybe this will drive it home. "She hits them till their legs are purple and swollen." Jennifer is shaking her head in disbelief. I can't talk anymore. The words are useless; they sound so barren and impotent. The more I talk the less real it feels. Hearing my words echo back at me feels like great terrible lies—lies because the things she has really done, the wounds that still pain me like fresh stripes, are impossible to describe; they remain hidden deep inside. I only have the outward story; the inward story refuses to be brought to light.

"Why doesn't anybody stop her?" Jennifer asks innocently.

"Who is going to stop her? Everyone pretends it isn't happening."

"Why can't you stop her?" Jennifer questions.

"It wouldn't do any good. Albert tried to stop her once by taking Jonathon, when he was a toddler, right out of Mother Kay's arms while she was hitting him with the stick. Albert protected him until Mother Helen came home from work. What happened? Jonathon's life became a living hell and Albert ran away from home. Others have tried; it's always the same."

I know this isn't the whole truth even as the words come out of my mouth. I don't know what would happen if I really tried to stop her because I have never tried, not outright. I am afraid. The coward inside of me doesn't want to be found. I don't want to look at the blackness inside of me.

"I'm sorry." Jennifer is sincere.

"It's okay. I'm going to get married someday and leave that house and all that it means behind me forever. Just you wait and see."

LXXIX

I hate this red dirt. It gets into everything. It stains my shoes and clothes and no amount of bleach can get it out. I am by myself tonight. Jennifer has gone to Flagstaff with her father. Claire and Lillian are helping Mother Kay hang wallpaper in the upstairs bedrooms. Mother looked a little suspicious when I told her I wanted to go by myself for a walk. I can't imagine what trouble I could get into here; that is, if I wanted to get into trouble. I just want to get away from the house. That's something Mother would never understand. It feels like this place wants to keep me, to bury me under the shifting red dirt and sand. But I can't be buried if I keep moving.

The winding dirt roads, with deep ruts in some places, lead to rows of houses or clusters of trailers. There is a little bundle of houses right where we live, some finished but most of them still in progress. There are fences around the yards, or goats in barns bleating to be milked. Only the occasional car, stirring up a spot of dust behind it, rumbles down the quiet road. It gets especially quiet in the evenings with only the snort of horses in the distance, silhouettes in the setting sun. Sometimes in the mornings I can hear a rooster crow, or a dog bark, or the sound of wings from a flock of pigeons that belongs to one of the neighbors. If I look out of the upstairs window I can see a Jensen girl carrying a pail of slop to the pigs, her long dress flapping to the side of her. Her brother is stooped with a hose in his hand, watering fragile trees in the wind. There is some quiet activity all around me. It's a small oasis of people in what feels like a sea of sagebrush and clouds and dirt.

But toward the east is the giant red mountain with its point sawed off. It looks as if it has been clawed by enormous hands, and juniper trees shoot up from the ravines. It casts a long devilish shadow over the land. The sun must climb this cliff, just as I must climb the rugged road to consciousness every morning. When I see it perched on the top of the mountain and rising still, I know that I too must make the journey of living. There is phrase that keeps churning in my head, a phrase I understand like never before: grim reality. It is not to be contested or proved, it simply is.

The sun is nearly down and darkness is near. The clouds are harboring the last bit of pink light. I can see the school in the distance. It is actually a beautiful place with its curbs and sidewalks and a nice, graded parking lot. There are evergreens in front, hugging the yellow walls and touching the tip of the red-tiled roof. There are large swatches of lawn dotted with honey locust trees waving their lacy fronds in the wind. It is a sanctuary, a place to go. I reach the school and walk the perimeter. I try one of the doors but it is locked.

I found a door open once and walked through the entire school, looking into classrooms and imagining the thrill of getting up in the mornings and going to a real school to be with others my own age and discover what there was to be had in such a place.

Today it is locked—every door. I sit in the shade of a locust tree and listen to the wind. Next to me is a trash can, full of the discards of school. The papers at the top are rattling in the breeze. Lying between me and the trash can is a paper, folded in quarters as though it had been purposefully placed for me to find. I ignore it. I look in the trash can at old homework assignments that I might have done if I were going to school. I imagine what it might be like while I sift through soda cans for students' work. When a car comes rumbling down the road I realize how pathetic I must look, going through a trash can like a beggar. I hide myself under the eaves of the school until the sound of the motor is far in the distance. The paper on the ground calls me again. I pick it up and unfold it, wanting something but expecting nothing. It has words on it and a title. Not a poem exactly, but written in stanzas. The first word is completely foreign. *Desiderata.* Underneath this it reads:

Go placidly amid the noise and the haste, and remember what peace there may be in silence.

What peace there may be. Peace. I don't know what peace is. Not this peace. I know the peace that is silent when there should be words, the peace that is hiding a secret when there should be truth. But this peace? I don't know of it, except I can feel it, right now. I can feel it like the breeze on my face; I can feel it like a warm bowl of stew in my stomach; I can feel it like being replete with sunshine all the way to the top of my head. Remember what peace there may be, in silence, in knowing, in remembering that I am this peace. I don't have to fight for anything. I don't have to fight for what is already mine. I merely have to go to this place. It is my peace, my own oasis and sanctuary.

I hold my breath and read the words again, tracing my finger over them. I have known this; it's as if I have extracted a forgotten truth from an unknown reservoir inside myself. I can see myself moving calmly through my life, through the drudgery and the injustice, like Moses parting the Red Sea, two rumbling chaotic walls of death on either side while crossing safely to the other side. Moses walked through it. He walked through it on dry ground. I will walk through my life just like Moses walked through the sea. It is just as daunting and feels just as impossible to cross through this place. But these words are like a key, a map to the way out. It is the only way. I thought that running away would bring me freedom. I thought escape in any of its various forms would lead to my freedom. I understand now. I will not leave my life. I will live it. I will live every hour and every minute of it until I have fulfilled my purpose. I don't know what the purpose of my life is, but when it is fulfilled I will know it. This is the freedom I have been longing for. Freedom isn't something I will find outside the walls of my life, outside the house in some far away place, or even outside of my body. Freedom is something inside of me; it is a power that grows outward until it destroys the guarded prison walls around me. There is peace. I can be at peace with what I have been given. I will accept this life and walk through it. I don't know what lies ahead but I know that there is a way to go through it. In silence.

Today I will take a step forward—not to survive but to live, to grow, to walk in the path upright, the path I have always been walking.

I fold the paper back into quarters and tuck it securely in my skirt pocket. There are many more words on the paper, words that are both inspiring and poetic, but I have what I need.

LXXX

It was my birthday today. I'm seventeen years old. I can't believe I made it to seventeen. I look down at my body and I am shocked because it isn't the little-girl body I used to have; it's a grown-up stranger's body and I am quite interested by it. I look at my face in the mirror and wonder what it will look like when I am twenty or even thirty. I close my eyes. When I open them my face is brand new. I am not the *me* that I suppose myself to be. I don't see the quirky and crooked smile but a straight one, with white shiny teeth. I see perfectly arched eyebrows, not the ones that want to turn down like a sad little puppy. I feel different.

I don't have to imagine the straight, dark hair that frames my oval face perfectly. I take out the braid and brush it smooth. It softens all the features of my face that I don't care for. My nose seems more sculpted and my eyes more blue standing in the light of the bedroom lamp with my hair around my jaw and over my ears. I can feel it swishing as I tie my robe tightly around my waist and walk downstairs to say good-bye to my birthday and say hello to a new and mysterious beginning. The kitchen is dark and I can hear the TV on in Father's bedroom. But for all intents and purposes I am alone. The kitchen stove light is on and it is enough light for me to see my full body image in the tall kitchen windows, another shadowy image like the pictures in my head. I walk mindfully across the cool kitchen floor and over to the sink. There I am again in the small window. I think about the birthdays of the past and where I am today. This has been a good one.

For the most part, birthdays are like any other day of the week. Mother said "Happy birthday" first thing in the morning as she has on all my birthdays since I can remember. She has never forgotten one. Father told me too after Mother reminded him at the breakfast table. He didn't actually say "Happy birthday" but it was as close as I could expect from Father. I was on kitchen this morning and was pouring milk on the baby's mush when I caught Mother whispering to Father out of the corner of my eye. I pretended I didn't see, and when I had finished taking care of the baby I began filling the sink up with hot water.

"Susanna?" Father's voice quieted the table of kids.

"Yeah?" I said in a clipped voice.

"Is it your birthday today?"

"Yep." I turned back to the sink and poured a generous amount of dishwashing liquid into the steaming water. I couldn't decide if I wanted Father to leave me alone or come and grab me around the waist and do a little dance with me across the kitchen floor in front of the family.

"How old are you? Fifteen?" he said, knowing full well I wasn't fifteen. Or did he?

I turned around and looked directly at Father, pleased to hear my own mouth claiming my place in the world, my years on the earth.

"I'm seventeen." I looked in Father's eyes, trying to determine if he knew me the way I had once believed he did. He looked surprised.

"You're really seventeen?" I hoped I wasn't falling for one of his pranks.

"I am." Father's face seemed genuine and he looked at Mother who confirmed the information. Father got up from his chair and brought his emptied plate and glass and slipped them into the water where my hands were. He put one hand firmly on my shoulder, "You're practically an old spinster. We're gonna have to bump you out of the nest soon."

"You're not getting rid of me that easily," I said in desperate seriousness. But Father laughed and grabbed me in a big hug. It felt good but I withheld something from him. I don't know what it was or why I did it but I knew I wasn't Father's little girl and perhaps I never had been. It was a moment of sadness and liberation all at once. From the window I watched Father climb into his truck and I felt love for him because he is my father, because he works for the food on the table and he comes home every night, because I can claim him, whether or not he claims me. There is only one of him. I release my grasp on him, full of hope and disappointment, and let him go.

I was surprised to see a gift on the kitchen table. I tried not to wonder if it might be for me. There was a pink card taped to the top of the package. I was alone in the kitchen so I peeked at it to see if there was a name on the card. My name was written in careful cursive handwriting that I recognized immediately. I still didn't dare open the present. Mother appeared from the hallway.

"Jennifer dropped that off for you about an hour ago." I touched the silver wrap and was about to turn away to hide the tear in my eye when I heard Mother Kay's voice.

"I don't know about birthday presents," she said, her voice full of disapproval. I ignored her comment and began preparing dinner. "Well, aren't you going to open it?" Mother Kay said.

"I'd rather ... I thought maybe tonight." I didn't want to open it in front of Mother Kay and I didn't know how to have a plausible excuse for it.

"Don't be silly. Open it. Don't you think the rest of us want to see what it is?"

I shrugged and began untying the silver ribbon and removed the card from the top. This was the first birthday present I had ever received and I felt a bit ceremonious about it. I was careful to keep the wrapping paper in one piece, noticing that Mother Kay was getting annoyed. I wasn't prepared for what Jennifer had done for me. Inside the box was a beautiful dress. It was white with a concourse of embroidered cobalt blue twigs and flowers. It had a dropped waist and princess seams on the bodice. It looked like something Jennifer would wear, something that accentuated the natural curves of my new seventeen-year-old body. I did my best to hide the emotion that swelled inside of me.

"I hope you don't intend on wearing that thing," Mother Kay said. I didn't answer her but folded the lovely dress back into the box and carried it to my bedroom. I noticed that Mother hadn't said anything about the dress. I took it out again and held it up to myself. I imagined feeling beautiful in it, feeling proud to be me, to have a friend that would spend her own money and time on me. I opened the card and read it slowly, holding the delicious words in my heart and my hands.

Dear Susanna,
Every now and then we meet someone
Who makes life more worthwhile
Who makes our journey brighter
By the sunshine of a smile
Who seems to understand us
In a way few people do
And I met someone just like that
On the day that I met you!

Thanks for being such a good friend.
Happy Birthday!

With Love,
Jennifer

Jennifer's words held more power for me than the gift itself and I savored them alone in my room until I heard Mother Kay calling me.

"Just because it's your birthday, that doesn't make you special. We still need to eat, birthday or not."

"I'm coming," I called back, undeterred. Mother Kay's words carried no sting and I hurried downstairs to make dinner.

It's over now, my birthday. I feel so different, like have I slipped out of one costume in exchange for a new one. A better one.

"What are you still doing up?" Mother says, startling me.

"I just came downstairs to get a drink," I say, filling me a glass of water.

Mother stands next to me at the sink. "Did you have a nice birthday?"

"I did."

Mother puts her arms around me and hugs me tight. "You know I love ya, don't ya?" she whispers in my ear.

"Yeah, I know."

I can see my reflection in the window, hugging my mother, my long hair down my back. I see two women in an embrace, one of them observing from a distance.

LXXXI

There's a division going on in the Work. I don't really understand what is happening except that people are divided over who has the authority to perform marriages. Brother Coleman ordained several men to apostleship, including one of his sons. There seems to be a lot of people upset about it and they are selling their houses and moving back to where they came from. Father announced last Sunday after dinner that we would be moving back to Fifth East. All the adults have been rattled by the division. It's hard taking sides, proclaiming your allegiance to one man over another. This place was supposed to be some kind of Zion where all of God's people came together in one place, a place where not only did everyone share religious beliefs, but also the hopes and dreams of each other. It was to be a place where no one stared at you, a place without classes and cliques where the world remained far away in cities and paved roads.

The dream of a united people hasn't exactly lived up to everyone's hopes. I thought I would feel terrible about another split in the group but I feel strangely detached. Maybe I'm not supposed to be here. Maybe there is something up ahead that is waiting for me. Perhaps this place is just a stopping point along the road to wherever it is I am going.

Father told me I had to stay Down South while the rest of the family went back to Fifth East. He will be selling the house to William Baum and someone needs to stay and take care of it until the paperwork is done and the sale is final. Of course that would be me. I am left alone … again. This time, I don't mind it. It has given me the chance to see who I am, to decide what I believe in and where I am going with the rest of my life.

I am not supposed to go to Meeting on Sunday, but I still go. Everyone there thinks I have rebelled and I have chosen to follow them instead of going back to Fifth East with the rest of my family. All the girls at the sewing factory are acting really strange. They act like I am their friend now that they think I'm going to be on their side. At Meeting they come up to me and say "Hi, Susanna, how are you!" The hypocrisy both surprises and angers me. I realize now that I was better off being rejected by those kinds of people. They will certainly be surprised when I'm gone.

Living down here by myself has shown me that I am a complete person. I can make my own decisions without Father's endorsement or Mother's approval. I'm not sure what has happened to me. I feel like I just broke out of my cocoon. Mother said I finally matured. I don't know what it is except that the sun has come out from behind the clouds and is lighting the way before me. I feel like I am a whole person with all the tools I need to navigate my way through whatever lies up ahead. Maybe I have matured.

I am going take a walk alone tonight. The evenings are cool and the days are getting shorter. I will be going back to Fifth East soon. I need to say good-bye to this place, to the great night sky and the big gold sun that is slipping behind the western fields, which will rise again tomorrow. I will say good-bye to Meg, whose bones lie naked in the fields far to the south. I will say good-bye to the cracker box house while I am still in its shadow, and to Chanta, the horse who whinnies and prances in the ever-blowing wind, who taught me that there is no shame in being who you are. I will say good-bye to Valentine, my old withered friend who finally gave up but left his mark on my soul. I will say good-bye to myself, the part of me that died here, that was buried in the red sands of this desert.

I have heard people who have lived here all their lives talk about how much they love it here. I don't love it, but I've come to appreciate it; even the red sand has its own unique beauty. It is a place of great consistency. I know each day that the wind will blow and blow and that sagebrush will grow and the sky will open itself up like a giant mouth, a great blue sky which no amount of clouds can encompass. There will always be stars present every night and a deep quiet that calms even the wild jackrabbits scurrying across the road in the moonlight. Such a place cannot be tamed.

LXXXII

October 27, 1990: I started a diary today. So many things have changed. I will be leaving in another week. Father is coming down to get me. Claire and Lillian send me letters almost every day keeping me updated on the goings on at Fifth East. Mother Kay had her baby last week. A little girl. Mother Beverly is due with hers in about six weeks. Mother Laverna is going to have her baby in March. There will be a lot for me to do when I return.

It's really funny, because everyone seems to want me to come back. When the family moved Down South and left me alone at Fifth East I felt orphaned and deserted. I find myself in the exact same situation and yet I feel needed and important. Nothing has changed except for me. It's as if when I changed the world changed with me. When I saw myself in a new light, others saw it too. I didn't know I had so much power over my circumstances. I am actually excited about going back and trying out my new self.

I remember being very young, four or five years old. I was oblivious to others' intents and I forgave without thought or question. I can look back and still feel the things I felt at that young age. I remember knowing Mother Kay wasn't a safe person to be around, so I avoided her. It was as simple as that. I did whatever I needed to do to preserve my sense of self and my dignity. I felt happiness. That was a long, long time ago. I built myself a bubble of protection that turned into a citadel and then a prison.

But I have found a window in that prison and I can see outside the walls and into my own future. I am here for a reason, I have to believe that. Everything I have experienced must be for something. I have to find meaning out all of this. I will stay here with my family but someday I will get married. I will marry a man of my own choosing.

I will not run away from who I am in this world. I'll find a way to live in spite of things. I will create a life that I can be proud of. Someday I will be an old woman; at least I believe that I will. At the end of those years, I will feel no regret.

Mother told me once that spirits on the other side come down to earth at many levels of experience. Some are young and some are old. I've thought very often about my spirit, who I am inside of this body, who my essence is, entangled with this identity. I feel like an old spirit lives inside this body, an old spirit with some unfinished business. I will leave this life someday, but not before I make my peace with it.

I've been home for a couple of weeks now. Things are going as well as can be expected. I drove back with Father. We talked some of the time but mostly we both rode in a comfortable silence. I found myself looking at my face in the passenger-side mirror. The shape has changed: elongated, with a clean jaw line and noticeable cheekbones. My skin is finally smooth again since it's been a few years since I had my face slapped. I am happy with what I see in the mirror. In the eyes of the body I see myself, a deep well of remembrance and an unchangeable security. It feels good. It feels right.

Today I decided to do something I never thought I could do. I'm a little nervous but I am prepared to do it. I am making a new beginning, a first wobbly step toward a change and wholeness, a first step toward the truth. I have spent my life thus far hiding, pretending and running needlessly. I don't know why I have been given this lot, and I no longer need to know why. I am prepared to make my life anew, to be the one directing its path, cutting this path through the jungle of misperception and confusion. Today, this moment with a pay phone cradled to my ear and the sound of traffic in the distance, I take the first step of my life, the first real decision I have ever made. I dial. It rings and an old friendly voice comes on the line.

"Hello, Joe?" My voice is shaky and I try to regain my confidence.

"Hello, Susanna! It's so good to hear your voice again! It's been a long time." I close my eyes and smile, a smile that I can feel all the way down to my stomach.

"It's good to talk to you again too." There's a unanimous silence between us. "Joe … I need to tell you something."

"Okay," he says. "What is it?"

"I need to tell you the truth."

EPILOGUE

It is a long walk down the driveway and it is very cold tonight. I wrap my winter parka tightly around me. I make the first footprints in the snow, a two-inch blanket resting on everything. A deep silence surrounds me and for the first time today I can hear my own breathing with an awareness that surprises me. My breath becomes alive in the frigid air, a swirling white before my face. The front door opens and Audrie pokes her head out into the silent night, her light brown pigtails bouncing in the porch light.

"Mom, where are you going?"

"I'm just getting the mail. I'll be right back. Go back inside with the other kids, okay?"

Audrie gives me an enthusiastic wave.

"Bye, Mom!" she yells into the night air. The door slams shut and I am once more engrossed in the moment of perfect quiet.

When I reach the mailbox it is frozen shut and it takes a few hard pulls to loosen it up. I rarely come and get the mail myself, but today, for some reason, I wanted to do it. With my arms full I begin the walk back home. I am with myself, warm, like a friend nearby who doesn't need to speak to feel comfortable. I look at the house in front of me, growing larger in the moonlight. My home sits flat and long in front of me. Four windows, two on either side of a solid front door with a wreath hung in the middle. A tall sloping green roof caps the brick and stucco walls. The light from the windows glows and twinkles in the darkness, like four happy eyes. Inside that home is everything I could ever want or hope for. It is a symbol of triumph and relief. I draw in a great breath of peace, the peace that I know is mine.

I stop halfway up the driveway, the snow collecting on the top of my head. I can hear the silence of the snow falling. I can hear the silence of my own peace like the soft layer of snow that mutes the night sounds. This peace settles around me, softening all the hard edges.

I look forward to walking through the front door, to the sounds of children on all fours pretending to be a family of dogs. I know my husband is somewhere nearby and will come and rest with me on the couch. I will read C.S. Lewis by lamplight while the kids sit in a circle around me, their wet hair and clean-smelling skin an intoxication I cannot get enough of.

I begin to run home, my feet sinking into the fresh snow on the driveway, the cold air burning my lungs. Once more I am running. The familiarity startles me, like a forgotten memory excavated by accident. I am running toward home. My home. A place I long to be. I do not question the hearts of the souls that live in my home. I do not question my own heart. I feel safe in my own space and it belongs to me and I belong to it.

There is a joy that awaits me, as well as the joy that I feel in this moment. I have a home. I am welcome here. I am loved and safe and wanted. The past no longer haunts me, but provides me with a perspective and a depth that makes every moment a spark of possibility.

AUTHOR'S NOTE

All of my life I have tried to write my story. Journals and papers fill my closet as evidence of this need. Even as a small child I tried in vain to put the words of my life on paper to bring them to life. But it felt as though my fingers were frozen and my mouth stopped shut. It wasn't time. Now it is time and this book is my mouth finally opened. All that I am begins with the choice to speak honestly and with integrity.

It took many false starts and much mental and emotional wrestling before I allowed this book, these words, to come out of me. To speak the unspoken, to lay bare the secrets that wavered between truth and lies, broke the bonds that held me captive in my own life. It was the beginning of a journey, a journey that I am still discovering.

Most of the names in this book have been changed out of respect for the privacy of my family. It is the only privacy I can afford them. Although this book is the truest thing I have ever written, I realize that it is a narrow truth. It is only a thin slice in a very large and complicated pie. I don't claim it as anything other than my view, my story.

In my own final analysis, this book is my burial ground, where the fragments of the past come together to form a broken and incomplete thing. Like old bones finally found, I laid them out together the best I knew how. I humbly accept these small, unfinished memories as they are. I bury them and free them all at once. May they finally rest in peace.

NOTE TO THE READER

In an effort to clear up possible confusion I want to state a few things.

Polygamy and Mormonism are not the same thing. I am not a Mormon although I was raised and bred on Mormon theology and basic Christian beliefs. Most of my ancestors were converted to the LDS Church during the 1850s and beyond. In my house the Book of Mormon and the Bible were nearly synonyms. That said, I did not consider myself a Mormon. My family on both sides had disassociated themselves from the church and embraced a more fundamental way of life. I believed that the LDS Church was as much my enemy as the rest of the world.

While this book was written about polygamy, it was not written against polygamy. While I have chosen not to practice that lifestyle myself, many of my friends and loved ones live it honestly and decently, and, I dare say, are some of the best people I know. There are plenty of honorable people who raise balanced and healthy children, who have also chosen to practice polygamy. I respect their choices.

I specifically chose not to use the word polygamy in telling my story. It wasn't something any of us in the family talked about. It was simply our life. Nevertheless, it was a life of secrets. This book was written in an effort to unveil those secrets—to rob them of their power. I finally exposed, even if only for myself, all the things that couldn't be said for so many years. Thank you for reading.

978-0-595-40777-4
0-595-40777-3

Printed in the United States
136235LV00005B/15/A